PREDICTIVE ANALYTICS AND ITS APPLICATIONS

Matthew N. O. Sadiku
Abayomi J. Ajayi-Majebi
Paul A. Adekunte

PREDICTIVE ANALYTICS AND ITS APPLICATION

ISBN: 9798240871252

Edition: Paperback

Copyright: 115247066881

Permissions Notice: write to the author at: sadiku@ieee.org

Printed and published in the USA

Author's Website: https://matthew-sadiku.com/

Publisher Information:

SELFPUBLISHINGLLC

Published by Self-Publishing LLC | SelfPublishingLLC.com

Credits

Publisher: Steve Martin

DEDICATED
TO OUR SIBLINGS:

Moses, David (late), James, and Julius

Olusegun (late), Abiodun, Kolawole, Kayode, Yetunde

Emmanuel, Florence, Samson, and Bunmi

PREFACE

Predictive analytics is a data science discipline that utilizes predictive models to forecast future outcomes using historical data. It is one of the advanced technologies being used in the modern world. It is a powerful technique that "predicts" the future, in a sense. Predictive analytics can help predict the future growth of any real-life entity with the help of advanced modern technologies such as machine learning, big data, statistical models, artificial intelligence, etc. Predictive analytics looks for past patterns to measure the likelihood that those patterns will reoccur. Unlike traditional analytics, which relies on human-defined algorithms, predictive analytics uses artificial intelligence to identify patterns and anomalies independently.

This book examines predictive analytics and its applications in various industries such as healthcare, business, marketing, finance, manufacturing, supply chain, insurance, customer care, human resources, fraud detection, risk management, consumer relationship management, and entertainment. It is organized into fourteen chapters that summarize predictive analytics and its applications in a concise manner.

Chapter 1 - Introduction: In this chapter, we will go over predictive data analytics and provides some of its applications. The chapter serves as introduction to the entire book. Traditional forecasting methods often rely on historical trends and simple statistical models, which can be prone to errors, particularly in volatile markets. Predictive analytics involves looking at historical data to predict future outcomes. It is a data science that involves collecting and using current data to predict future outcomes in various industries.

Chapter 2 - Healthcare: In this chapter, we will provide an introduction to the use of predictive analytics in healthcare. In the dynamic, unpredictable landscape of healthcare, the ability to foresee future events is becoming increasingly crucial. Predictive analytics has emerged as a transformative tool in the healthcare sector. AI-powered predictive analytics enables healthcare professionals to anticipate and address medical issues before they escalate, thereby improving patient outcomes and optimizing the overall efficiency of healthcare systems. By enabling earlier diagnoses, personalizing treatments, and streamlining operations, it offers a path toward a more efficient and effective healthcare system.

Chapter 3 - Business: This chapter explores how predictive analytics is reshaping business strategy across industries. Business predictive analytics enables businesses to anticipate trends, behaviors, and outcomes by analyzing historical and current data. Predictive analytics provides a critical edge in navigating the uncertainties of the business world, allowing companies to anticipate changes, optimize operations, and capitalize on emerging opportunities. In the business world, predictive analytics' ability to identify patterns and make data-based predictions can lead to drastically improved decision-making. Without leveraging predictive analytics, businesses risk missing out on opportunities, failing to anticipate market trends, and being unprepared for potential disruptions.

Chapter 4 - Marketing: This chapter examines the significant role of predictive analytics in transforming marketing. In the modern marketing landscape, data is the new currency. Predictive analytics in marketing (or predictive marketing) implies using data mining, artificial intelligence, and statistical modelling for data analysis to generate predictions, like campaign outcomes, customer behavior, and industry trends forecasts, to help marketers make proactive decisions. Marketing professionals who want to remain relevant and competitive in their field should be prepared to apply predictive analytics in their own marketing strategies.

Chapter 5 - Finance: This chapter provides useful information into how predictive analytic techniques are used in finance sector. Predictive analytics for the finance industry uses machine learning and artificial intelligence to forecast future outcomes, driving financial forecasting and risk management. It allows institutions and investors to make smarter decisions by predicting trends like stock market movements, credit events, and key economic indicators such as GDP growth, unemployment, and inflation rates. Predictive analytics in finance equips finance leaders with the ability to manage risks proactively, improve accuracy in planning, optimize investments, and create better customer experiences.

Chapter 6 - Manufacturing: In this chapter, we examine how predictive analytics is transforming manufacturing processes. In manufacturing, predictive analytics has been widely used for improving operational efficiency, minimizing expenses, and enhancing overall decision-making. The goal is to predict future outcomes, identify potential issues, and uncover opportunities for improvement. Predictive analytics offers a powerful solution to the common challenges faced by manufacturing companies. Adopting predictive analytics in manufacturing is no longer an option but a necessity to stay competitive in the market.

Chapter 7 - Supply Chain: This chapter aims to explore the role of predictive analytics in supply chain management. Predictive analytics has emerged as a key success factor in supply chain management, using historical data and machine-learning to turn uncertainty into actionable insights. When combined with artificial intelligence (AI), predictive analytics is set to redefine how supply chains operate, shifting them from reactive to proactive and even prescriptive models. Predictive analytics in the supply chain refers to the use of data, statistical algorithms, and machine learning techniques to forecast future events and trends within the supply chain. Its introduction is helping logistics and supply chain companies meet increasing demands.

Chapter 8 - Insurance: This chapter delves into how predictive analytics is revolutionizing the insurance sector. At its heart, the insurance industry depends on the ability to predict outcomes and behavior changes. Predictive analytics is all about forecasting the likelihood of future events. This technology enables insurers to forecast future events and behaviors with unprecedented accuracy. With rising claims volumes, fraud risks, and customer demands, predictive analytics is no longer a “nice-to-have” but a core capability. Predictive analytics has become foundational for insurers facing climate volatility, margin pressure, and increasing risk complexity.

Chapter 9 - Customer Service: In this chapter, we will explore the transformative impact of predictive analytics on customer service. Predictive analytics in customer service refers to the use of historical data, artificial intelligence, statistical algorithms, and machine learning to anticipate future customer behaviors, potential issues, and service needs. It helps you anticipate what customers need – before they ask. It is about using data to personalize support, resolve issues early, and boost customer satisfaction. Predictive analytics in customer service uses data from past support interactions, including tickets, chat logs, call transcripts, feedback, and agent actions, to identify trends and customer behaviors.

Chapter 10 - Human Resources: This chapter explores the role of predictive analytics in human resources (HR). Predictive HR analytics, also known as predictive people analytics or workforce analytics, refers to the use of data, statistical algorithms, and machine learning techniques to identify the likelihood of future outcomes based on historical data. By leveraging predictive analytics, HR professionals can move beyond traditional methods and gain insights from historical data on hiring outcomes, employee turnover, and performance. Predictive analytics applications in human resources have gained significant attention as organizations seek to move beyond historical reporting toward forward looking insights. It is helping companies plan their workforce more effectively.

Chapter 11 - Fraud Detection: In this chapter, we examine the multifaceted impact of predictive analytics on the fight against fraud or deceitful online activities. Fraud is a global problem that affects nearly every industry. Fraud detection through predictive analytics has become a critical defense mechanism in today's digital landscape. Predictive analytics plays a transformative role in fraud detection and prevention by enabling organizations to identify, predict, and respond to fraudulent activities with greater precision and speed. Predictive analytics in fraud detection has revolutionized the way financial institutions preemptively address and mitigate cyber threats, reducing the incidence of breaches and saving millions in potential losses.

Chapter 12 - Risk Management: This chapter will explore how predictive analytics has revolutionized risk management across various industries. Risk is an inherent and inevitable part of every business operation. Predictive analytics has emerged as a transformative force in risk management. Unlike traditional models that focus on risk mitigation after an event occurs, predictive analytics proactively identifies patterns and anomalies that signal potential threats. From financial institutions assessing credit risk to healthcare providers predicting disease outbreaks, predictive analytics is reshaping the way organizations approach uncertainty. Predictive analytics empowers financial institutions to take a proactive approach to risk management.

Chapter 13 - Customer Relationship Management: This chapter explores the transformative role of predictive analytics in customer relationship management (CRM) systems. CRM has become the cornerstone of modern business strategy, playing a critical role in achieving long-term success and sustainability. Traditional CRM systems often fall short in accurately forecasting future customer actions. The integration of AI-powered predictive analytics fundamentally reshapes CRM capabilities, offering a multitude of benefits that address the shortcomings of traditional systems. Predictive analysis in CRM has been widely explored in recent years, driven by the increasing need for companies to harness large datasets and derive actionable insights for customer engagement. It is transforming how businesses understand and engage customers.

Chapter 14 - Entertainment: This chapter examines the transformation role of predictive analytics on entertainment. With data science, entertainment companies can rely on objective data to drive their decision-making. By analyzing vast amounts of data, entertainment companies can gain valuable insights into audience preferences and tailor their content accordingly. Predictive analytics has undoubtedly become an indispensable tool in the entertainment industry, offering a bridge between the unpredictability of human creativity and the demands of commercial viability. The integration of predictive analytics has provided the entertainment industry with a robust framework for navigating an increasingly complex and competitive market.

This is a comprehensive introductory text on the issues, ideas, theories, and applications of predictive analytics. It provides an overview of various applications in simple terms so that beginners can understand it. It is a must-read book for anyone who wants to learn predictive analytics, which is an important emerging technology today.

M. N. O. Sadiku, A. J. Ajayi-Majebi, and P. A. Adekunte

ABOUT THE AUTHORS

A. Matthew N. O. Sadiku received his B. Sc. degree in 1978 from Ahmadu Bello University, Zaria, Nigeria and his M.Sc. and Ph.D. degrees from Tennessee Technological University, Cookeville, TN in 1982 and 1984 respectively. From 1984 to 1988, he was an assistant professor at Florida Atlantic University, Boca Raton, FL, where he did graduate work in computer science. In total, he received seven college degrees. From 1988 to 2000, he was at Temple University, Philadelphia, PA, where he became a full professor. From 2000 to 2002, he was with Lucent/Avaya, Holmdel, NJ as a system engineer and with Boeing Satellite Systems, Los Angeles, CA as a senior scientist. He is presently a Regents professor emeritus of electrical and computer engineering at Prairie View A&M University, Prairie View, TX.

He is the author of over 1,660 professional papers and over 170 books including “Elements of Electromagnetics” (Oxford University Press, 7th ed., 2018), “Fundamentals of Electric Circuits” (McGraw-Hill, 7th ed., 2020, with C. Alexander), “Computational Electromagnetics with MATLAB” (CRC Press, 4th ed., 2019), “Principles of Modern Communication Systems” (Cambridge University Press, 2017, with S. O. Agbo), and “Emerging Internet-based Technologies” (CRC Press, 2019). In addition to the engineering books, he has written Christian books including "Secrets of Successful Marriages" (with J. O. Sadiku), "How to Discover God's Will for Your Life," and commentaries on all the books of the New Testament Bible. Some of his books have been translated into ten languages: French, Korean, Chinese (and Chinese Long Form in Taiwan), Italian, Portuguese, Spanish, German, Dutch, Polish, and Russian.

He was the recipient of the 2000 McGraw-Hill/Jacob Millman Award for outstanding contributions in the field of electrical engineering. He was also the recipient of Regents Professor award for 2012-2013 by the Texas A&M University System. He is a registered professional engineer and a life fellow of the Institute of Electrical and Electronics Engineers (IEEE) "for contributions to computational electromagnetics and engineering education." He is a fellow of the Nigerian Academy of Engineering. He was the IEEE Region 2 Student Activities Committee Chairman. He was an associate editor for IEEE Transactions on Education. He is also a member of Association for Computing Machinery (ACM). His current research interests are in the areas of computational electromagnetic, computer science/networks, engineering education, and marriage counseling. His works can be found in his autobiography, "My Life and Work" (Trafford Publishing, 2024) or his website: www.matthew-sadiku.com. He can be reached via email at sadiku@ieee.org

B. Abayomi Ajayi-Majebi is a full-time professor and past chairman of the Manufacturing Engineering Dept. at Central State University (CSU). A baccalaureate degree graduate (1976) of the University of Lagos, College of Engineering (Civil), Akoka Campus in Lagos, West Africa, he is an alumnus and three-time graduate (PhD, MS, MA) of The Ohio State University (OSU), Columbus, Ohio, where he received the doctoral degree in Engineering in 1983. His areas of professional engineering interests and research include: predictive analytics, manufacturing productivity improvement studies, quality and reliability engineering studies, renewable energy studies, nuclear engineering studies, reliability based probabilistic design optimization, design of engineering experiments, statistical modeling and data analysis, computer aided design, finite element analysis, reliability and safety engineering, Weibull Failure Analysis Modeling, materials testing for impact strength, fatigue and creep research, temperature and humidity testing, polymer aging studies under ultraviolet radiation, manufacturing systems operations analysis, creativity and innovation methodologies, systems thinking, and discrete-event-based systems simulation modeling, especially applied to Manufacturing Systems. He is a Summer 2016, 2014, 2011 and also 2010 National Aeronautics and Space Administration (NASA) Summer Faculty Fellow at the NASA Glenn Research Center in

Cleveland, Ohio. For over 41 years, he has supported the professional development of about 400 graduate Manufacturing Engineers and over 700 CSU STEM and non-STEM students. In February 2015, he was honored by the White House President Obama's Administration as a Champion of Change in Higher Education among Historically Black Colleges/Universities (HBCUs). He was subsequently honored with a citation by the Ohio Senate.

He has served as Director of the Minor in Nuclear Engineering program at Central State University and oversaw the development and implementation of the program teaching four (4) nuclear engineering courses to undergraduate engineering students. He is a Life member of the National Society of Black Engineers (NSBE), a Senior and Endowed Member of the Society of Manufacturing Engineers (SME) and a Senior Member of the American Society for Quality (ASQ), he is a Life Member of the American Nuclear Society (ANS). He is a member of the American Society of Civil Engineers (ASCE) and the Society for the Advancement of Materials and Process Engineering (SAMPE). He is the Vice President of the Dayton, Ohio Chapter 18 of the Society of Manufacturing Engineers (SME). He has served as a past National Chairman of the Board of the African Christian Fellowship USA (ACF-USA). He is affiliated with and / or has worshipped God with other Congregants in many church organizations across the World.

He has in the past been a CESSNA 152 and 172 single-engine airplane pilot flying from the Xenia and Springfield Airports in Greene County, Ohio. He is an avid moderate and bridled athlete and enjoys such sports as swimming, jogging, basketball, soccer, table tennis, lawn tennis, badminton, racquetball, volleyball, hiking, cross-country racing, shot put, high-jumping, long-jumping. cycling, motorcycle riding. He holds a U. S. Class A Commercial Driver's License with four endorsements.

He is a registered Professional Engineer (PE) with the State of Ohio and is a Certified Manufacturing Engineer, so certified by the Society of Manufacturing Engineers (SME). He is also an American Society for Quality (ASQ) Certified Quality Engineer (CQE) and is also an ASQ Certified Reliability Engineer (CRE). He is a faculty adviser for both the CSU Student Chapter of the National Society for Black Engineers (NSBE) and the CSU chapter of the Society of Manufacturing Engineers (SME). He has for approximately thirty (30) years served the State of Ohio Residents as a Notary Public being duly registered with the Greene County Clerk of Courts in discharging the duty which service he performs free of charge to the public.

C: Paul A. Adekunte received his B.Sc in zoology from Ahmadu Bello University, Zaria, Nigeria in 1983 and master's degree in crime management and prevention from Bayero University, Kano, Nigeria in 2011. He got his postgraduate degree in Biology in 2005 from the Federal College of Education (Technical) Akoka, Lagos, Nigeria. He also obtained certificates in public relations and computer studies. He is a professional educator in biology at the secondary and advanced levels as well a security expert. He is a member of several professional bodies. His current areas of research interests include management, educational guidance and counseling, conflict and crisis resolution, and security matters. He has published several professional papers. He currently resides with his wife in Lagos, Nigeria and can be reached via email at adekuntepaul@gmail.com.

Brief Table of Contents

CHAPTER 1 INTRODUCTION....................................1

CHAPTER 2 PREDICTIVE ANALYTICS IN HEALTHCARE....................................29

CHAPTER 3 PREDICTIVE ANALYTICS IN BUSINESS....................................64

CHAPTER 4 PREDICTIVE ANALYTICS IN MARKETING....................................97

CHAPTER 5: PREDICTIVE ANALYTICS IN FINANCE....................................127

CHAPTER 6: PREDICTIVE ANALYTICS IN MANUFACTURING....................................160

CHAPTER 7: PREDICTIVE ANALYTICS IN SUPPLY CHAIN....................................191

CHAPTER 8: PREDICTIVE ANALYTICS IN INSURANCE....................................223

CHAPTER 9: PREDICTIVE ANALYTICS FOR CUSTOMER SERVICE....................................258

CHAPTER 10: PREDICTIVE ANALYTICS FOR HUMAN RESOURCES....................................285

CHAPTER 11: PREDICTIVE ANALYTICS IN FRAUD DETECTION... 317

CHAPTER 12: PREDICTIVE ANALYTICS IN RISK MANAGEMENT 343

CHAPTER 13: PREDICTIVE ANALYTICS IN CUSTOMER RELATIONSHIP MANAGEMENT.. 374

CHAPTER 14: PREDICTIVE ANALYTICS IN ENTERTAINMENT 400

INDEX.. 423

Detailed Table of Contents

CHAPTER 1 INTRODUCTION....................................1

1.1 INTRODUCTION....................................1

1.2 WHAT IS PREDICTIVE ANALYTICS?....................3

1.3 APPLICATIONS OF PREDICTIVE ANALYTICS.9

1.4 BENEFITS....................................18

1.5 CHALLENGES....................................21

1.6 CONCLUSION....................................23

REFERENCES....................................25

CHAPTER 2 PREDICTIVE ANALYTICS IN HEALTHCARE....................................29

2.1 INTRODUCTION....................................29

2.2 WHAT IS PREDICTIVE ANALYTICS?....................31

2.3 PREDICTIVE ANALYTICS IN HEALTHCARE.36

2.4 APPLICATIONS OF PREDICTIVE ANALYTICS IN HEALTHCARE....................................39

2.5 BENEFITS....................................46

2.6 CHALLENGES....................................51

2.7 FUTURE OF PREDICTIVE ANALYTICS IN HEALTHCARE....................................56

2.8 CONCLUSION....................................57

REFERENCES....................................59

CHAPTER 3 PREDICTIVE ANALYTICS IN BUSINESS 64

3.1 INTRODUCTION 64

3.2 WHAT IS PREDICTIVE ANALYTICS? 66

3.3 PREDICTIVE ANALYTICS IN BUSINESS 71

3.4 APPLICATIONS OF PREDICTIVE ANALYTICS IN BUSINESS 73

3.5 BENEFITS 81

3.6 CHALLENGES 84

3.7 FUTURE OF PREDICTIVE ANALYTICS IN BUSINESS 89

3.8 CONCLUSION 89

REFERENCES 92

CHAPTER 4 PREDICTIVE ANALYTICS IN MARKETING 97

4.1 INTRODUCTION 97

4.2 WHAT IS PREDICTIVE ANALYTICS? 99

4.3 PREDICTIVE ANALYTICS IN MARKETING 104

4.4 APPLICATIONS OF PREDICTIVE ANALYTICS IN MARKETING 106

4.5 BENEFITS 113

4.6 CHALLENGES 118

4.7 FUTURE OF PREDICTIVE ANALYTICS IN MARKETING 120

4.8 CONCLUSION 121

REFERENCES 123

CHAPTER 5: PREDICTIVE ANALYTICS IN FINANCE 127

5.1 INTRODUCTION 127

5.2 WHAT IS PREDICTIVE ANALYTICS? 129

5.3 PREDICTIVE ANALYTICS IN FINANCE 134

5.4 APPLICATIONS OF PREDICTIVE ANALYTICS IN FINANCE 137

5.5 BENEFITS 145

5.6 CHALLENGES 149

5.7 FUTURE OF PREDICTIVE ANALYTICS IN FINANCE 152

5.8 CONCLUSION 153

REFERENCES 155

CHAPTER 6: PREDICTIVE ANALYTICS IN MANUFACTURING 160

6.1 INTRODUCTION 160

6.2 WHAT IS PREDICTIVE ANALYTICS? 162

6.3 PREDICTIVE ANALYTICS IN MANUFACTURING 167

6.4 APPLICATIONS OF PREDICTIVE ANALYTICS IN MANUFACTURING 169

6.5 BENEFITS 175

6.6 CHALLENGES 179

6.7 FUTURE OF PREDICTIVE ANALYTICS IN MANUFACTURING 183

6.8 CONCLUSION 185

REFERENCES 187

CHAPTER 7: PREDICTIVE ANALYTICS IN SUPPLY CHAIN 191

7.1 INTRODUCTION 191

7.2 WHAT IS PREDICTIVE ANALYTICS? 193

7.3 PREDICTIVE ANALYTICS IN SUPPLY CHAIN 198

7.4 APPLICATIONS OF PREDICTIVE ANALYTICS IN SUPPLY CHAIN 201

7.5 BENEFITS 208

7.6 CHALLENGES 212

7.7 FUTURE OF PREDICTIVE ANALYTICS IN SUPPLY CHAIN 216

7.8 CONCLUSION 217

REFERENCES 219

CHAPTER 8: PREDICTIVE ANALYTICS IN INSURANCE..223

8.1 INTRODUCTION..223

8.2 WHAT IS PREDICTIVE ANALYTICS?.............225

8.3 PREDICTIVE ANALYTICS IN INSURANCE ..230

8.4 APPLICATIONS OF PREDICTIVE ANALYTICS IN INSURANCE...232

8.5 BENEFITS 242

8.6 CHALLENGES...246

8.7 FUTURE OF PREDICTIVE ANALYTICS IN INSURANCE...250

8.8 CONCLUSION 252

REFERENCES...254

CHAPTER 9: PREDICTIVE ANALYTICS FOR CUSTOMER SERVICE...258

9.1 INTRODUCTION..258

9.2 WHAT IS PREDICTIVE ANALYTICS?.............260

9.3 PREDICTIVE ANALYTICS IN CUSTOMER SERVICE...266

9.4 APPLICATIONS OF PREDICTIVE ANALYTICS IN CUSTOMER SERVICE.....................................268

9.5 BENEFITS 272

9.6 CHALLENGES...275

9.7 FUTURE OF PREDICTIVE ANALYTICS IN CUSTOMER SERVICE 278

9.8 CONCLUSION 279

REFERENCES 281

CHAPTER 10: PREDICTIVE ANALYTICS FOR HUMAN RESOURCES 285

10.1 INTRODUCTION 285

10.2 WHAT IS PREDICTIVE ANALYTICS? 287

10.3 PREDICTIVE ANALYTICS IN HUMAN RESOURCES 292

10.4 APPLICATIONS OF PREDICTIVE ANALYTICS IN HUMAN RESOURCES 294

1-0.5 BENEFITS 299

10.6 CHALLENGES 304

10.7 FUTURE OF PREDICTIVE ANALYTICS IN HUMAN RESOURCES 310

10.8 CONCLUSION 311

REFERENCES 313

CHAPTER 11: PREDICTIVE ANALYTICS IN FRAUD DETECTION 317

11.1 INTRODUCTION 317

11.2 WHAT IS PREDICTIVE ANALYTICS? 319

11.3 PREDICTIVE ANALYTICS IN FRAUD DETECTION 324

11.4 APPLICATIONS OF PREDICTIVE ANALYTICS IN FRAUD DETECTION..327

11.5 BENEFITS..331

11.6 CHALLENGES..333

11.7 FUTURE OF PREDICTIVE ANALYTICS IN FRAUD DETECTION..336

11.8 CONCLUSION..338

REFERENCES..340

CHAPTER 12: PREDICTIVE ANALYTICS IN RISK MANAGEMENT..343

12.1 INTRODUCTION..343

12.2 WHAT IS PREDICTIVE ANALYTICS?...........345

12.3 PREDICTIVE ANALYTICS IN RISK MANAGEMENT..350

12.4 APPLICATIONS OF PREDICTIVE ANA LYTICS IN RISK MANAGEMENT........................352

12.5 BENEFITS..359

12.6 CHALLENGES..362

12.7 FUTURE OF PREDICTIVE ANALYTICS IN RISK MANAGEMENT..367

12.8 CONCLUSION..368

REFERENCES..370

CHAPTER 13: PREDICTIVE ANALYTICS IN CUSTOMER RELATIONSHIP MANAGEMENT .. 374

13.1 INTRODUCTION 374

13.2 WHAT IS PREDICTIVE ANALYTICS? 376

13.3 PREDICTIVE ANALYTICS IN CUSTOMER RELATIONSHIP MANAGEMENT 381

13.4 APPLICATIONS OF PREDICTIVE ANALYTICS IN CUSTOMER RELATIONSHIP MANAGEMENT 383

13.5 BENEFITS 387

13.6 CHALLENGES 391

13.7 FUTURE OF PREDICTIVE ANALYTICS IN CUSTOMER RELATIONSHIP MANAGEMENT .. 394

13.8 CONCLUSION 395

REFERENCES 397

CHAPTER 14: PREDICTIVE ANALYTICS IN ENTERTAINMENT 400

14.1 INTRODUCTION 400

14.2 WHAT IS PREDICTIVE ANALYTICS? 402

14.3 PREDICTIVE ANALYTICS IN ENTERTAINMENT 407

14.4 APPLICATIONS OF PREDICTIVE ANALYTICS IN ENTERTAINMENT 409

14.5 BENEFITS 412

14.6 CHALLENGES 414

14.7 FUTURE OF PREDICTIVE ANALYTICS IN ENTERTAINMENT....417

14.8 CONCLUSION....418

REFERENCES....420

INDEX

CHAPTER 1 INTRODUCTION

"Change is the law of life. And those who look only to the past or the present are certain to miss the future." – John F. Kennedy.

1.1 INTRODUCTION

Predictive analytics is a subset of advanced analytics that uses machine learning, data modeling, artificial intelligence, deep learning algorithms, and data mining to forecast outcomes based on patterns in vast historical datasets. It uses statistical algorithms and machine learning to forecast outcomes based on historical data, helping businesses anticipate and prepare for future events with a high degree of accuracy. Companies rely on predictive analytics to detect patterns in data that identify risks and opportunities. Predictive analytics is no longer a futuristic concept; it is a powerful tool reshaping the business landscape. It is a transformative technology revolutionizing businesses across sectors. Its ability to extract valuable insights from data and predict future trends empowers businesses to make more informed decisions, optimize operations, and ultimately drive significant growth [1].

Predictive analytics is an advanced technology used in the modern world. It is a powerful technique that "predicts" the future, in a sense. It can help answer key questions, such as how many products a business could sell in the next three months and how much profit it is likely to make. Predictive analytics goes beyond productivity limits. Nowadays, it is used across major industries, including healthcare, finance, insurance, retail, and manufacturing. Predictive analytics techniques are also used for many applications, such as weather forecasting, translation, decision-making, and video games. Predictive analytics can help forecast the future growth of any real-world entity using advanced technologies such as machine learning, big data, statistical models, and artificial intelligence. Figure 1.1 shows the word cloud for predictive analytics [2].

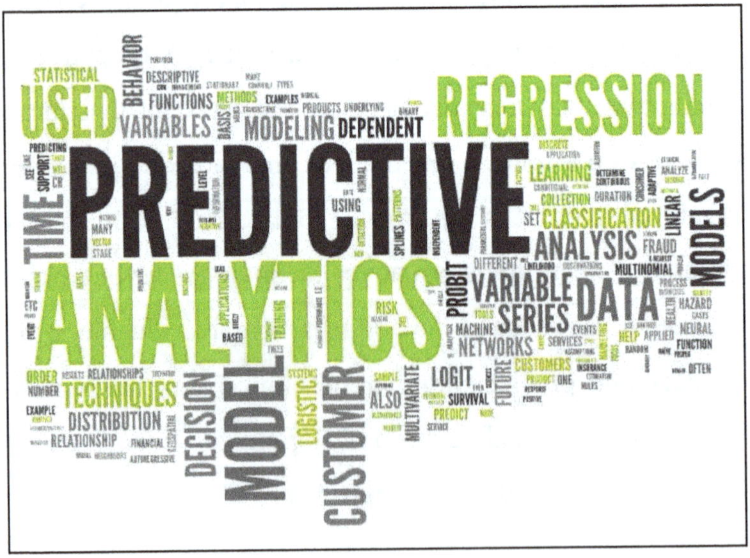

Figure 1.1: The word cloud for predictive analytics [2].

Predictive analytics involves looking at historical data to predict future outcomes. It is a branch of data science that involves collecting and using current data to predict future outcomes across various industries. It uses data mining techniques, machine learning, and statistical modeling to find patterns in data and identify risks and opportunities. This powerful tool has become necessary in today's world, enabling organizations to predict trends, reduce risks, and make informed decisions. You can use predictive analytics to analyze historical data, uncover patterns, and forecast future outcomes. These forecasts predict industry trends and behaviors, guide informed business and investment decisions, and are sometimes used to boost efficiency, increase profits, and protect information [3].

In this chapter, we will go over predictive data analytics and provide some of its applications. The chapter begins with explaining predictive analytics. It provides some applications of predictive analytics. It highlights some benefits and challenges of predictive analytics. The last section concludes with comments.

1.2 WHAT IS PREDICTIVE ANALYTICS?

As its name implies, predictive analytics involves forecasting future trends, such as sales demand and exchange rates. and other important metrics. The technique relies on applying statistical modeling and regression analysis to historical data to identify and understand trends and forecast future ones. Strictly speaking, predictive analytics does not predict the future; rather, it uses probability theory to determine what is likely to happen based on patterns and trends revealed by analyzing historical data [4]. Predictive analytics accurately anticipates customer demand, preventing overstocking and stockouts while adapting to market changes. Figure 1.2 illustrates predictive analytics [5], while Figure 1.3 shows different components of predictive analytics [6].

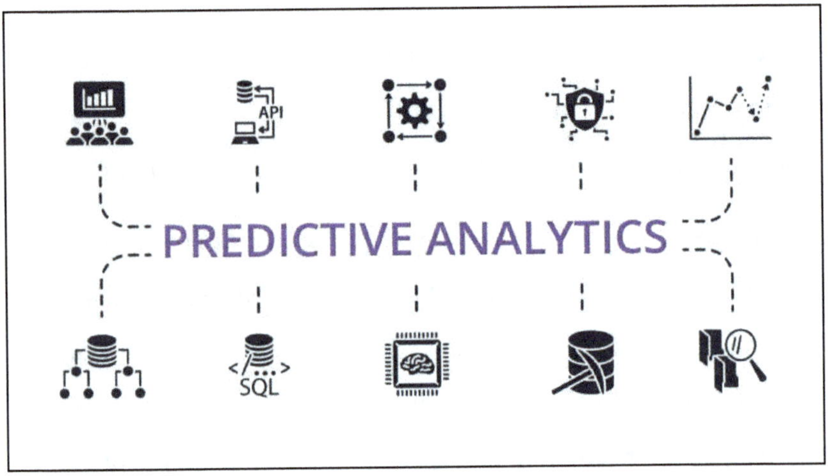

Figure 1.2 Predictive analytics [5].

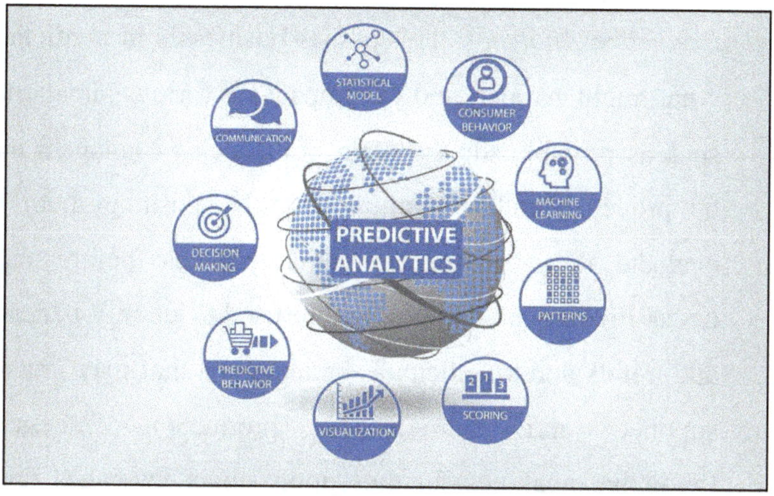

Figure 1.3 Different components of predictive analytics [6].

In general, analytics provides an efficient way to improve planning by giving you better forecasts. There are different types of data analytics. They are briefly explained as follows [7]:

- *Descriptive Analytics*: Descriptive analytics examines what has happened over the years. They are capable of detecting trends in historical data. Analytics can uncover trends and propose probable reasons for change by comparing the same data across different periods. It can be seen as the industry baseline, which assesses past and current data to generate more meaningful insights and delivers them to people so they can use their own intelligence and knowledge to make decisions.

- *Predictive Analytics*: This assists businesses in predicting what might happen and the impact of various situations, such as possible supply chain bottlenecks. Managers can be proactive rather than reactive by pushing them to evaluate these prospective circumstances before they occur. Predictive analytics may be used to identify patterns and trends and to anticipate breakdowns that may impact suppliers and, consequently, production processes. Predictive analytics for the supply chain leverages data, statistical algorithms, and machine learning techniques to identify the likelihood of future outcomes.
- *Prescriptive Analytics*: Prescriptive analytics builds on predictive analytics and dives deeper into predicting future insights on what can be done next. Prescriptive analytics uses the findings of descriptive and predictive analytics to recommend what measures a business should take to achieve its objectives. Because prescriptive analytics is increasingly complex, it requires more powerful software capable of rapidly processing and interpreting large amounts of data.
- *Cognitive Analytics:* Cognitive analytics attempts to mimic human thought and behavior, and they can assist companies in answering challenging, complex problems. Cognitive analytics does this by leveraging artificial intelligence (AI), enabling it to improve over time. Using

AI in the industry to answer complex questions and draw contextual conclusions about how humans would have interacted with the situation. It helps with more meaningful data, scaled experience, and knowledge, leading to better decisions.

- *Diagnostics Analytics*: This gives the ability to identify the root cause. It is characterized by techniques such as drill-down, data discovery, data mining, and correlations. It involves analyzing overall performance and figuring out why errors, mistakes, and delays occur. It lets the manager know the delays, breakdowns, and disruptions in the demand and supply processes and the reasons behind them.

Figure 1.4 shows these major types of data analytics [8]. Unlike diagnostic and descriptive analytics, which analyze situations after they occur, predictive analytics uses advanced techniques to forecast future outcomes. In the supply chain, it is time to shift from mere descriptive and diagnostic analytics to predictive and prescriptive analytics. Predictive analytics is a branch of data analytics that uses historical data, statistical modeling, data mining techniques, and machine learning to predict future outcomes. Figure 1.5 shows the predictive analytics process [9].

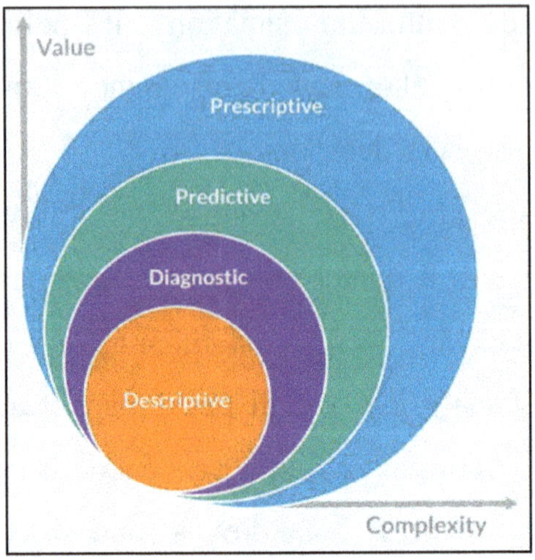

Figure 1.4 Types of data analytics [8].

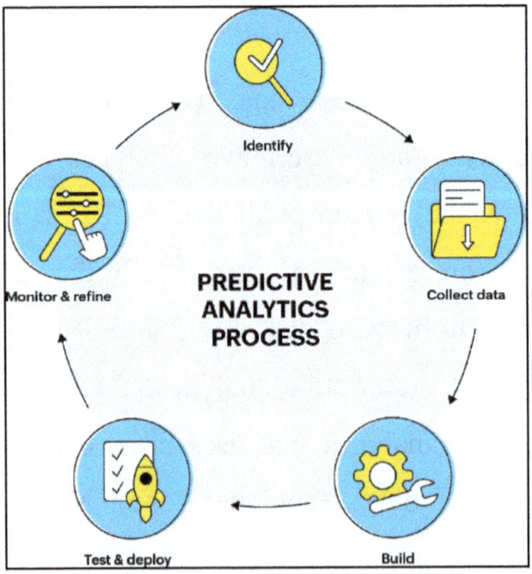

Figure 1.5 Predictive analytics process [9].

1.3 APPLICATIONS OF PREDICTIVE ANALYTICS

The predictive analytics capabilities are vast but primarily used to anticipate potential issues in the near and distant future. Some of the applications of predictive analytics are shown in Figure 1.6 [9]. Predictive data analytics is used across many industries to anticipate future outcomes of a given scenario. Predictive analytics is playing an increasingly important role in a wide range of industries, including retail, healthcare, finance, risk management, and manufacturing. Common applications include the following [10-13]:

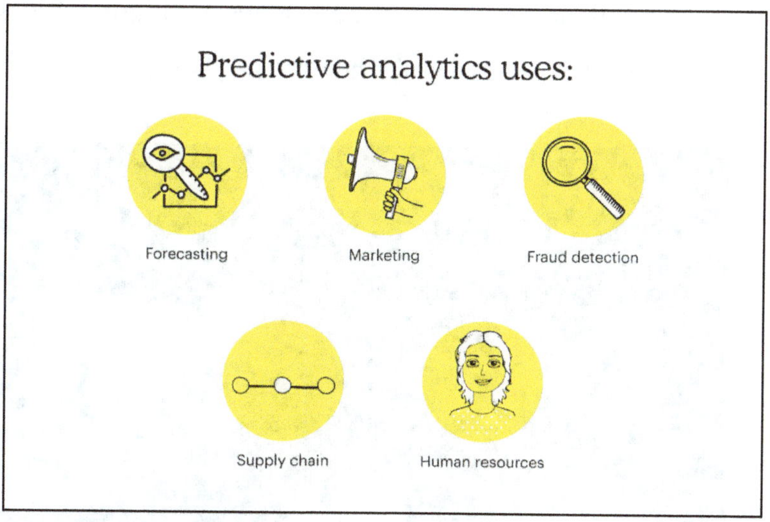

Figure 1.6 Some applications of predictive analytics [10].

- *1. Healthcare:* An example of using algorithms for rapid, predictive analytics for prevention comes from the healthcare industry. Predictive analytics is used to analyze vast amounts of patient records, medical images, genetic information, and administrative data, leading to enhanced patient care and better patient outcomes. Healthcare applications include medical diagnosis, disease prediction and prevention, and clinical trials. Many healthcare facilities nowadays use advanced software systems to perform various medical processes using available datasets from medical institutions and predictive analytics. With the help of predictive analytics in healthcare, diseases can be easily predicted based on symptoms, and preventive treatments, medication testing, and their results can be suggested. Figure 1.7 shows predictive analytics for healthcare [14].

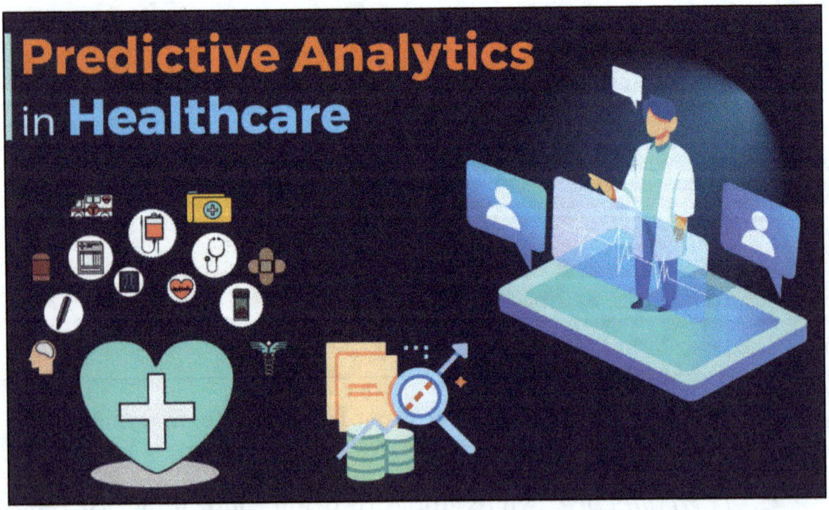

Figure 1.7 Use of predictive analytics in healthcare [14].

- *2. Business*: As we move into a world of technological advances where more and more data is created and stored digitally, businesses are looking for ways to take advantage of this opportunity and use this information to help generate profits. Businesses can use big data to their advantage by applying predictive analytics effectively. Predictive analytics can provide many benefits to a wide range of businesses, including asset management firms, insurance companies, and communications companies. It is a set of business intelligence (BI) technologies that uncover relationships and patterns in large volumes of data, enabling the prediction of behavior and events. Unlike other BI technologies, predictive analytics is forward-looking, using past events to anticipate the future. In business, predictive models exploit patterns found in historical and transactional data to identify risks and opportunities. Predictive analytics enables businesses to make informed decisions by analyzing trends and patterns in historical data. By leveraging advanced statistical techniques and machine learning algorithms, businesses can glean invaluable insights from historical data to anticipate future trends, optimize operations, and ultimately, drive significant growth. Figure 1.8 shows predictive analytics for business [15].

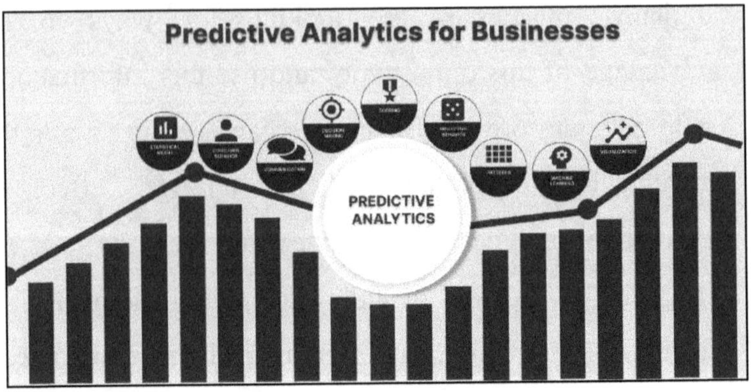

Figure 1.8 Predictive analytics for business [15].

- *3. Retail:* Companies in the retail industry make use of predictive analytics to study extensive datasets, including sales transactions, customer demographics, inventory levels, and market trends. The insights help retailers prepare for shifts in consumer behavior, tailor offerings to customer preferences, and drive higher sales while providing a more satisfying shopping experience. Tableau is a well-known data visualization tool that comes with powerful predictive analytics capabilities. It simplifies data processing to make decision-making more efficient and offers time-series analysis, letting users perform predictive analytics, such as forecasting, within a visual analytics interface. Predictive analytics, enabled by machine learning, helps retailers understand customers' preferences. It works by analyzing users' browsing patterns and how frequently a product is clicked on on a website.

- *4. Marketing:* In marketing, consumer data is abundant and leveraged to create content, advertisements, and strategies to reach better potential customers where they are. By examining historical behavioral data and using it to predict future outcomes, you engage in predictive analytics. Predictive analytics can process large datasets containing customer information, purchasing behavior, demographics, and engagement metrics to help marketers anticipate trends, target audiences, and allocate resources, driving higher ROI on marketing investments. Marketers use predictive analytics to answer questions about marketing campaigns, such as how a consumer might react to a new type of visual branding. A good example of predictive analytics in marketing is the toy industry. Predictive analytics techniques can help the toy maker gain deeper insight into consumers' most likely reactions. Figure 1.9 shows predictive analytics for marketing [16].

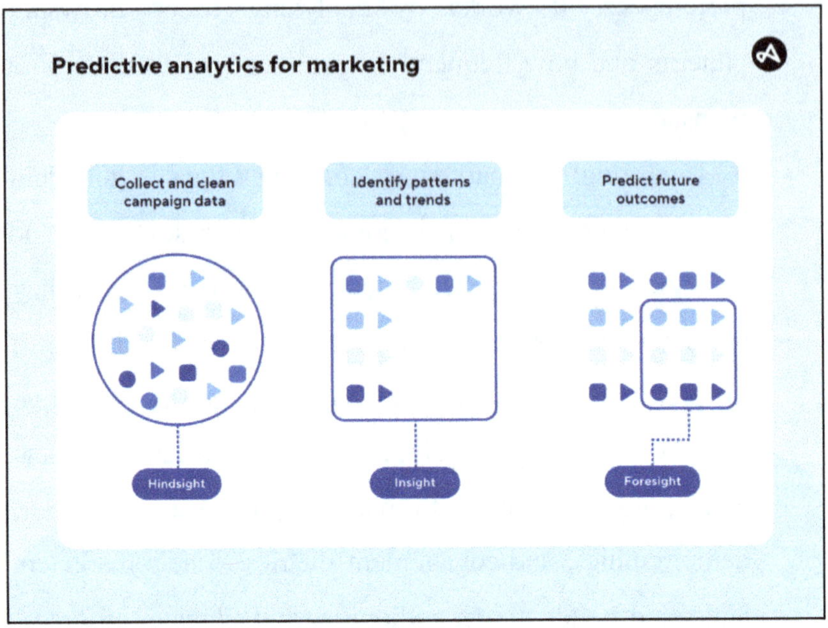

Figure 1.9 Predictive analytics for marketing [16].

- *5. Finance:* Every business needs to keep periodic financial records, and predictive analytics can play a big roleb in forecasting your organization's future health. Using historical data from previous financial statements, as well as data from the broader industry, you can project sales, revenue, and expenses to craft a picture of the future and make decisions.

- *6. Manufacturing:* In the manufacturing industry, predictive analytics can process sensor data, equipment logs, maintenance records, and production metrics. Predictive models are then developed to minimize stockouts, reduce maintenance costs, and optimize inventory levels. In manufacturing, algorithms can be trained on historical data to accurately predict when a piece of machinery is likely to malfunction. Manufacturing applications include inventory management, predictive maintenance, quality control, and defect detection.
- *7. Supply Chains:* Supply chains are under constant pressure to anticipate various issues, such as a spike in fuel costs, fewer drivers available to deliver goods, and a shortage of goods to satisfy an order. Using predictive models enables players in the supply chain to anticipate potential problems and minimize their impact on the steady flow of goods. Predictive analytics leverages historical data from sales, inventory levels, transportation routes, weather conditions, and supplier performance to anticipate changes in demand. It is transforming supply chain management by enabling businesses to forecast demand more accurately.
- *8. Forecasting:* Some of the most common uses of predictive modeling techniques are using past data to

create accurate forecasts about future inventories, demand, and the need for services or supplies. In forecasting, historical data is retrieved from a database to examine past performance and anticipate what is most likely to happen next.

- *9. Fraud Detection:* Fraud is typically detected by looking for patterns of activity over a period of time. Someone engaging in fraud has identified the best time or window of opportunity to commit fraud. Predictive analytics techniques can be used to identify fraud patterns in an organization. By detecting unusual patterns or anomalies in transaction data, predictive analytics uncovers fraudulent activity and helps prevent financial losses. One predictive analytics example is identifying customer fraud and determining whether there is a pattern of bad orders or a fluke in purchasing patterns. Sifting through the data helps uncover issues and prevent them from recurring.
- *10. Insurance:* Similar to fraud, unexpectedly high and suspicious claims are the bane of insurance companies. They would like to avoid paying such claims. Though the objective is simple enough, predictive modeling has had only partial success in eliminating this source of significant losses for companies.
- *11. Customer Relationship Management (CRM):* One of the most impactful applications of predictive analytics lies

in enhancing customer relationship management. Instead of relying on generic marketing strategies, businesses can utilize predictive models to understand individual customer behavior, preferences, and needs with unprecedented accuracy. It involves predicting customer churn (customer leaving), recommending products based on past purchases, and personalizing marketing campaigns. CRM uses predictive analysis in applications for marketing campaigns, sales, and customer service.

- *12. Risk Management:* In today's interconnected world, businesses face a multitude of risks, ranging from financial fraud to operational disruptions. Predictive analytics plays a vital role in mitigating these risks by identifying potential threats and vulnerabilities before they materialize. By analyzing historical data on fraudulent activities, predictive models can identify patterns and anomalies that indicate potential fraud.
- *13. Customer Service:* Customer segmentation is performed based on insights from predictive analytics. Customers are grouped into segments based on their purchase patterns. For example, book buyers will form one cluster while t-shirt buyers will constitute another. Tailored marketing strategies are then developed for each segment based on its characteristics. Predictive analytics using machine learning can also identify dissatisfied

customers and help sellers design products to retain existing customers and attract new ones.

- *14. Human Resources:* Predictive analytics using machine learning identifies employee churn rate and keeps human resources (HR) departments informed of the same. Models can be trained with datasets that have details such as an employee's monthly income, allowances, increments, insurance, and so on. The models learn from records of ex-employees and find patterns to understand the reasons for leaving. They then predict whether new employees are likely to resign, empowering HR to minimize the risk.

Other applications include government, entertainment and hospitality, weather forecasting, Internet of Things, cybersecurity, demand forecasting, and e-commerce.

1.4 BENEFITS

Predictive analytics has become part of mainstream business. By using data to forecast future trends, companies gain the insights needed to make better decisions. Other benefits of predictive analytics include the following [17,18]:

- *Improved Decision-making*: Through predictive analytics, businesses improve their decision-making process. This allows organizations to develop market strategies tailored to insights from data analysis, leading to more effective decision-making. From personalized healthcare and education to urban planning and environmental sustainability, data-driven insights will guide decision-making for a better future. For example, e-commerce companies can make informed decisions about their inventory by predicting which products are likely to be in demand. Figure 1.10 shows how predictive analytics helps in making better decisions [1].

Figure 1.10 How predictive analytics helps in making better decisions [1].

- *Enhanced Efficiency:* Predictive analytics also drives operational efficiency by automating processes. By leveraging predictive analytics, businesses can optimize their operational processes and allocate resources more efficiently. This leads to cost savings, improved productivity, and better utilization of available resources.

- *Enhanced Customer Experience:* Predictive analytics enables businesses to enhance the customer experience by providing personalized product recommendations based on user behavior. By analyzing customer data, businesses can understand individual preferences and tailor their offerings accordingly, leading to increased customer satisfaction and loyalty.
- *Personalization*: Predictive analytics are widely used to personalize customer experiences. Netflix, for example, uses predictive algorithms and data from a user's viewing history to recommend movies and shows.
- *Risk Reduction:* The likelihood of default by a buyer or a consumer of a service may be assessed in advance by the credit score, applying predictive analytics. The credit score is generated by the predictive model using all the data related to the person's creditworthiness. Credit card issuers and insurance companies apply this to identify fraudulent customers.

Figure 1.11 shows some benefits of predictive analytics [10].

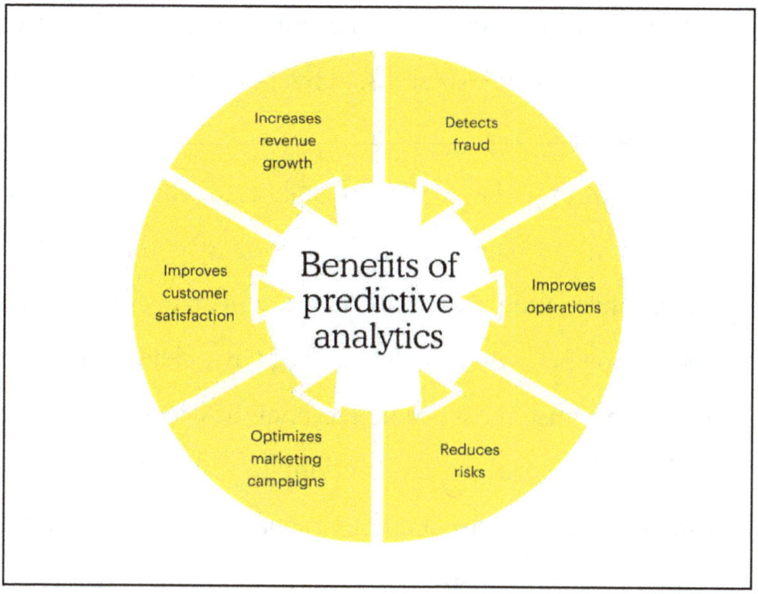

Figure 1.11 Some benefits of predictive analytics [10].

1.5 CHALLENGES

While the challenges and risks associated with predictive analytics can seem daunting, they can be avoided if those behind predictive models are well-trained and knowledgeable in data. Other challenges of predictive analytics include the following [9,13]:

- *Ethical Concerns:* Predictive analytics often uses personal data, and it is important to handle this information responsibly. As the use of personal data in analytics grows, ensuring data privacy and security will be paramount. Regulations and best practices will continue to evolve to protect individuals. Mitigating bias in data and algorithms will be crucial to ensuring the fair and responsible use of predictive analytics across diverse demographics and social groups.

- *Data Quality:* The quality of data used, for example, can present a problem since if the data is inaccurate or incomplete, the predictions made will likely be that way, too. Using poor-quality data will always yield poor-quality results because most predictive analytics models are literal in how they process data. Ultimately, the quality of the data delivered from predictive analytics depends on the quality of the data source.
- *Data Bias:* If the data used to train a model contains biases, then those biases can carry over into the predictions. This can lead to unfair or harmful outcomes, which are especially problematic in areas such as hiring, lending, or law enforcement. People are prone to putting their inherent biases into their queries, no matter how hard they try to keep them out. These biases then become part of the modeling process, resulting in data that is less accurate than it could be.
- *Privacy and Security:* Privacy and security are two major issues businesses face when using predictive analytics. The data analytics process sometimes involves reviewing user accounts for data, which users agree to when they sign up. However, the business is responsible for

maintaining account security and must handle the resulting data responsibly. Personal information is easily misused for fraudulent activities, and the business can be held liable for its failure to maintain privacy and security.

- *Interpretability:* The effectiveness of the data that is delivered by predictive analytics is dependent on the person who is reading the data. The data derived from the model may be excellent, but if the person reading the results doesn't have a good idea of what they are looking for, the data is essentially useless. Whoever prepares the data needs to make it accessible for readers who can understand the results, but may not be able to parse the syntax, so the data makes sense.

1.6 CONCLUSION

Predictive analytics is the practice of using statistical algorithms and machine learning techniques to analyze historical data, identify patterns, and predict future outcomes. It is an advanced branch of data science that uses historical data, statistical modeling, and machine learning to answer the question, “What might happen next?” It is the process of using data to forecast future outcomes with high precision. It is used to predict future events. It facilitates visualizing the future and is more reliable and accurate than previous tools.

Traditional forecasting methods often rely on historical trends and simple statistical models, which can be prone to errors, particularly in volatile markets. Predictive analytics, however, leverages more sophisticated algorithms, incorporates a wider range of data sources, and accounts for external factors that might influence demand. More information on the applications of predictive analytics is available from the books in [19-24].

REFERENCES

[1] "Amazing predictive analytics: 5 Ways to revolutionize your business,"

https://techaku.com/amazing-predictive-analytics-5-ways-to-revolutionize-your-business/

[2] "How to use the new predictive analytics in your budgeting process,"

https://verdivision.com/2019/08/12/predictive-analytics-budgeting-process/

[3] M. N. O. Sadiku, S. A. Ajayi, and J. O. Sadiku, "Applications of predictive analytics," *International Journal of Trend in Scientific Research and Development*, vol. 10, no. 2, March-April, 2026, pp. 1045-1054.

[4] "Supply chain predictive analytics: What is it and who's doing it?"

https://riverlogic.com/?blog=supply-chain-predictive-analytics-what-is-it-and-whos-doing-it

[5] N. Babin, "AI and predictive analytics: Revolutionizing demand forecasting in supply chain management,"

https://www.linkedin.com/pulse/ai-predictive-analytics-revolutionizing-demand-supply-nicolas-babin-xrj2e/

[6] “The role of analytics in marketing: Types of analytics, marketing analytics process and tools,” February 2024,

https://www.sprinkledata.com/blogs/the-role-of-analytics-in-marketing-types-of-analytics-marketing-analytics-process-and-tools

[7] “An overview of supply chain analytics,” February 2023, Unknown Source.

[8] I. Tymchuk, “Big data and predictive analytics in supply chain: Success stories and tips,” November 2020,

https://www.n-ix.com/big-data-predictive-analytics-supply-chain-case-study/

[9] “Examples of predictive analytics in the travel industry at Jordan Judah,”

https://asktheman.xyz/

[10] “The basics of predictive analytics: From data to insights,”

https://mailchimp.com/resources/predicitve-analytics/

[11] L. Ticong, “6 Industry-leading predictive analytics examples & applications,” April 2024,

https://www.datamation.com/big-data/predictive-analytics-examples/

[12] C. Yun et al., "Predictive analytics: A survey, trends, applications, opportunities, and challenges for smart city planning," *International Journal of Computer Science and Information Technology*, vol. 23, no. 56, May 2022, pp. 226-231.

[13] "How can you improve your predictive analytics with ML?" July 2022,

https://www.turing.com/kb/predictive-analytics-with-ml

[14] K. Lewis, "Predictive analytics in healthcare: Current & future uses," April 2024,

https://www.linkedin.com/pulse/predictive-analytics-healthcare-current-future-uses-kevin-lewis-gyckc

[15] "Predictive analytics for businesses: Why is it important?"

https://visiochart.com/blog/predictive-analytics-business/

[16] "What is predictive analytics?"

https://www.adjust.com/glossary/predictive-analytics/

[17] "What is predictive analytics and how does it work?"

https://www.geeksforgeeks.org/data-analysis/what-is-predictive-analytics-and-how-does-it-work/

[18] "What is predictive analytics and why it matters,"
https://ischool.syracuse.edu/what-is-predictive-analytics/

[19] E. Siegel, *Predictive Analytics: The Power to Predict Who Will Click, Buy, Lie, or Die.* Wiley, 2016.

[20] N. A. Ali, *Predictive Analytics for the Modern Enterprise: A Practitioner's Guide to Designing and Implementing Solutions.* O'Reilly Media, 2024.

[21] A. Bari, M. Chaouchi, and T. Jung, *Predictive Analytics For Dummies*. For Dummies, 2nd edition, 2016.

[22] D. T. Larose, *Data Mining and Predictive Analytics.* Wiley, 2025.

[23] I. D. Dinov, *Data Science and Predictive Analytics: Biomedical and Health Applications using R*. Springer, 2nd edition, 2023.

[24] D. Abbott, *Applied Predictive Analytics: Principles and Techniques for the Professional Data Analyst.* Wiley, 2014.

CHAPTER 2
PREDICTIVE ANALYTICS IN HEALTHCARE

"I have a dream that my four little children will one day live in a nation where they will not be judged by the color of their skin but by the content of their character."

– Martin Luther King, Jr.

2.1 INTRODUCTION

In the dynamic, unpredictable landscape of healthcare, the ability to foresee future events is becoming increasingly crucial. The shift from reactive to proactive care represents one of the most significant advancements in the industry. At the heart of this transformation is predictive analytics, a branch of advanced data science. By leveraging vast amounts of data and sophisticated algorithms, AI-powered predictive analytics enables healthcare professionals to anticipate and address medical issues before they escalate, thereby improving patient outcomes and optimizing the overall efficiency of healthcare systems. The primary goal is to identify patterns and forecast future events, such as disease outbreaks, patient readmission risks, or the effectiveness of specific treatments [1].

Predictive analytics has emerged as a transformative tool in the healthcare sector, enabling the use of vast amounts of patient data to predict and prevent disease, optimize treatment plans, and enhance healthcare services. Predictive analytics in healthcare is a type of analytics that evaluates current and historical data to predict future events. For example, recent research has shown that predictive analytics using social and environmental patient data provides better risk estimates for cardiovascular disease [2].

The healthcare landscape is undergoing a data-driven revolution, with predictive analytics reshaping how we approach healthcare delivery and management. Predictive analytics, a powerful branch of data science, is transforming how healthcare providers, payers, and researchers approach patient care, operational efficiency, and strategic planning. In healthcare, this means moving beyond simply treating existing conditions to anticipating patient needs, preventing complications, and optimizing the entire delivery system. By turning vast amounts of clinical and administrative data into actionable insights, predictive analytics is redefining what is possible in-patient care and organizational efficiency. The promise of predictive analytics in healthcare is nothing short of revolutionary [3].

In this chapter, we will provide an introduction to the use of predictive analytics in healthcare. The chapter begins by explaining predictive analytics. It describes predictive analytics in healthcare and provides some of its applications. It highlights some benefits and challenges of predictive analytics in healthcare. It predicts the future of predictive analytics in healthcare. The last section concludes with comments.

2.2 WHAT IS PREDICTIVE ANALYTICS?

As its name implies, predictive analytics involves forecasting future trends, such as sales demand and exchange rates. and other important metrics. The technique relies on applying statistical modeling and regression analysis to historical data to identify and understand trends and forecast future ones. Strictly speaking, predictive analytics does not predict the future; rather, it uses probability theory to determine what is likely to happen based on patterns and trends revealed by analyzing historical data [4]. Predictive analytics accurately anticipates customer demand, preventing overstocking and stockouts while adapting to market changes. Figure 2.1 illustrates predictive analytics [5], while Figure 2.2 shows different components of predictive analytics [6].

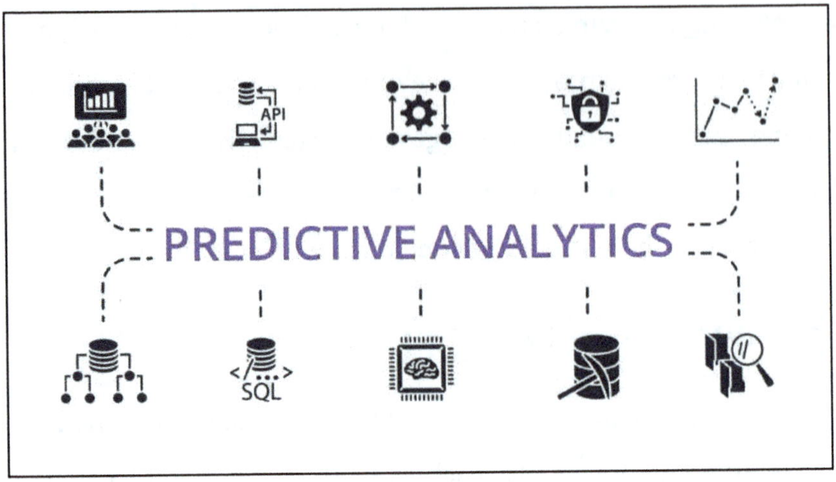

Figure 2.1 Predictive analytics [5].

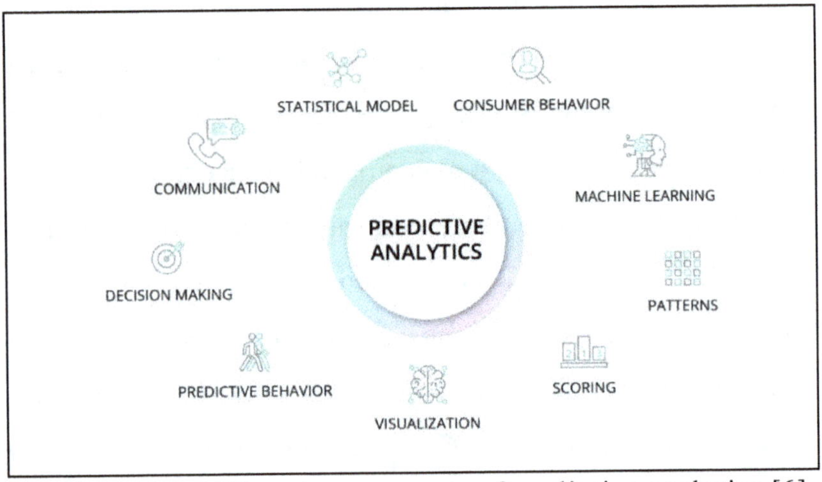

Figure 2.2 Different components of predictive analytics [6].

In general, analytics provides an efficient way to improve planning by giving you better forecasts. There are different types of data analytics. They are briefly explained as follows [7]:

- *Descriptive Analytics:* Descriptive analytics examines what has happened over the years. They are capable of detecting trends in historical data. Analytics can uncover trends and propose probable reasons for change by comparing the same data across different periods. It can be seen as the industry baseline, which assesses past and current data to generate more meaningful insights and delivers them to people so they can use their own intelligence and knowledge to make decisions.
- *Predictive Analytics:* This assists businesses in predicting what might happen and the impact of various situations, such as possible supply chain bottlenecks. Managers can be proactive rather than reactive by pushing them to evaluate these prospective circumstances before they occur. Predictive analytics may be used to identify patterns and trends and to anticipate breakdowns that may impact suppliers and, consequently, production processes. Predictive analytics for the supply chain leverages data, statistical algorithms, and machine learning techniques to identify the likelihood of future outcomes.
- *Prescriptive Analytics:* Prescriptive analytics builds on predictive analytics and dives deeper into predicting future

insights on what can be done next. Prescriptive analytics uses the findings of descriptive and predictive analytics to recommend what measures a business should take to achieve its objectives. Because prescriptive analytics is increasingly complex, it requires more powerful software capable of rapidly processing and interpreting large amounts of data.

- *Cognitive Analytics:* Cognitive analytics attempts to mimic human thought and behavior, and they can assist companies in answering challenging, complex problems. Cognitive analytics does this by utilizing artificial intelligence (AI), which enables it to improve over time. Using AI in the industry to answer complex questions and draw contextual conclusions about how humans would have interacted with the situation. It helps with more meaningful data, scaled experience, and knowledge, leading to better decisions.
- *Diagnostics Analytics:* This gives the ability to identify the root cause. It is characterized by techniques such as drill-down, data discovery, data mining, and correlations. It involves analyzing overall performance and figuring out why errors, mistakes, and delays occur. It lets the manager know the delays, breakdowns, and disruptions in the demand and supply processes and the reasons behind them.

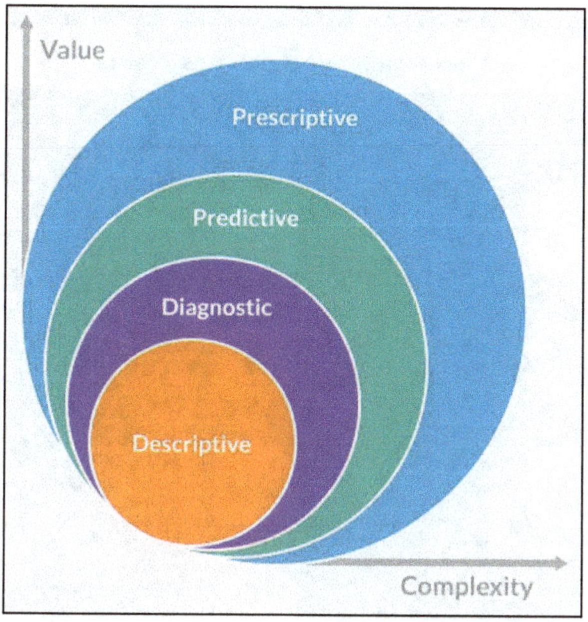

Figure 2.3 Types of data analytics [8].

Figure 2.3 shows these major types of data analytics [8]. Unlike diagnostic and descriptive analytics, which analyze situations after they occur, predictive analytics uses advanced techniques to forecast future outcomes. In the supply chain, it is time to shift from mere descriptive and diagnostic analytics to predictive and prescriptive analytics. Predictive analytics is a branch of data analytics that uses historical data, statistical modeling, data mining techniques, and machine learning to predict future outcomes. Figure 2.4 shows how predictive analytics works [9].

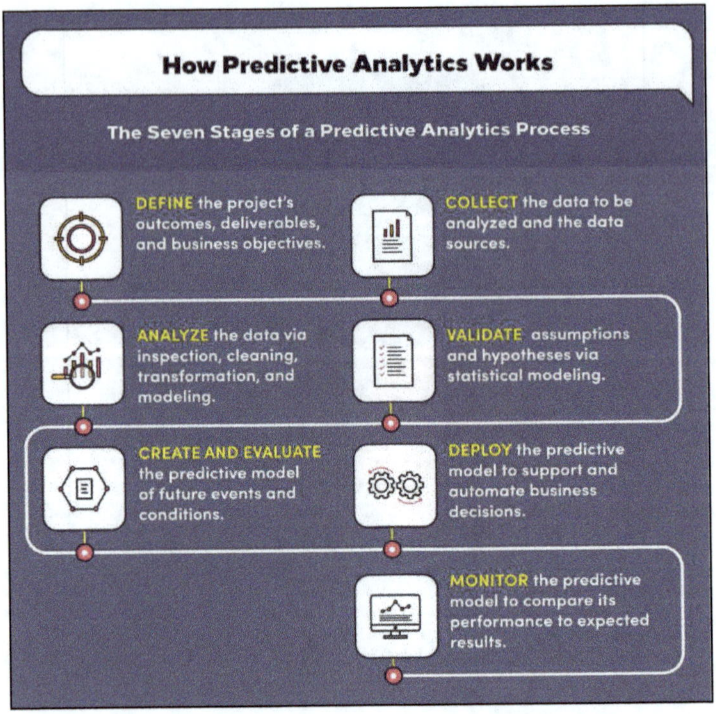

Figure 2.4 Predictive analytics process [9].

2.3 PREDICTIVE ANALYTICS IN HEALTHCARE

In the unpredictable and often emergent environment of the healthcare industry, teams across the care continuum need proactive approaches to stay ahead. Predictive analytics is a key component of success across teams, enhancing patient outcomes, financial performance, and operational efficiency. It is undeniably transforming healthcare, offering unprecedented opportunities for proactive patient care, operational optimization, and the advancement of precision medicine. By analyzing historical and real-time data, healthcare providers can forecast high-risk clinical events, allowing for early intervention that improves patient survival rates and reduces the financial burden on the healthcare system. The journey of predictive analytics in healthcare involves four stages: data collection, preprocessing, modeling, and interpretation of results [10].

Interest in predictive analytics has grown alongside pressures affecting healthcare systems globally. Demand is increasing, driven by aging populations, escalating operational costs, resource scarcity, and a higher prevalence of chronic conditions. Predictive analytics aims to alert clinicians and caregivers to the likelihood of events and outcomes before they occur, helping them prevent health issues rather than merely cure them. Figure 2.5 shows predictive analytics in healthcare [11], while Figure 2.6 shows some healthcare analysts [12].

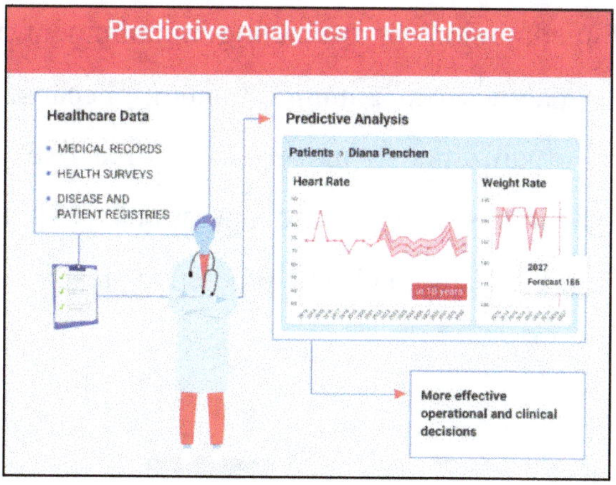

Figure 2.5 Predictive analytics in healthcare [11].

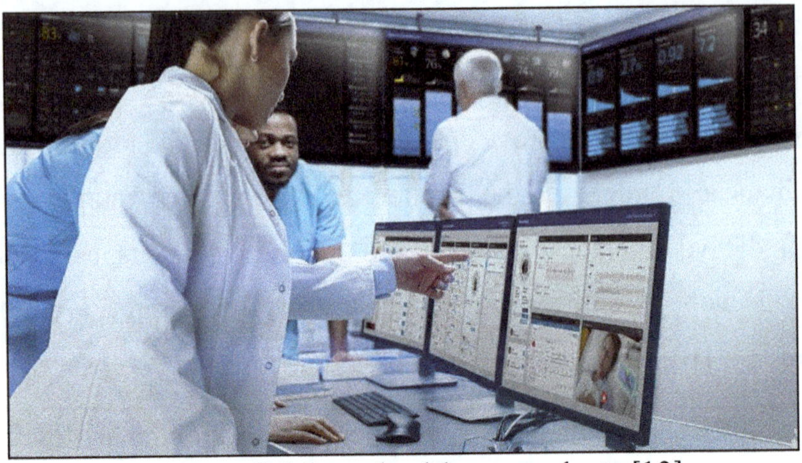

Figure 2.6 Some healthcare analysts [12].

In a healthcare context, predictive analytics refers to the use of historical and real-time data to estimate the likelihood of future events. Predictive models typically combine statistical modeling, machine learning, and data analysis techniques to identify patterns that are not readily apparent through manual review. The value comes from relatively focused models applied to well-defined problems, such as identifying patients at risk of readmission or predicting appointment no-shows. Predictive analytics is gaining traction because it helps healthcare organizations move from reactive to more anticipatory models of care and operations [13]. Figure 2.7 presents both the traditional and predictive treatment methods [14].

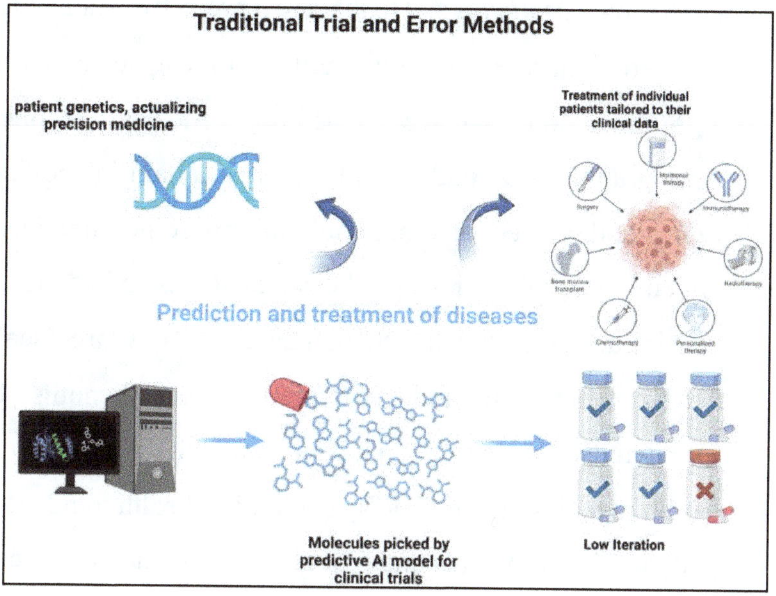

Figure 2.7 Traditional and predictive methods of treatment [14].

2.4 APPLICATIONS OF PREDICTIVE ANALYTICS IN HEALTHCARE

Predictive analytics impacts every facet of healthcare and opens up exciting possibilities, from earlier interventions to a more customized, thoughtful, and engaging patient experience. It is already being applied across a range of clinical and operational settings. From preventing costly readmissions and optimizing clinical decisions to managing population health and accelerating drug discovery, the applications of predictive analytics are vast and impactful. Common applications of predictive analytics in healthcare include the following [1,11,13,15-17]:

- *Predictive Modeling*: Healthcare predictive analytics software analyzes current and historical data using algorithms and statistical methods. Medical records, demographic data, and patient histories all aid in spotting trends and connections that could otherwise go unnoticed. By taking a global view, predictive analytics in healthcare can influence global health management and large-scale health trends, in addition to providing benefits to individuals. Predictive analytics can help guide public health planning and policy by examining health trends and patterns. Governments and global health organizations can use this information to plan immunization campaigns, allocate funds, and implement preventive health initiatives. Clinical treatment and operational effectiveness both benefit from predictive analytics.
- *Patient Care:* The most direct impact of predictive analytics is felt at the point of care. One of its primary clinical applications is early diagnosis and risk stratification. By analyzing patterns in electronic health records (EHRs), lab results, and even wearable device data, predictive models can identify patients at high risk for developing chronic conditions such as diabetes, heart disease, or sepsis long before clinical symptoms become severe. For instance, sepsis—a leading cause of hospital mortality—can often be predicted hours in advance

through real-time monitoring of vital signs, allowing clinicians to intervene during the critical "golden hour." Beyond individual patient care, predictive analytics can optimize hospital operations and resource management. Figure 2.8 shows a clinical trial [18], while Figure 2.9 shows some caregivers [12].

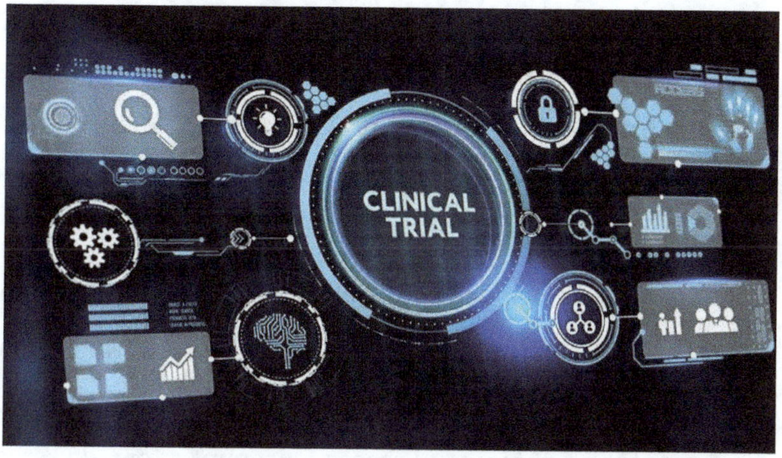

Figure 2.8 A representation of a clinical trial [18].

Figure 2.9 Some caregivers [12].

- *Personalized Medicine:* Predictive analytics is a cornerstone of personalized medicine. Traditional "one-size-fits-all" treatment protocols are being replaced by tailored approaches that consider a patient's unique genetic profile, lifestyle, and medical history. Predictive models can forecast how a specific individual might respond to a particular medication or treatment plan, reducing the need for trial and error and minimizing adverse drug reactions. This precision not only improves recovery rates but also enhances the overall patient experience by providing truly individualized care.
- *Disease Management:* Chronic diseases are the leading causes of death and disability in the US, as well as the main drivers of the country's $3.5 trillion in annual health costs. Five chronic diseases account for 75% of healthcare spending: cancer, cardiovascular disease, diabetes, obesity, and kidney disease. Chronic disease management depends on the ability of healthcare professionals to prevent their development and control them. Predictive analytics is particularly valuable in managing chronic diseases such as diabetes and heart disease. By continuously monitoring patient data, AI can detect early signs of disease exacerbation and prompt timely interventions. For conditions like diabetes and heart disease, predictive models can analyze blood sugar

levels, heart rate, and other vital signs to predict potential complications and recommend preventive measures.

- *Population Health Management:* Predictive analytics is not only applicable at the individual level. Healthcare organizations can also use it for population health management. When they have data on patients' conditions, medications, and personal histories, analytics can be used to identify similar patients within a population cohort. It can also help identify cohorts at risk of a potential disease outbreak. In such a scenario, healthcare professionals can start looking at treatments immediately, which improves people's chances of survival. With predictive analytics, it is possible to extrapolate data from an individual level to a population cohort with similar characteristics. This way, it is possible to treat a patient using a cross-patient pool of consolidated data.
- *Resource Optimization:* Efficient resource allocation is a critical concern in healthcare management. Predictive analytics plays a crucial role in enhancing operational efficiency and optimizing resource allocation within healthcare facilities. Operationally, predictive analytics helps optimize resources. Hospitals can forecast patient admission rates, emergency department surges, and even the demand for specific medical supplies. This foresight allows administrators to schedule staff more effectively

and manage inventory with greater precision, reducing wait times for patients and lowering the facility's overhead costs.

- *Patient Stratification:* Predictive analytics enables early diagnosis and preventive care by identifying health risks before they escalate. Identifying high-risk patients before their health issues escalate is crucial, especially for managing chronic conditions like heart disease and cancer, which are leading causes of death and disability. Predictive analytics enables patient stratification, allowing for proactive interventions and preventive care tailored to individual risk profiles.
- *Risk Prediction*: One of the most established uses of predictive analytics in healthcare is identifying patients at risk of deterioration before it becomes clinically obvious. Predictive models are used to flag risks such as sepsis, cardiac events, hospital readmission, or complications linked to chronic conditions. These predictions are based on patterns found in vital signs, laboratory results, medical history, and wider behavioral or social data. If a patient at risk can be identified earlier, clinicians have more scope to intervene before the situation escalates. This can reduce avoidable admissions, shorten recovery times, and improve outcomes. By identifying risk earlier, predictive

analytics gives clinicians a better chance to act before a situation escalates into something more serious.

- *Fraud Detection:* Fraud in healthcare is a common problem. The financial implications of healthcare fraud are staggering. Predictive analytics can be used to detect fraudulent claims and billing practices. Data-driven fraud detection systems have been widely implemented in healthcare, resulting in significant cost savings. Predictive analytics plays a vital role in fraud detection, combating the estimated $300 billion lost annually to healthcare fraud. In the realm of health insurance, predictive tools are used for fraud detection and cost forecasting, identifying suspicious claims patterns and helping payers manage risk more accurately. Payers can analyze claims data to identify fraudulent behavior patterns, detect them early, and prevent insurance abuse. This significantly impacts healthcare costs.
- *Insurance Claims:* Another use of predictive analytics in healthcare is the ability to calculate the accurate cost of health insurance for each specific individual based on age, gender, medical history, insurance case history, heredity, etc. The use of predictive analytics in health insurance is rapidly expanding. To accurately predict a patient's health risks and determine insurance premiums, insurers are leveraging this technology. In the healthcare industry,

advanced analytics has also been instrumental in revolutionizing the claim reimbursement procedure. Hospitals can benefit from faster insurance reimbursements by having better financial flow. It can assist companies in managing operating costs, providing high-quality patient care, and streamlining administrative processes. Healthcare companies can review their applications before submission by using predictive analysis. Predictive analytics can help calculate the cost of health insurance for a specific person with higher precision by cross-analyzing data such as age, gender, genetics, and medical history.

- *Demand Forecasting:* Giving the right medicines at the right time to a patient suffering from a disease is crucial for doctors in saving lives. A healthcare project aims to estimate the demand for healthcare products using predictive analytics. It will guide you in drawing various plots and deducing insightful conclusions from them.

2.5 BENEFITS

By leveraging predictive analytics in healthcare, organizations can experience many benefits. Predictive analytics offers benefits to many teams across the care continuum. Care managers and clinical teams can use predictive models to create treatment plans tailored to each patient's profile and allocate time and resources where they are most needed. As shown in Figure 2.10, predictive analytics improves patient outcomes [19]. Other benefits of predictive analytics in healthcare include the following [1,2,10,18]:

Figure 2.10 Predictive analytics improves patient outcomes [19].

- *Cost Reduction:* The financial implications of predictive analytics in healthcare are profound. By preventing diseases, reducing hospital readmissions, and optimizing treatment plans, predictive analytics can significantly lower healthcare costs. For example, predictive models can identify patients at high risk of readmission and recommend follow-up care or lifestyle changes to prevent unnecessary hospital stays. This not only improves patient outcomes but also reduces the financial burden on healthcare systems. A patient's expected healthcare costs can be forecast by understanding their past utilization and treatment needs. By calculating the likely cost of care, health plans can set appropriate premiums and manage risk proactively to help minimize unnecessary spending.

- *Resource Allocation*: Healthcare organizations have successfully used predictive analytics to optimize resource allocation. By effectively allocating healthcare resources, providers reduce burnout and maximize their capacity – a critical benefit for any provider facing a staff shortage. Predictive analytics solutions can also identify patients likely to miss their appointments, helping prevent that time slot from going to waste. Over time, effective resource allocation will lead to cost savings for the organization and improve profitability.
- *Disease Prevention:* Research studies have shown that predictive analytics can improve early disease detection. Healthcare professionals and health insurance companies use predictive algorithms to assess the likelihood that a patient will develop an illness. Once healthcare providers detect this risk, they can offer treatment plans to help the patient. Predictive models can also be applied to detect early disease symptoms, enabling care before the onset of

more severe symptoms that require more expensive treatments.

- *Readmission Prevention:* One of the most successful use cases of predictive analytics is readmission prevention. Hospital readmissions pose a substantial challenge to healthcare systems, leading to poorer patient outcomes and considerable financial burdens. They are not only detrimental to patient health but also a significant financial burden on the healthcare system, costing billions of dollars annually. Predictive models can identify patients at high risk of readmission upon discharge, enabling care teams to implement targeted follow-up plans, such as home health visits or medication reconciliation, to support a successful recovery.
- *Clinical Decision Support:* Predictive analytics empowers clinicians with real-time insights to make more informed decisions. This includes early diagnosis of conditions by detecting subtle signs of diseases, forecasting a patient's response to specific treatments to avoid trial-and-error approaches, and continuously monitoring critical conditions to spot early warning signs.
- *Disease Prevention:* One of the most profound impacts of predictive analytics lies in its ability to facilitate early disease prevention and detection. Physicians and nurses must act fast to identify any deterioration in a patient's

health in both conventional hospital wards and intensive care units. By analyzing a patient's comprehensive medical history, laboratory results, and demographic information, predictive models can generate risk scores that identify individuals at risk of developing chronic conditions such as diabetes or heart disease. This proactive identification allows healthcare providers to intervene earlier, thereby significantly improving long-term health outcomes and potentially averting severe health crises.

- *Enhanced Cybersecurity:* Cyberattacks are common in the medical field. According to the research, hacking was the most frequent cause of the more than 82.6 million compromised medical records between January and October 2023. Cybersecurity predictive analytics has the potential to improve healthcare. Real-time risk scores for various online transactions can be computed by healthcare companies using predictive analytics and artificial intelligence solutions for the medical industry. Based on these scores, events can be responded to.

Figure 2.11 shows some benefits of predictive analytics in healthcare [11].

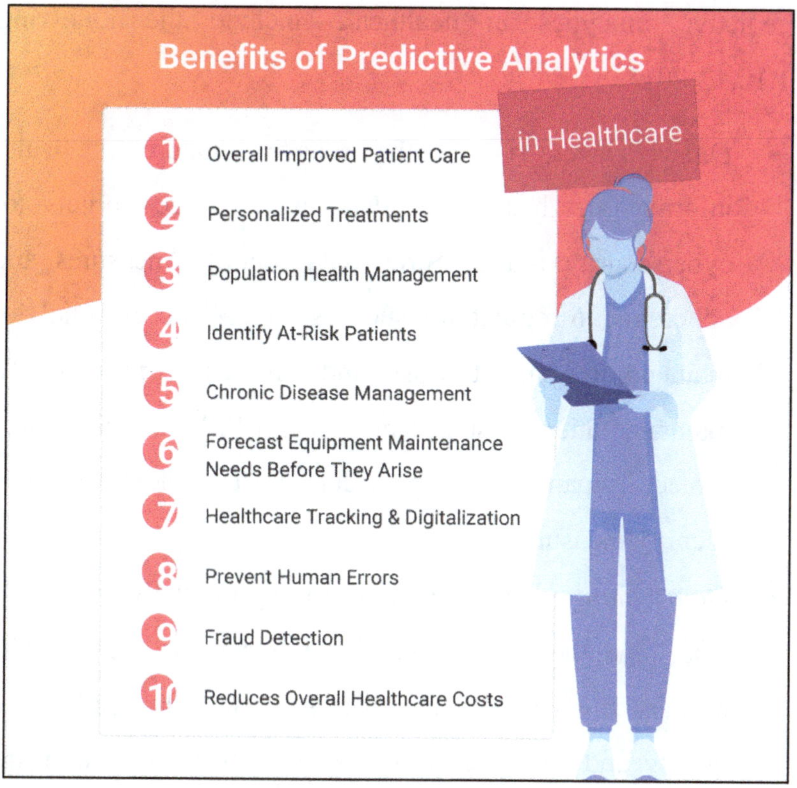

Figure 2.11 Some benefits of predictive analytics in healthcare [11].

2.6 CHALLENGES

Despite its immense potential, implementing predictive analytics in healthcare is not without challenges and risks. Data privacy, data quality, algorithmic bias, accuracy, ethical considerations, interoperability, and security remain paramount concerns, as the use of sensitive patient information requires robust protection against breaches. Other challenges of predictive analytics in healthcare include the following [1,10,13,20]:

- *Data Privacy:* Given the sensitive nature of health information, healthcare data is a huge target for cybersecurity issues. Strict data security measures and adherence to regulations such as HIPAA are essential for maintaining patient trust and protecting privacy. To maintain patient trust, comply with HIPAA regulations, and protect human privacy, providers must employ strict data security measures.
- *Data Quality:* The foundation of any predictive model is data, and healthcare data is notoriously messy. The primary challenge is not accessing data, but rather the quality and consistency of that data. In many healthcare environments, data is incomplete, inconsistently recorded, or spread across multiple systems that do not integrate easily. Missing values, duplicate records, inconsistent coding, and unstructured free-text clinical notes often plague healthcare datasets. Electronic health records, diagnostic platforms, administrative systems, and remote monitoring tools often operate in silos rather than within a unified data environment. This fragmentation affects both accuracy and timeliness.

- *Ethical Concerns*: Addressing bias and ethical concerns in predictive analytics is essential. Ethical considerations, including data privacy, bias, and accountability, are vital to the responsible implementation of AI in healthcare. Implementing fairness-aware AI and bias mitigation techniques can help create more equitable and transparent predictive models. Ethical considerations, such as addressing healthcare disparities and mitigating bias in data and algorithms, also need ongoing attention.
- *Bias:* The issue of algorithmic bias has gained significant attention. Predictive analytics algorithms can inadvertently perpetuate or amplify existing implicit biases present in historical data, leading to unfair outcomes or exacerbating healthcare disparities for certain demographic groups. If the historical data used to train these models contains biases related to race, gender, or socioeconomic status, the resulting predictions may inadvertently perpetuate health disparities. Ensuring that models are fair, transparent, and validated across diverse populations is a critical step for the industry. Continuous critical examination of algorithmic outputs and proactive measures to mitigate bias are necessary to ensure equitable care.
- *Accuracy:* Predictive analytics reflects the data it learns from. If that data is skewed or unrepresentative, the outputs will be too. Predictive models are under constant

scrutiny to avoid potential misdiagnoses, biases, or treatment errors. They must be rigorously validated to prevent misdiagnoses, biases, or treatment errors. A lack of trust in the model due to inaccuracies can hinder its adoption and impact patient safety.

- *Economic Reality:* The economic realities of implementing predictive analytics cannot be ignored. Developing and deploying large-scale predictive systems requires significant financial investment. Costs for comprehensive implementations are high. The long-term return on investment—through reduced readmissions, optimized staffing, and better patient outcomes—can be substantial. The high upfront costs and the risk of project failure deter many organizations from pursuing advanced analytics initiatives.
- *Organizational Culture:* Perhaps the most significant barrier to the successful adoption of predictive analytics is organizational culture and workflow integration. If a predictive tool requires clinicians to log in to a separate system, manually enter data, or disrupt their established routines, it will face steep resistance. To be effective, predictive insights must be delivered seamlessly within the clinician's existing workflow, providing actionable recommendations at the point of care.

- *Physician Adoption:* Physician adoption is another critical hurdle. Many healthcare professionals are unfamiliar with AI-driven tools or are skeptical of their clinical validity. There is a strong desire to maintain clinical autonomy, and clinicians may resist tools that appear to dictate patient care, especially if the model operates as a "black box" where the reasoning behind a prediction is not transparent.
- *Regulatory Compliance:* The integration of predictive analytics into healthcare raises profound ethical and legal questions. Patient privacy and data security are paramount concerns. Healthcare organizations must navigate complex regulations, such as the Health Insurance Portability and Accountability Act (HIPAA) in the United States, to ensure that the use of extensive data complies with strict privacy standards.
- *Interoperability:* Encouraging interoperability and data sharing among healthcare systems and institutions is crucial. It enables the creation of more comprehensive datasets and more accurate predictive models.
- *Explainability:* For predictive analytics to be used in practice, clinicians and operational teams need to trust the output. This becomes more complex as models increase in sophistication. Some machine learning systems operate as "black boxes," where the reasoning behind a prediction is not easily explained. In clinical settings, it is more

problematic. Decisions that affect patient care require strict transparency, or at least a level of interpretability that allows professionals to understand and challenge the output.

- *Human Errors*: The impact that human errors could have on healthcare could be fatal. Providing real-time, accurate insights to guide medical professionals' actions, data can help flag potential errors and prevent fatal mistakes.

2.7 FUTURE OF PREDICTIVE ANALYTICS IN HEALTHCARE

Predictive analytics can have a huge impact on the healthcare sector as technology advances. It holds the potential to transform healthcare from a reactive system to a proactive, data-driven enterprise. As the healthcare industry continues its journey towards a more proactive, personalized, and efficient model, predictive analytics will undoubtedly serve as a cornerstone, empowering stakeholders to deliver higher-quality care, improve patient outcomes, and build a healthier future for all. The continued integration of artificial intelligence and machine learning, which promises to refine predictive capabilities further, is vital. These innovations will drive significant improvements in patient care, operational efficiency, and overall healthcare outcomes. As we move forward, the goal of predictive analytics in healthcare remains clear: to harness the power of data to save lives, reduce costs, and ensure that the right care reaches the right patient at the right time [1].

As the healthcare industry continues to evolve, predictive analytics stands at the forefront of innovation, offering the promise of improved patient outcomes, reduced costs, and better resource allocation. Imagine a world where doctors can anticipate medical issues before they arise, treatments are tailored to individual patients' unique needs, and healthcare resources are allocated precisely. This is not a distant future; it is the reality that predictive analytics in healthcare is creating today [16].

2.8 CONCLUSION

Predictive analytics is no longer a futuristic concept; it is a powerful tool currently reshaping the healthcare industry. By enabling earlier diagnoses, personalizing treatments, and streamlining operations, it offers a path toward a more efficient and effective healthcare system. Predictive analytics in healthcare refers to using statistical algorithms and machine learning methods to detect patterns in data and predict future events. Using large-scale data from multiple sources, healthcare data analysis can provide invaluable insights into patient health, disease progression, and treatment efficacy. The use of predictive analytics provides healthcare organizations with a better understanding of how a patient will respond to treatment and whether they are at a higher risk of developing complications. Researchers and hospitals that have used predictive analytics have gained important insights and seen meaningful improvements in patient outcomes.

Predictive analytics in healthcare uses technology to create more effective, economical systems and to enhance the health of individuals and the community as a whole. Predictive analytics is becoming a more visible part of decision-making across healthcare systems. It is changing health outcomes through personalized care delivery, proactive risk identification, and improved operational outcomes. Health systems have used it to create platforms for predicting and preventing the most common and costly diagnoses, provide enhanced accuracy in predicting length of stay, and help providers personalize treatments. Applied properly, it can help organizations identify risk earlier, reduce avoidable readmissions, improve capacity planning, and make more effective use of limited resources. More information on the use of predictive analytics in healthcare is available from the books in [21-32].

REFERENCES

[1] https://manus.im

[2] "Predictive analytics in healthcare: Use cases & examples," https://www.twilio.com/en-us/resource-center/predictive-analytics-healthcare

[3] M. N. O. Sadiku, M. Oteniya, and J. O. Sadiku, "Predictive analytics in healthcare," *International Journal of Trend in Scientific Research and Development*, vol. 10, no.3, May-June 2026, pp. 269-280.

[4] "Supply chain predictive analytics: What is it and who's doing it?"

https://riverlogic.com/?blog=supply-chain-predictive-analytics-what-is-it-and-whos-doing-it

[5] N. Babin, "AI and predictive analytics: Revolutionizing demand forecasting in supply chain management,"

https://www.linkedin.com/pulse/ai-predictive-analytics-revolutionizing-demand-supply-nicolas-babin-xrj2e/

[6] "From insight to innovation: Why data analysis will define industry leaders in 2025," https://www.inkl.com/news/from-insight-to-innovation-why-data-analysis-will-define-industry-leaders-in-2025

[7] "An overview of supply chain analytics," February 2023, Unknown Source.

[8] I. Tymchuk, "Big data and predictive analytics in supply chain: Success stories and tips," November 2020,

https://www.n-ix.com/big-data-predictive-analytics-supply-chain-case-study/

[9] "Predictive analytics in insurance: Types, tools, and the future," October 2020,

https://online.maryville.edu/blog/predictive-analytics-in-insurance/

[10] L. Masta, "Predictive analytics in healthcare: A comprehensive guide," March 2026,

https://arcadia.io/resources/predictive-analytics-healthcare

[11] B. Petrova, "Predictive analytics in healthcare," November 2025,

https://www.revealbi.io/blog/predictive-analytics-in-healthcare

[12] "Predictive analytics in healthcare: Three real-world examples," June 2020,

https://www.philips.com/a-w/about/news/archive/features/20200604-predictive-analytics-in-healthcare-three-real-world-examples.html

[13] "Predictive analytics in healthcare: Benefits, uses & risks," April 2026,

https://groupsolutions.three.com/insights/predictive-analytics-in-healthcare

[14] D. Dixon et al., "Unveiling the influence of AI predictive analytics on patient outcomes: A comprehensive narrative review," *Cureus*, vol. 16, no. 6, May 2024.

[15] "How is predictive analytics in healthcare revolutionizing it?"

https://nextgeninvent.com/blogs/predictive-analytics-in-healthcare-revolutionizing-it/

[16] "Predictive analytics in healthcare: How AI is improving patient outcomes,"

https://demolobby.com/veritisbeta/blog/predictive-analytics-in-healthcare-how-ai-is-improving-patient-outcomes/

[17] Manika, "Top 5 predictive analytics in healthcare projects," October 2024,

https://www.projectpro.io/article/predictive-analytics-in-healthcare-projects/732

[18] S. L. Karthika, "AI-powered predictive analytics in health care: Transforming patient outcomes!" May 2024,

https://www.linkedin.com/pulse/ai-powered-predictive-analytics-health-care-transforming-karthika-s-l-rip2c

[19] S. Olumide, "Predictive analytics in healthcare: Improving patient outcomes," https://www.kdnuggets.com/predictive-analytics-in-healthcare-improving-patient-outcomes

[20] M. Nnamdi, "Predictive analytics in healthcare," April 2024, https://www.researchgate.net/publication/379478196_Predictive_Analytics_in_Healthcare

[21] A. Singhal et al. (eds.), *Prediction in Medicine: The Impact of Machine Learning on Healthcare.* Bentham Science Publishers, 2024.

[22] A. Bari, M. Chaouchi, and T. Jung, *Predictive Analytics For Dummies*. For Dummies, 2nd edition, 2016.

[23] V. Subbhuraam (ed.), *Predictive Analytics in Healthcare, Volume 1: Transforming the Future of Medicine.* Institute of Physics Publishing, 2021.

[24] V. Subbhuraam (ed.), *Predictive Analytics in Healthcare: Transforming the Future of Medicine, Volume 2*. Iop Publishing Ltd, 2025.

[25] J. W. Nelson, J. Felgen, and M. A. Hozak (eds.), *Using Predictive Analytics to Improve Healthcare Outcomes*. Wiley, 2021.

[26] G. Ikwe, *Healthcare Analytics for Professionals: Harnessing Data Insights to Transform Patient Care and Operational Excellence.* Independently Published, 2024.

[27] G. Blokdyk, *The Operational Excellence Library; Mastering Predictive Analytics in Healthcare.* 5STARCooks, 2024.

[28] B. Kelley, *Healthcare Data Analytics: Primary Methods and Related Insights.* Independently Published, 2019.

[29] Innoware PJP, *AI and Predictive Analytics in Population Health Management: Transforming Healthcare for the Future.* Independently Published, 2024.

[30] C. E. Morr and H. Ali-Hassan, *Analytics in Healthcare: A Practical Introduction*. Springer, 2019.

[31] C. Chakraborty, K. Dasgupta, and S. Banerjee (eds.), *Green Computing and Predictive Analytics for Healthcare.* Boca Raton, FL: CRC Press, 2020.

[32] G. D. Miner et al., *Practical Predictive Analytics and Decisioning Systems for Medicine.* Academic Press, 2014.

CHAPTER 3 PREDICTIVE ANALYTICS IN BUSINESS

"The best way to predict your future is to create it." - Abraham Lincoln

3.1 INTRODUCTION

In the modern business landscape, data is not just numbers; it is the very essence of innovation. We are in a data-driven world, where information is one of the most valuable assets a business can have. This has given rise to big data analytics, which helps businesses extract meaningful patterns from vast volumes of data. The rise of big data has been a game-changer for predictive analytics, providing the vast amounts of data necessary for accurate predictions. Business predictive analytics enables businesses to anticipate trends, behaviors, and outcomes by analyzing historical and current data. Predictive analytics provides a critical edge in navigating the uncertainties of the business world, allowing companies to anticipate changes, optimize operations, and capitalize on emerging opportunities [1].

Predictive analytics looks for past patterns to measure the likelihood that those patterns will recur. It uses statistical algorithms and machine learning techniques to estimate the likelihood of future outcomes based on historical data. Unlike traditional analytics, which relies on human-defined algorithms, predictive analytics uses artificial intelligence to identify patterns and anomalies independently. Executives and business owners can use this type of statistical analysis to understand customer behavior. Predictive analytics is used in a variety of industries, including finance, healthcare, manufacturing, telecommunications, marketing, and retail [2]. Predictive analytics helps in credit scoring, fraud detection, and investment strategies in finance.

Predictive analytics is the use of statistics and modeling techniques to forecast future outcomes. It uses historical statistics and modeling techniques in forecasting. The goal of predictive analytics is to make predictions about future events, then use those predictions to improve decision-making. By embracing this technology, organizations can tap into its diverse capabilities to drive efficiency and growth in an increasingly data-driven world. Predictive analysis can be used in several different applications—industries from insurance to marketing use predictive techniques to make important decisions. Businesses use predictive analytics to fine-tune their operations and decide whether new products are worth the investment. Investors use predictive analytics to decide where to put their money. Predictive analytics has become a pivotal tool for gaining a competitive advantage [3].

This chapter explores how predictive analytics is reshaping business strategy across industries. It begins by explaining predictive analytics. It describes predictive analytics in business and provides some of its applications. It highlights some benefits and challenges of predictive analytics in business. It predicts the future of predictive analytics in business. The last section concludes with comments.

3.2 WHAT IS PREDICTIVE ANALYTICS?

As its name implies, predictive analytics involves forecasting future trends, such as sales demand and exchange rates. and other important metrics. The technique relies on applying statistical modeling and regression analysis to historical data to identify and understand trends and forecast future ones. Strictly speaking, predictive analytics does not predict the future; rather, it uses probability theory to determine what is likely to happen based on patterns and trends revealed by analyzing historical data [4]. Predictive analytics accurately anticipates customer demand, preventing overstocking and stockouts while adapting to market changes. Figure 3.1 illustrates predictive analytics [5], while Figure 3.2 shows different components of predictive analytics [6].

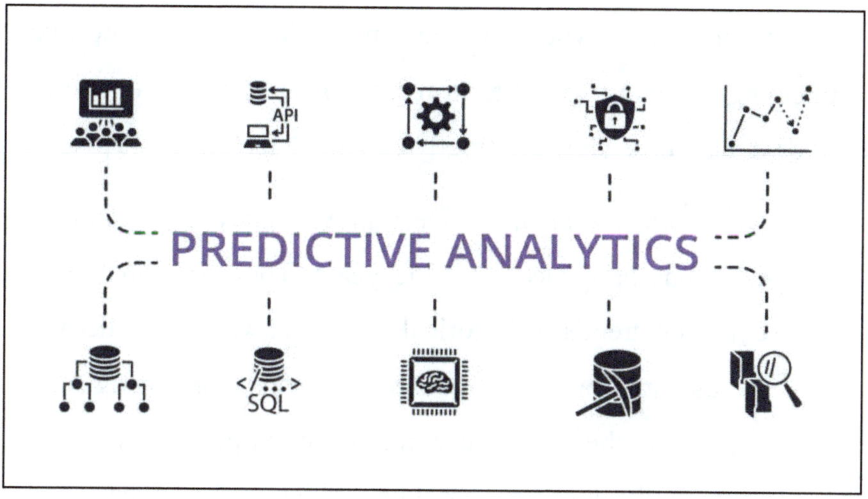

Figure 3.1 Predictive analytics [5].

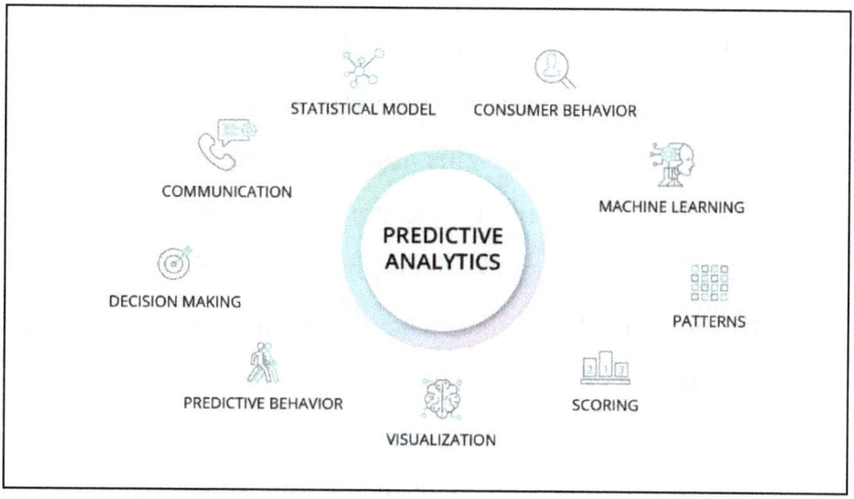

Figure 3.2 Different components of predictive analytics [6].

In general, analytics provides an efficient way to improve planning by giving you better forecasts. There are different types of data analytics. They are briefly explained as follows [7]:

- *Descriptive Analytics:* Descriptive analytics examines what has happened over the years. They are capable of detecting trends in historical data. Analytics can uncover trends and propose probable reasons for change by comparing the same data across different periods. It can be seen as the industry baseline, which assesses past and current data to generate more meaningful insights and delivers them to people so they can use their own intelligence and knowledge to make decisions.
- *Predictive Analytics:* This assists businesses in predicting what might happen and the impact of various situations, such as possible supply chain bottlenecks. Managers can be proactive rather than reactive by encouraging them to evaluate these prospective circumstances before they arise. Predictive analytics may be used to identify patterns and trends and to anticipate breakdowns that may impact suppliers and, consequently, production processes. Predictive analytics for the supply chain leverages data, statistical algorithms, and machine learning techniques to identify the likelihood of future outcomes.
- *Prescriptive Analytics:* Prescriptive analytics builds on predictive analytics and dives deeper into predicting future

insights on what can be done next. Prescriptive analytics uses the findings of descriptive and predictive analytics to recommend what measures a business should take to achieve its objectives. Because prescriptive analytics is increasingly complex, it requires more powerful software capable of rapidly processing and interpreting large amounts of data.

- *Cognitive Analytics:* Cognitive analytics attempts to mimic human thought and behavior, and it can assist companies in answering challenging, complex problems. Cognitive analytics does this by leveraging artificial intelligence (AI), enabling it to improve over time. With the use of AI in industry, it is possible to answer complex questions and draw contextual conclusions about how humans would have interacted with the situation. It helps with more meaningful data, scaled experience, and knowledge, leading to better decisions.
- *Diagnostic Analytics:* This gives the ability to identify the root cause. It is characterized by techniques such as drill-down, data discovery, data mining, and correlations. It involves analyzing overall performance and figuring out why errors, mistakes, and delays occur. It lets the manager know the delays, breakdowns, and disruptions in the demand and supply processes and the reasons behind them.

Figure 3.3 shows these major types of data analytics [8]. Unlike diagnostic and descriptive analytics, which analyze situations after they occur, predictive analytics uses advanced techniques to forecast future outcomes. In the supply chain, it is time to shift from mere descriptive and diagnostic analytics to predictive and prescriptive analytics. Predictive analytics is a branch of data analytics that uses historical data, statistical modeling, data mining techniques, and machine learning to predict future outcomes. Figure 3.4 shows the predictive analytics process [9].

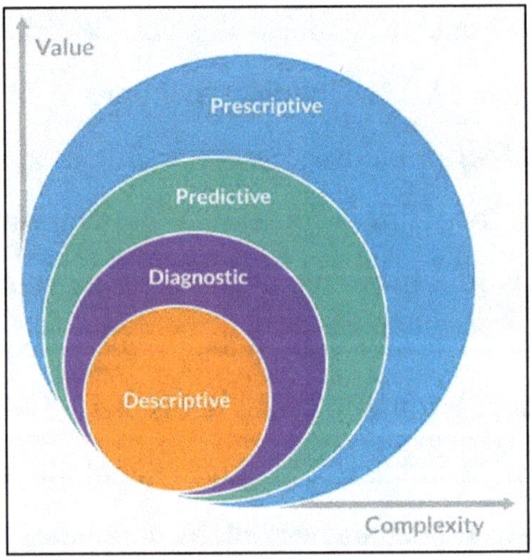

Figure 3.3 Types of data analytics [8].

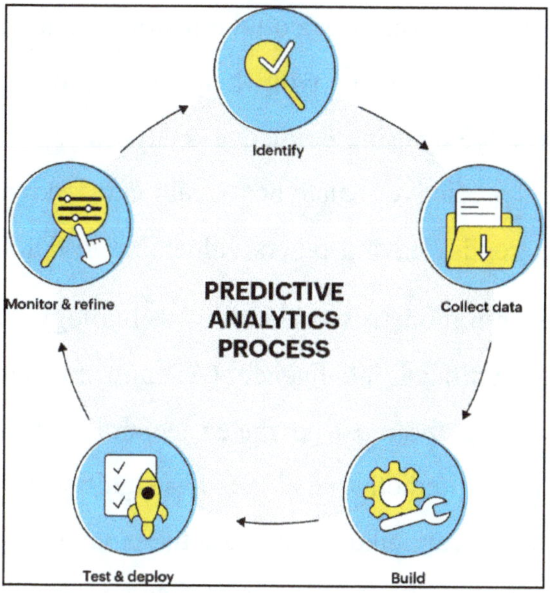

Figure 3.4 Predictive analytics process [9].

3.3 PREDICTIVE ANALYTICS IN BUSINESS

The business environment in which we live today is dynamic. It faces fierce competition and has to handle massive data sets. Data can only be meaningful if coupled with predictive analytics. Predictive analytics is the process of analyzing historical data using statistical algorithms and machine learning techniques to predict future outcomes. It only focuses on forecasting the future. It calculates the probability of future results based on records using data, statistical algorithms, and machine learning methods. Predictive analytics has made businesses smarter and equipped them with better decision-making capabilities by turning vast data into accurate, future-oriented insights. Businesses could transform their insights into stronger decisions that will help them maintain their competitive edge by using predictive analytics [9]. Competitors embracing predictive analytics gain an advantage by forecasting trends, leaving others vulnerable to falling behind.

We live in a modern world full of technology; it advances day by day. Artificial intelligence (AI) and machine learning (ML) are among the most advanced technologies. Integrating AI and ML into predictive analytics has significantly enhanced the technology's capabilities. In predictive analytics, AI and ML are used to analyze large volumes of data and identify patterns that humans may miss. Businesses can use AI and ML to make more accurate predictions and better-informed decisions. One of the main benefits of using AI and ML in predictive analytics is the ability to process large amounts of data quickly and accurately. Traditional predictive analytics techniques are often limited by the amount of data they can process, but AI and ML algorithms can handle much larger datasets. Artificial intelligence in predictive analytics is no longer an emerging trend; it is now a building block of how intelligent businesses operate. Many industries are using predictive analytics to gain a competitive edge. Predictive analytics can help businesses identify new opportunities, mitigate risks, and improve overall performance. For example, retailers can use predictive analytics to optimize pricing strategies, while manufacturers can use it to predict equipment failure and prevent downtime [11]. Figure 3.5 shows predictive analytics for business [12].

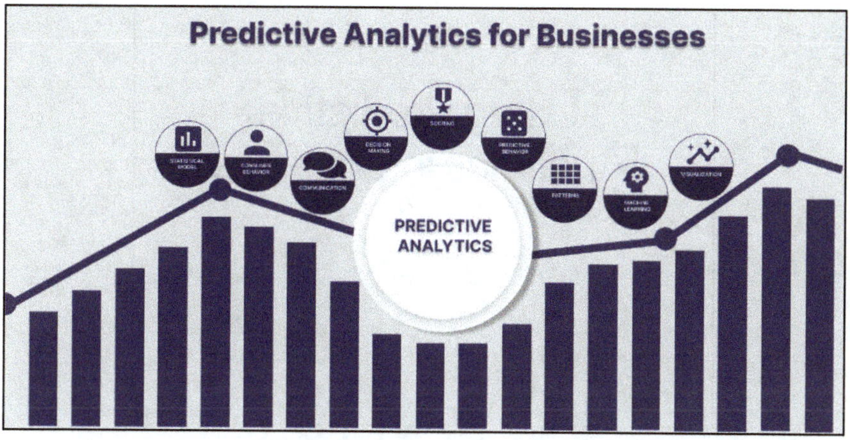

Figure 3.5 Predictive analytics for business [12].

3.4 APPLICATIONS OF PREDICTIVE ANALYTICS IN BUSINESS

Predictive analytics can be applied to any industry that deals with data and is willing to embrace it. Predictive models are used for many applications, including weather forecasting, video game development, voice-to-text translation, customer service, and investment portfolio strategies. Some uses of predictive analytics in business are shown in Figure 3.6 [13]. Common applications of predictive analytics in business include the following [2,11,14,15]:

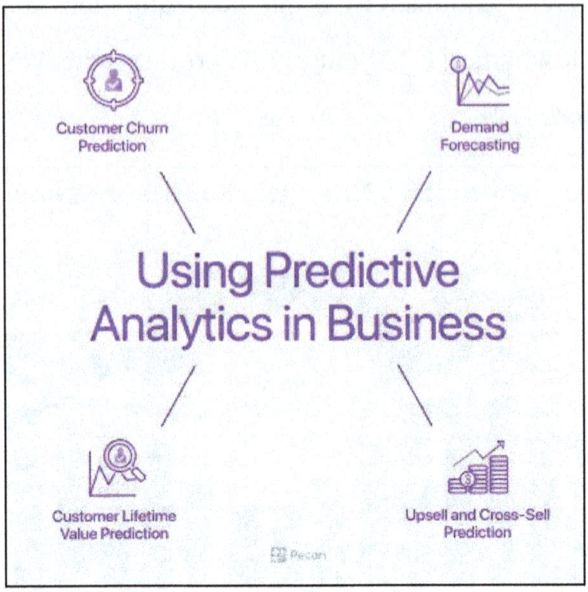

3.6 Some uses of predictive analytics in business [12].

- *Retail*: Retail is a huge industry with a lot of moving parts. That is why it can be difficult to figure out how to make the most of your business. Predictive analytics is revolutionizing the retail industry by offering businesses the tools to anticipate customer needs, optimize inventory, and refine marketing strategies. It can optimize pricing strategies, predict consumer behavior, and personalize marketing campaigns. A retail chain can predict which products will be in high demand during a holiday season and adjust inventory and marketing campaigns accordingly. For example, Walmart, the world's largest retailer, has been leveraging AI and machine learning across its operations, including its online grocery service. The online grocery service allows customers to place grocery orders online and either pick them up at their local Walmart store or have them delivered to their homes.

- *Banking and Finance*: Predictive analytics can identify fraudulent transactions, predict loan defaults, and optimize investment portfolios. Predicting loan defaults is another way for banking and finance companies to save money. In finance, predictive analytics is extensively used for risk management and fraud detection. By identifying high-risk borrowers early on, you can ensure that those loans do not go through—and if they do, you know how much risk is involved in them. The bank's implementation of AI and machine learning in its fraud detection system is just one example of how businesses can use these technologies to improve their operations and protect against fraud. For example, JPMorgan Chase, one of the world's largest banks, has been using AI and machine learning to prevent card-testing attacks. Card testing attacks are a type of fraud in which criminals use small transactions to test the validity of stolen credit card information before using it for larger transactions.
- *Marketing and Sales:* As we step into a data-driven future, AI is ushering in a new era of marketing. Predictive analytics plays a key role in advertising and marketing. It

can improve lead generation by identifying which customers are likely to buy your products or services. It can also optimize marketing campaigns based on customer behavior patterns and preferences. Sales forecasting is often a guessing game without data. Predictive analytics brings accuracy and clarity by combining historical sales, market trends, seasonal patterns, and customer behavior. Accurate sales forecasts also help businesses set realistic targets, plan budgets, and allocate resources more efficiently, giving sales teams a clear roadmap to meet company goals.

- *Accounting:* Predictive accounting shifts the focus from what has happened to what could happen in the future, necessitating marginal expense analysis. It integrates historical data to forecast future resource demands and associated costs, helping managers make informed decisions about adjustments and resource management. A shift from historical to predictive accounting enables organizations to assess and respond to future demands by employing various costing methods for different purposes.
- *Supply Chain:* Supply chain analytics is used to manage inventory levels and set pricing strategies. Supply chain predictive analytics use historical data and statistical models to forecast future supply chain performance, demand, and potential disruptions. This helps businesses

proactively identify and address risks, optimize resources and processes, and improve decision-making. Inventory management and supply chain planning are often full of guesswork. Overstocking ties up capital and increases storage costs, while stockouts lead to lost sales and unhappy customers.

- *Forecasting:* Human-guided forecasting is bounded by time and mental bandwidth. Even conventional statistical models have limits on the number of variables they can process without becoming irrelevant or noisy. Business forecasting uses historical data and patterns to predict future trends, such as seasonal sales increases and decreases. Predicting future demand for products or services can help businesses optimize inventory levels and improve sales. Predictive models help make weather forecasts, develop video games, translate voice-to-text messages, make customer service decisions, and develop investment portfolios.
- *Fraud Detection:* Identifying fraudulent activities can help businesses reduce losses and improve security. Financial services use predictive analytics to examine transactions for irregular trends and patterns. The irregularities pinpointed can then be examined as potential signs of fraudulent activity.

- *Risk Assessment:* Every business faces risks, including financial, operational, and fraudulent activities. Risk assessment enables users to identify and assess the potential hurdles associated with any given business. Predictive analytics can also enable early detection of problems, helping businesses improve their risk mitigation strategies. Investors, financial professionals, and business leaders use predictive models to help reduce risk. Assessing the risk of a particular event can help businesses make informed decisions and minimize losses. For example, an investor or an advisor can use predictive models to help craft an investment portfolio with an appropriate level of risk, considering factors such as age, family responsibilities, and goals.
- *Predictive Maintenance:* Predictive maintenance is a perfect example of operational efficiency made possible through machine learning models. It is a technique that uses data and analytics to predict when equipment will need repairs or maintenance before a failure occurs. Predicting when equipment will need repairs can help businesses reduce downtime and increase efficiency. For example, General Electric (GE), a multinational conglomerate, has been investing in AI and machine learning to improve the performance of its products and

services. One area where GE has been using AI and machine learning is predictive maintenance.

- *Business Intelligence*: Business intelligence (BI) differs from predictive business analytics (PBA). BI involves querying and reporting on data, while analytics seeks to understand the reasons behind past occurrences and project future outcomes. In the ever-evolving landscape of business intelligence, a groundbreaking transformation is underway, powered by AI-driven predictive analytics. This remarkable shift is reshaping how organizations glean insights, make decisions, and seize opportunities. Successful PBA implementation requires committed teams and structured practices to analyze critical drivers of business decisions. Figure 3.7 shows predictive analytics in business intelligence [16].

Figure 3.7 Predictive analytics in business intelligence [16].

- *Insurance:* Companies are under pressure to produce effective and marketable drugs that insurers will cover. Data and predictive analytics play an important role in underwriting. Insurance companies examine applications for new policies to determine the likelihood of paying out on a future claim. The analysis is based on the current risk pool of similar policyholders as well as past events that have resulted in payouts.
- *Credit Scoring:* Credit scoring makes extensive use of predictive analytics. When a consumer or business applies for credit, data on the applicant's credit history and on the credit records of borrowers with similar characteristics are used to predict the risk that the applicant might fail to repay any new credit approved for them.
- *Stock Trading*: Active traders look at a variety of historical metrics when deciding whether to buy a particular stock or other asset. Moving averages, bands, and breakpoints are all based on historical data and are used to forecast future price movements.
- *Customer Relationship Management* (CRM): Predictive analytics enables groups to predict purchaser behaviors, preferences, and desires. By analyzing historical client data, businesses can create personalized advertising and marketing strategies, optimize pricing, and enhance average customer satisfaction.

3.5 BENEFITS

The advantages of predictive analytics are multifaceted. It elevates decision-making by offering unparalleled accuracy and insights derived from vast data pools. When the data is available in real time, predictive analytics empowers businesses to respond instantly. The insights generated by predictive analytics can help businesses and organizations make more informed decisions, improve their operations, and, ultimately, drive growth and success. Knowing what your customers are likely to do next is one of the biggest advantages of predictive analytics. Other benefits include the following [11,17,18]:

- *Automation:* An advantage of using AI and ML in predictive analytics is automation. Predictive models can be trained and run automatically without human intervention. Predictions can be generated quickly and without errors, resulting in more efficient decision-making. Tasks such as data pre-processing, feature selection, and model selection can be automated using AI and ML, saving time and resources.
- *Cost-effectiveness:* Using AI and ML in predictive analytics can also be cost-effective. Predictive models can be trained and run on cloud-based platforms, eliminating the need for expensive hardware and software. AI and ML can help businesses identify cost savings opportunities and

optimize their operations, ultimately reducing overall costs.

- *Proactive Decision-making*: Effective strategic decision-making has a profound impact on business performance. Traditional decision-making processes rely on intuition, past experiences, or incomplete data, leading to suboptimal outcomes. The ability to predict future outcomes can help companies make better decisions about where they should invest their resources and which customers could be profitable down the road. Predictive analytics helps companies make proactive rather than reactive decisions. Formulating proactive plans helps retailers predict demand and prevent stockouts, whereas marketers may employ predictive analytics to forecast which leads are most likely to convert. The failures of once-successful companies such as Wang Labs, Digital Equipment, Borders, and Blockbuster raise critical questions about organizational decision-making. Irrational decision-making affects corporate success or failure.
- *Enhanced Operational Efficiency:* Predictive analytics optimizes efficiency by foreseeing production issues or supply chain delays. When you successfully predict outcomes using predictive analytics, you can optimize your business processes. For example, airlines use predictive analytics to determine optimal flight schedules.

In contrast, manufacturers can utilize it to schedule maintenance and minimize downtime.

- *Improved Accuracy:* One of the main advantages of using AI and ML in predictive analytics is the improvement in accuracy. These technologies enable predictive models to learn from vast amounts of data and make more accurate predictions. They can also identify patterns and trends that humans may miss, leading to more accurate predictions. By harnessing the predictive power of analytics, businesses can tailor their strategies with unparalleled precision. Integrating AI with predictive analytics enhances its accuracy and power, allowing businesses to make more informed decisions.
- *Competitive Advantage*: Predictive analytics has become essential for businesses looking ahead of their competition. There is no doubt that predictive analytics helps you anticipate market shifts and customer behavior before your competitors do. It gives your business a strategic edge by helping you stay ahead of competitors and uncover risks early.
- *Personalization:* One of the strongest applications of predictive analytics now is customer experience. AI can model a customer's past behavior and use it to predict what they will want next. This personalization is powered by AI-driven predictive analytics that continuously refine

the understanding of customers. With personalization at the forefront, predictive analytics allows companies to anticipate customer needs. By analyzing purchase and browsing behaviors, businesses deliver targeted recommendations, boosting satisfaction and loyalty.

- *Customer Churn:* Nobody likes losing a customer. But sometimes, it seems impossible to identify when and why different customers might slow down or stop interacting with your business. Fortunately, predictive analytics can help you identify which customers may be nearing the end of their relationships with your company. This method can also reveal why they may be likely to churn.
- *Scalability:* AI and ML also enable predictive analytics to be scaled to large datasets. Predictive models can be trained on massive amounts of data, and predictions can be generated for large numbers of customers or clients. This makes it possible to gain insights and make predictions at a large scale, which is helpful for businesses and organizations with large customer bases.

3.6 CHALLENGES

There are some challenges that you might face while working with predictive analytics. There are concerns about data privacy and security, as AI requires vast amounts of sensitive data. The initial investments for implementing AI

Analytics can be substantial, potentially posing financial challenges for smaller businesses. The human element remains essential, as AI cannot entirely replace human judgment and expertise. Other challenges include the following [17,19,20]:

- *Privacy Concerns*: AI algorithms can, unintentionally, absorb biases found in past data, and predicting based on personal data raises privacy issues. You must test for fairness (i.e., that models do not discriminate) and ensure compliance with data privacy regulations when working with customer or patient data. Establishing strict ethical frameworks and having checks and balances reduces these risks.
- *Ethical Concerns:* Ethical considerations and data governance will become more important as the usage of predictive analytics expands. The use of predictive analytics has been criticized and, in some cases, legally restricted due to perceived inequities in its outcomes. The technology may encounter issues with bias, as AI algorithms can perpetuate existing prejudices in the data they are trained on. It perpetuates bias and discrimination if the training data is not diverse or the algorithm is not adequately tested and validated. Predictive models may result in statistical discrimination against racial or ethnic groups in areas such as credit scoring, home lending, employment, or risk of criminal behavior.

- *Data Quality:* The effectiveness of predictive analytics depends on the quality of the data collected. Quality data means the presence of organized data, which is required to answer the questions expected for the analysis. To make accurate predictions, the data used to train the algorithms needs to be clean, accurate, and relevant. More data is not always better; better data is better. Ensure your data is clean, current, and relevant. Invest in data governance and encourage a culture of responsible data stewardship throughout your organization. Effective data governance frameworks ensure that data is managed securely and responsibly, in accordance with privacy regulations and organizational policies.
- *Complexity:* Predictive analytics is complex and requires specialized skills to implement and maintain. It is a sophisticated field of analytics that involves extracting valuable insights from historical and current data to predict future trends and outcomes. As businesses face increased competition and market complexity, predictive analytics has emerged as a strategic tool for anticipating customer behavior, optimizing operations, and guiding high-level decision-making. As complexity in business environments increases, adopting systematic thinking is essential.

- *Over-reliance:* Over-reliance on algorithmic outputs without contextual understanding can lead to flawed strategic decisions. Reliance on a loyalty card program may result in ineffective customer targeting.
- *Integration:* It can be challenging to integrate predictive models with your existing systems and processes. It may require some custom software development or process modifications to incorporate the solution into regular business processes. Integration of predictive analytics into business strategy is still in its evolutionary phase, offering vast potential for future exploration and innovation. The integration of predictive analytics with ESG (Environmental, Social, and Governance) metrics opens new strategic possibilities. Data integration is another crucial aspect, as it involves consolidating data from diverse sources such as databases, spreadsheets, and external data streams into a unified dataset. This integration enables a holistic view of the data, providing a comprehensive foundation for analysis. Transforming raw data into actionable insights involves a structured process integrating these analytical techniques with robust data visualization and reporting tools.
- *Transparency:* To mitigate risks, businesses must adopt robust data governance practices and ensure transparency in their analytics processes. As executives demand greater

transparency in decision support systems, future research can explore how machine learning models can not only predict outcomes but also explain underlying factors in human-understandable terms. This is crucial for increasing trust and adoption among decision-makers.

- *Global Reach:* As the business landscape becomes more global and interconnected, cross-border predictive systems and multi-lingual machine learning models will play an essential role in supporting international business strategy. A company deciding to enter a new international market must consider local consumer behavior, the regulatory environment, and the competitive landscape.
- *Skills Gap:* There is a high demand for data science and AI talent, and not all organizations have specialized expert teams available. You should train current analysts or hire specialists. Most companies opt to collaborate with seasoned AI developers to initiate their AI-driven predictive analytics initiatives and impart knowledge to their teams.
- *Collaboration:* Collaboration across departments is crucial. Your marketing, operations, and finance teams must all align on the goals and usage of AI tools. Once implemented, your predictive analytics solution should become a part of everyday decision-making, not just a one-time project.

3.7 FUTURE OF PREDICTIVE ANALYTICS IN BUSINESS

Predictive analytics is the use of data and algorithms to forecast potential future outcomes. It has evolved from a niche discipline into a mainstream necessity. It is not about fortune-telling. It is about leveraging the vast oceans of data we generate daily to identify patterns, trends, and probabilities of future outcomes. The evolution of predictive analytics has been driven by technological advancements and growing recognition of the value of data in decision-making. This technology's growing importance is underscored by its ability to provide insights that drive strategic decisions, optimize operations, and improve overall business performance. In the future, predictive analytics will rapidly integrate within AI ecosystems, promoting automated and intelligent decision-making. Predictive analytics is expected to drive success for businesses. As technology continues to advance, predictive analytics may play an increasingly important role in shaping the future of business methods and decision-making.

3.8 CONCLUSION

In the business world, predictive analytics' ability to identify patterns and make data-based predictions can lead to drastically improved decision-making. Predictive analytics can prove to be a game-changer for all sorts of businesses. It enhances decision-making capabilities, taking your business to new heights. Businesses can become proactive in improving efficiency, increasing customer satisfaction, and reducing costs. Adopting predictive analytics is necessary for sustainable growth and competitive advantage in today's data-driven business environment. This modern approach to data analysis has revolutionized the way businesses operate by forecasting trends, identifying risks, and optimizing various aspects of their operations. As businesses face fierce competition in today's data-driven landscape, predictive analytics is proving essential for strategic growth.

In recent years, the use of artificial intelligence (AI) and machine learning (ML) in predictive analytics has grown rapidly. When predictive analytics meets AI, it becomes a proactive decision engine that drives value, efficiency, and resilience. AI brings speed, scale, and sophistication to predictive analytics that were previously impossible. Traditional predictive models often required human-led feature selection, slow training times, and periodic manual tuning. Today's AI-driven platforms automate much of that process, learning from new data in real-time and improving continuously. Without leveraging predictive analytics, businesses risk missing out on opportunities, failing to anticipate market trends, and being unprepared for potential disruptions. Embracing predictive analytics is not merely a necessary option; it is a strategic imperative for corporations aiming to thrive in a dynamic and competitive business environment. More information on the use of predictive analytics in business is available in the books [21-28].

REFERENCES

[1] A. A. Adesina, T. V. Iyelolu, and P. O. Paul, "Leveraging predictive analytics for strategic decision-making: Enhancing business performance through data-driven insights," *World Journal of Advanced Research and Reviews*, vol. 22, no. 3, 2024, pp. 1927–1934.

[2] C. Halton, "Predictive analytics: Definition, model types, and uses," April 2025,

https://www.investopedia.com/terms/p/predictive-analytics.asp

[3] M. N. O. Sadiku, P. A. Adekunte, and J. O. Sadiku, "Predictive analytics in business," *International Journal of Trend in Scientific Research and Development*, vol. 10, no.2, March-April, 2026, pp. 1083-1093.

[4] "Supply chain predictive analytics: What is it and who's doing it?"

https://riverlogic.com/?blog=supply-chain-predictive-analytics-what-is-it-and-whos-doing-it

[5] N. Babin, "AI and predictive analytics: Revolutionizing demand forecasting in supply chain management,"

https://www.linkedin.com/pulse/ai-predictive-analytics-revolutionizing-demand-supply-nicolas-babin-xrj2e/

[6] "From insight to innovation: Why data analysis will define industry leaders in 2025,"

https://www.inkl.com/news/from-insight-to-innovation-why-data-analysis-will-define-industry-leaders-in-2025

[7] "An overview of supply chain analytics," February 2023, Unknown Source.

[8] I. Tymchuk, "Big data and predictive analytics in supply chain: Success stories and tips," November 2020,

https://www.n-ix.com/big-data-predictive-analytics-supply-chain-case-study/

[9] "Examples of predictive analytics in the travel industry at Jordan Judah,"

https://asktheman.xyz/

[10] "Transforming business insights with predictive analytics and AI,"

https://www.techprofree.com/transforming-business-insights-with-predictive-analytics-and-ai/#google_vignette

[11] "AI and machine learning for predictive analytics in business,"

https://malogica.software/blog/ai-and-machine-learning-for-predictive-analytics-in-business

[12] "Predictive analytics for businesses: Why is it important?"

https://visiochart.com/blog/predictive-analytics-business/

[13] S. C. Sivek, "3-Minute nutshell: Business uses of predictive analytics,"

https://www.pecan.ai/blog/business-uses-predictive-analytics/

[14] "Chapter 5 summary: Deploying the predictive business analytics function,"

https://cdn.bookey.app/files/pdf/book/en/predictive-business-analytics.pdf

[15] L. Gamerz, "Unveiling the power of predictive analytics in business," February, 2024,

https://ustudywith.blogspot.com/2024/02/unveiling-power-of-predictive-analytics.html

[16] P. Sinha, "5 Applications of predictive analytics in business intelligence,"

https://www.oodlestechnologies.com/blogs/5-Applications-of-Predictive-Analytics-in-Business-Intelligence/

[17] M. Mistry, "How does AI in predictive analytics transform business decisions and drive growth?" January 2026,

https://kodytechnolab.com/blog/ai-in-predictive-analytics/

[18] S. Beumont, "Predictive analytics: Leveraging data for business insights," https://codingcops.com/predictive-analytics/

[19] D. Henkin, "Predictive analytics—Why it matters and how AI supercharges it," https://www.forbes.com/sites/davidhenkin/2025/05/20/predictive-analytics-why-it-matters-and-how-ai-supercharges-it/

[20] A. Adwani, "Predictive analytics for business strategy: Leveraging machine learning for competitive advantage," *International Journal of Social Impact*, vol. 10, no. 3, July-September 2025, pp. 295-306.

[21] R. R. Barton, *Predictive Analytics for Business using R*. World Scientific Publishing Company, 2024.

[22] E. Siegel, *Predictive Analytics: The Power to Predict Who Will Click, Buy, Lie, or Die.* Wiley, 2016.

[23] N. A. Ali, *Predictive Analytics for the Modern Enterprise: A Practitioner's Guide to Designing and Implementing Solutions.* O'Reilly Media, 2024.

[24] A. Bari, M. Chaouchi, and T. Jung, *Predictive Analytics For Dummies*. For Dummies, 2nd edition, 2016.

[25] L. Maisel and G. Cokins, *Predictive Business Analytics: Forward-Looking Capabilities to Improve Business Performance.* Wiley, 2013.

[26] D. Covington, *Analytics: Data Science, Data Analysis, and Predictive Analytics for Business*. Lulu Press, 2019.

[27] A. Khang et al. (eds.), *Data-Driven Modeling and Predictive Analytics in Business and Finance: Concepts, Designs, Technologies, and Applications.* Boca Raton, FL: CRC Press, 2024.

[28] T. Miller, *Modeling Techniques in Predictive Analytics: Business Problems and Solutions with R, Revised and Expanded Edition.* Pearson Education, 2014.

CHAPTER 4 PREDICTIVE ANALYTICS IN MARKETING

"The Laws of Nature are just, but terrible. There is no weak mercy in them."

- Henry W. Longfellow

4.1 INTRODUCTION

In the modern marketing landscape, data is the new currency. Data science is a key aspect of decision-making for businesses in various industries. Artificial intelligence (AI) is transforming marketing through its capacity to analyze customer data and predict trends and preferences. AI technologies have emerged as essential tools for processing both structured and unstructured data with remarkable accuracy and speed. The incorporation of AI techniques, such as machine learning, into predictive analytics tools now enables companies to analyze massive amounts of data at high speed, boosting the accuracy and usefulness of predictive models. AI enhances predictive marketing by enabling advanced customer segmentation, churn prediction, personalized marketing, and dynamic pricing [1].

Predictive analytics in marketing (or predictive marketing) implies using data mining, artificial intelligence, and statistical modelling for data analysis to generate predictions, like campaign outcomes, customer behavior, and industry trend forecasts, to help marketers make proactive decisions. Predictive analytics empowers marketers to make important connections in their data to improve decision-making and planning. It helps marketers make better decisions today by providing insights into what is likely to happen in the future. With these insights, marketing teams optimize their campaigns to meet behavior, event-based, or revenue goals [2].

Predictive analytics, as its name implies, is the branch of advanced analytics that forecasts what is likely to happen based on patterns in the collected data. It uses patterns in historical data to forecast future outcomes or classify future events. It leverages AI to forecast future trends and customer behavior. In marketing, this means using data to predict consumer behavior, preferences, and trends. Predictive analytics provides a strategic advantage by enabling businesses to anticipate customer needs and tailor their marketing efforts accordingly. In the age of big data and AI, predictive analytics has emerged as a vital tool for data-driven marketing. Marketing is no longer about guessing what works. Using predictive analytics in marketing turns data into actionable insights [3].

This chapter examines the significant role of predictive analytics in transforming marketing. It begins by explaining predictive analytics. It describes predictive analytics in marketing and provides some of its applications. It highlights some benefits and challenges of predictive analytics in marketing. It predicts the future of predictive analytics in marketing. The last section concludes with comments.

4.2 WHAT IS PREDICTIVE ANALYTICS?

As its name implies, predictive analytics is about predicting future trends such as sales demand and exchange rates. and other important metrics. The technique relies on the application of statistical modeling and regression analysis to historical data to determine and understand trends and formulate future predictions. Strictly speaking, predictive analytics does not predict the future, but rather uses probability theories to determine what is likely to happen based on patterns and trends revealed by analyzing historical data [4]. Predictive analytics accurately anticipates customer demand, preventing overstocking and stockouts while adapting to market changes. Figure 4.1 illustrates predictive analytics [5], while Figure 4.2 shows different components of predictive analytics [6].

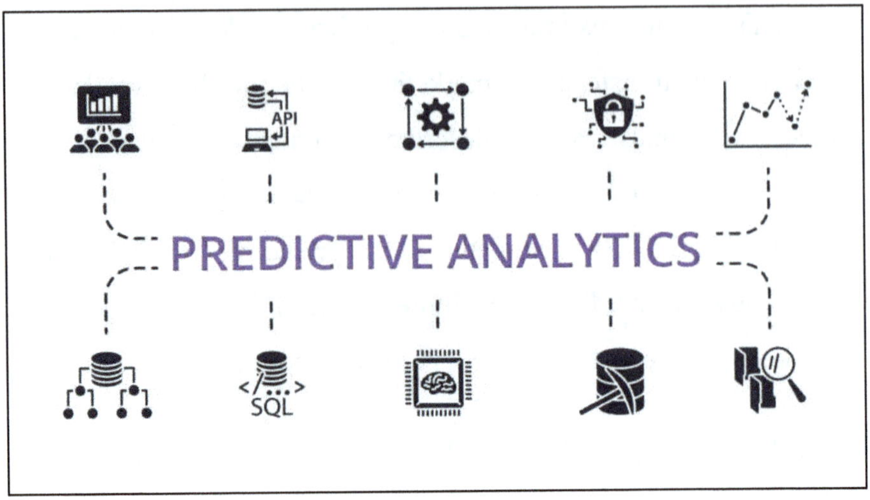

Figure 4.1 Predictive analytics [5].

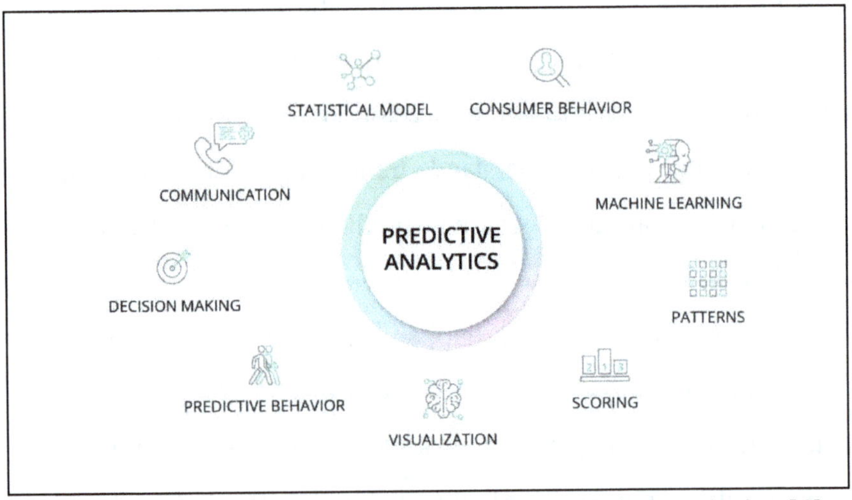

Figure 4.2 Different components of predictive analytics [6].

In general, analytics provides an efficient way to improve planning because it gives you better forecasts. There are different types of data analytics. They are briefly explained as follows [7]:

- *Descriptive Analytics:* Descriptive analytics examines what has happened over the years. They are capable of detecting trends in historical data. Analytics can uncover trends and postulate probable reasons for change by comparing the same data from various periods. It can be seen as the baseline of the industry, which basically assesses past and current data for more meaningful insights and delivers it to the people to use their own intelligence and knowledge to make decisions.
- *Predictive Analytics:* This assists businesses in predicting what might happen and the impact of various situations, such as possible supply chain bottlenecks. Managers can be proactive rather than responsive by pushing them to evaluate these prospective circumstances before they occur. Predictive analytics may be used to identify patterns and trends as well as anticipate breakdowns that may impact suppliers and, consequently, production processes. Predictive analytics for the supply chain leverages data, statistical algorithms, and machine learning techniques to identify the likelihood of future outcomes.
- *Prescriptive Analytics:* Prescriptive analytics builds on predictive analytics and dives deeper into predicting future insights on what can be done next. Prescriptive analytics uses the findings of descriptive and predictive analytics to recommend what measures a business should take to

achieve its objectives. Because prescriptive analytics is increasingly complicated, they need more powerful software capable of rapidly processing and interpreting large amounts of data.

- *Cognitive Analytics:* Cognitive analytics attempts to mimic human thought and behavior, and it can assist companies in answering challenging, complex problems. Cognitive analytics does this by utilizing artificial intelligence (AI), which allows it to improve over time. With the use of AI in the industry, answering complex questions and draw out contextual conclusions on how humans would have interacted with the situation. It helps with more meaningful data and scales experience and knowledge for better decisions.
- *Diagnostics Analytics:* This gives the ability to identify the root cause. It is characterized by techniques such as drill-down, data discovery, data mining, and correlations. It involves analyzing overall performance and figuring out why errors, mistakes, and delays occur. It lets the manager know the delays, breakdowns, and disruptions in the demand and supply processes and the reasons behind them.

Figure 4.3 shows these major types of data analytics [8]. Unlike diagnostic and descriptive analytics, which were designed to analyze situations after they happened, predictive analytics utilizes advanced data analytics techniques to forecast future outcomes. In the supply chain, the time has come to shift from mere descriptive and diagnostic analytics to predictive and prescriptive analytics. Predictive analytics is a branch of data analytics that makes predictions about future outcomes using historical data combined with statistical modeling, data mining techniques, and machine learning. Figure 4.4 shows the predictive analytics process [9].

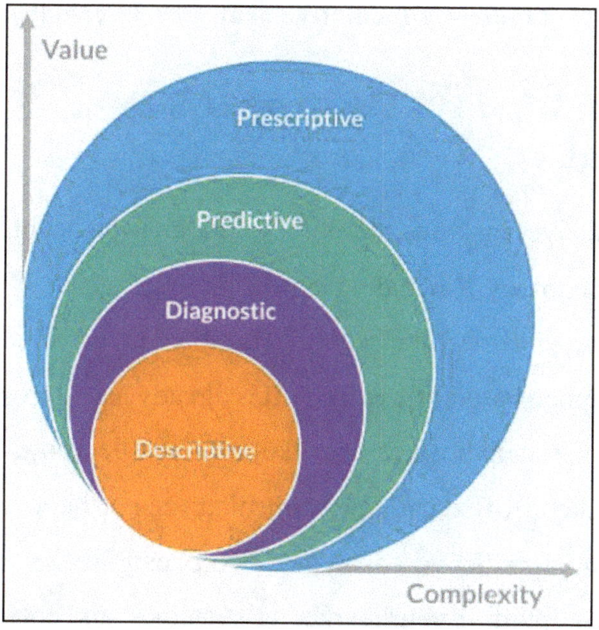

Figure 4.3 Types of data analytics [8].

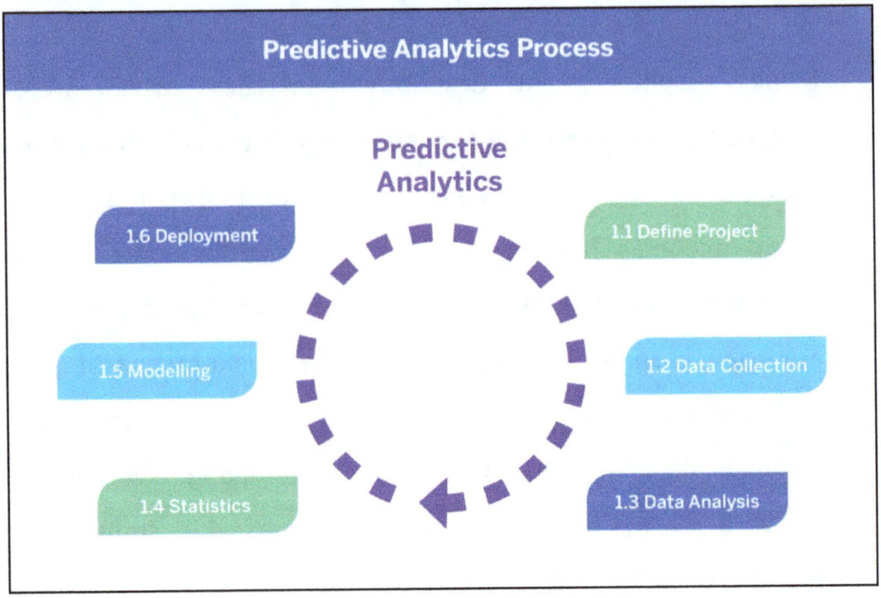

Figure 4.4 Predictive analytics process [9].

4.3 PREDICTIVE ANALYTICS IN MARKETING

Predictive analytics refers to a data analysis technique that uses technology (including artificial intelligence, statistical modeling, and machine learning) to predict or forecast what might happen based on raw data. It is already used across several industries to help businesses make informed decisions based on the likelihood of something happening (or not happening). By leveraging predictive analytics, you can make informed decisions, optimize your marketing strategies, and enhance your customers' experiences. Anticipating future actions and reactions is at the heart of predictive analytics. In marketing, predictive analytics helps you determine who is most likely to be converted or take other relevant actions. Predictive analytics in marketing (or predictive marketing) relies on a suite of powerful tools and technologies. It allows marketing specialists to use predictive analytics solutions to remove guesswork and proactively plan promotional activities and customer engagement efforts, ensuring their higher effectiveness. Figure 4.5 shows a marketing analyst [10].

Figure 4.5 A marketing analyst [10].

Predictive marketing is a data-driven strategy that leverages advanced analytics, machine learning, and AI to forecast future customer behaviors, preferences, and market trends. It is marketing that uses big data to develop accurate forecasts of future customer behavior. It is driving decisions in a big way. Instead of relying on guesswork, marketers can now make informed adjustments to their strategies based on what customers are likely to do next. Predictive marketing takes the guesswork out of your marketing strategy and allows you to respond dynamically to customer behavior observed across multiple channels [10]. It is revolutionizing the way businesses connect with their audience. Figure 4. 6 shows how to implement predictive analytics in marketing [12].

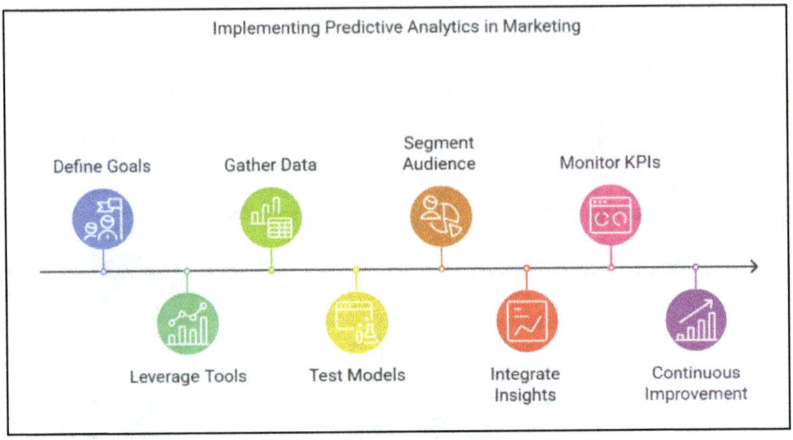

Figure 4.6 How to implement predictive analytics in marketing [12].

4.4 APPLICATIONS OF PREDICTIVE ANALYTICS IN MARKETING

Predictive analytics leverages historical data, artificial intelligence (AI), and machine learning (ML) to forecast future consumer actions and trends. Marketers can use predictive analytics to predict customer behavior, personalize experiences, and optimize campaigns with unparalleled precision. Predictive analytics has a wide range of applications in marketing. Marketing uses predictive analytics to acquire new customers, retain existing customers, and maximize sales. Common applications of predictive analytics in marketing include the following [11,13-18].

- *Retail:* A data-driven approach is the prime power of the modern retail market. Information and data analytics fuel every aspect of retail, from inventory management to pricing and marketing, and serve as a basis for predicting future trends. To build an effective strategy and drive sales, retailers must consider many variables, such as market trends, demand, competition, etc. This task becomes much easier with predictive analytics solutions. Predictive analytics models provide retailers with relevant information on which to base their strategies and tactics. They can also be used to determine the long-term popularity of a product or service, allowing retailers to concentrate on those that will deliver the highest profit. Figure 4.7 shows the benefits of predictive analytics in retail [19].

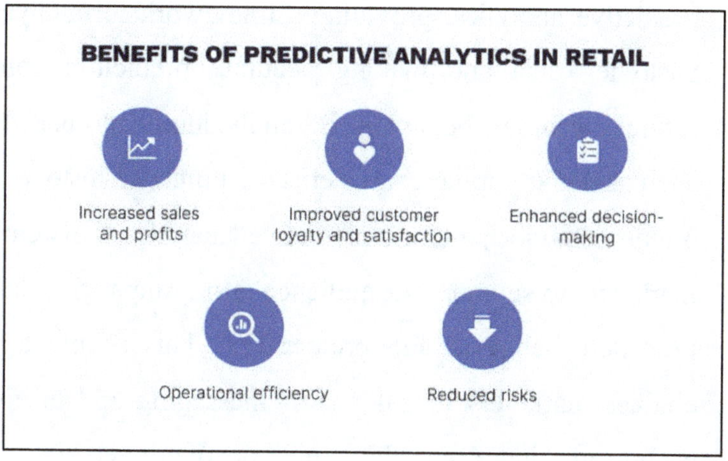

Figure 4.7 Some benefits of predictive analytics in retail [19].

- *Advertising:* As a subset of marketing, advertising can benefit from a predictive marketing strategy. Predictive advertising uses the marketing data collected from various sources to segment potential clients into very specific interest groups and demographics. It identifies which advertisements would be most successful with which groups, delivering personalized ad content promoting products or services that the specific client might be inclined to buy, even if they have not bought something like it before.
- *Customer Segmentation:* There is no denying that customer segmentation is important. Customer segmentation is the process of grouping customers based on shared traits or behaviors, such as demographics, past purchases, or internet activity. It is a critical component of predictive analytics, providing a framework for analyzing customer data and making accurate predictions about future customer behavior. By analyzing customer data, such as demographic characteristics, purchase history, and online behavior patterns, predictive analytics tools enable marketers to segment the audience into groups with shared predicted behavior and preferences. This segmentation enables marketers to tailor their messaging and offers to each group, increasing the likelihood of conversion.

- *Clustering Techniques:* Clustering is useful for segmentation, finding customers who behave similarly, so you can target them more accurately. Clustering is an unsupervised predictive analytics marketing technique. It involves grouping similar data points based on shared characteristics. What those shared characteristics will be is completely up to you. Audience segmentation is the most common way to utilize predictive analytics in marketing campaigns. "K" means clustering is the simplest and most efficient subtype, which is why it is the most popular method. For this, you set a "K" number of clusters, and each data point will be assigned to the cluster with the nearest mean.
- *Churn Prediction:* Customer churn is expensive, especially when you are blindsided by it. Predictive analytics in marketing helps you identify customers who are about to fall off the funnel. Predictive models can identify customers at risk of churning (leaving) and provide insights into the reasons behind their potential departure. By analyzing factors like purchase history, engagement, and feedback, you can take the necessary steps to prevent that from happening. This allows companies to take proactive measures to retain valuable customers. Companies like Verizon have done this well,

using churn models to identify at-risk subscribers and proactively keep them around.

- *Sentiment Prediction:* Marketing teams often face challenges with timing and messaging when rolling out campaigns. Traditional approaches often overlook real-time customer sentiment, which can lead to poorly timed messages that miss the mark, or worse, alienate the audience. Predictive analytics tools analyze comments and reviews left by current and potential clients on the company's website, app, and social media, as well as third-party review platforms and forums. This enables marketers to forecast how the launch of new campaigns or products will impact overall brand perception among the target demographic to adjust promotions to prevent reputational damage.
- *Pricing Optimization:* Predictive models can help companies optimize pricing strategies by analyzing market demand, competitor pricing, and historical sales data. This ensures that prices are competitive, yet profitable.
- *Predicting Customer Behavior*: Predictive models let you group people based on likely behavior, not just demographics or interests. One of the biggest wins here is knowing which customers are on the verge of dropping off. Instead of reacting after someone churns, predictive

analytics can flag them in advance. That gives marketers a chance to step in with the right message or incentive. When campaigns are powered by predictions- who is likely to buy, who is likely to bounce- you stop wasting time on the wrong audiences.

- *Demand Forecasting:* One of the biggest challenges for marketers is predicting what products or services will be in demand. Demand forecasting lets marketers accurately predict how much demand their campaigns will generate so they can ensure they have enough of their products or services at the right locations to meet the expected demand. Marketing professionals familiar with predictive analytics can use it to forecast demand and sales. Predictive analytics can forecast demand based on seasonality, trends, geography, and even weather. It helps by analyzing seasonal trends, market data, and customer behavior to forecast demand more accurately. Retailers like Walmart and platforms like Amazon rely on predictive analytics to manage inventory. It is not just about avoiding out-of-stocks (though that is important), but also aligning marketing efforts with what is actually available or about to be in demand.
- *Sales Forecasting:* Sales teams are constantly under pressure to hit their targets, but traditional forecasting methods often fall short of providing accurate guidance.

Many businesses still rely on intuition, historical averages, or basic trend projections to predict future sales. Predictive analytics takes sales forecasting to the next level by leveraging historical data to identify patterns that might otherwise go unnoticed. By analyzing variables like deal specifics, customer behavior, and market trends, these models deliver forecasts that are far more accurate than simple trend lines.

- *Lead Scoring:* Sales teams often struggle to manage a flood of leads, each with different levels of buying intent. Relying solely on basic demographics or engagement metrics does not provide the clarity needed to identify which leads are most likely to convert. Predictive analytics can identify which leads are most likely to convert, allowing you to prioritize your sales efforts. Predictive analytics tools determine which leads have the highest intention to buy, as well as calculate the perceived value of each lead based on their demographics, behavioral data, and interaction history with the company's representatives. Using these insights, marketing and sales teams direct their efforts to opportunities that have the best chance of converting to ensure higher revenue.
- *Predictive SEO:* Marketers who rely on traditional, reactive SEO often find themselves having to play catch-up. By the time they have all the data they need to make

an informed decision, that data may already be obsolete. Predictive SEO, on the other hand, anticipates trends and other issues before they begin to have an impact, ensuring that sites are optimized to take full advantage of what is to come. While traditional SEO relies on analyzing past data and making reactive changes, predictive SEO takes a forward-looking approach. Predictive SEO leverages advanced models to analyze patterns in search volumes, seasonal shifts, competitor strategies, and emerging topics. By tapping into data from search engines, social media discussions, news trends, and industry reports, these systems identify early signals of rising demand.

4.5 BENEFITS

The adoption of predictive analytics in marketing offers many benefits. Predictive analytics surpasses other modes of marketing analysis in terms of its depth, providing actionable insights and strategies. It is heavily focused on data as the sole source of accurate insights. By implementing predictive marketing strategies and tools, businesses can improve their overall marketing performance and unlock some specific benefits such as better targeting, improved ROI, smarter inventory planning, and higher engagement. Other benefits include the following [2,11,13,16]:

- *Automation:* Predictive analytics does not just stop at insights; it powers personalized, automated customer journeys. Look for something that can take all of the data points and send out marketing materials automatically. This is going to save you a lot of time. With predefined event triggers, software can send out material when you want to engage your customers.
- *Cost Savings:* The financial benefits of predictive analytics are evident. Predictive analytics can identify inefficiencies in marketing campaigns, helping companies allocate resources more effectively and reduce unnecessary spending.
- *Personalization:* Personalization involves tailoring marketing messages to each customer based on their preferences and behaviors. Advanced predictive modeling and AI tools are now being used by marketing teams to personalize the customer experience, which can lead to increased sales and a better ROI on individual marketing campaigns. By analyzing user behavior and preferences, predictive analytics can recommend personalized content, such as product recommendations, articles, or videos, to enhance user engagement and drive conversions. AI chatbots on websites can provide round-the-clock and personalized support to customers when they need it most.

- *Improved ROI:* It is well known that marketing campaigns can be costly, with some of them requiring significant up-front investments. Predictive analytics tools enable marketing teams to use their resources more efficiently while increasing return on investment (ROI). By targeting the right audience with personalized messages and optimizing marketing spend, companies can achieve a higher return on investment for their marketing campaigns. Predictive analytics tools enable marketing teams to use their resources more efficiently while increasing ROI.
- *Enhanced Customer Satisfaction:* As customer expectations continue to rise and competition intensifies, the ability to anticipate market trends and customer needs has become more crucial than ever. By forecasting what content, offers, and communication formats will be most impactful, marketing teams can adjust their messaging, propositions, and interactions across the company's websites, apps, and social media, leading to higher customer satisfaction and retention.
- *Enhanced Customer Experience*: Personalized marketing based on predictive analytics leads to improved customer experiences, as customers receive content and offers that are highly relevant to their needs and

preferences. Providing a seamless, engaging omnichannel experience is essential to retaining existing customers.

- *Enhanced Customer Retention:* Customer retention is often more cost-effective than acquisition, and predictive analytics plays a crucial role in identifying at-risk customers before they churn. By analyzing patterns in customer behavior, predictive models can flag warning signs that a customer might be considering leaving.
- *Improved Effectiveness:* By projecting customer preferences and needs as well as marketing campaign effectiveness, companies can fine-tune their promotional and customer communication strategies to improve marketing metrics, such as conversion and retention rates. By accurately predicting customer behavior and segmenting for personalization, marketers can create highly effective marketing campaigns targeted only to those most likely to take the desired action, and avoid marketing spend on those unlikely to convert.
- *Competitive Advantage:* Predictive marketing analytics allows businesses to get ahead of the competition by anticipating future trends, as well as by attracting new customers and retaining existing ones. Companies that leverage predictive analytics gain a competitive edge by staying ahead of market trends and responding to changes faster than their competitors.

- *Faster Decision-Making*: Making informed decisions in marketing can be a challenge because it requires an in-depth understanding of your target audience, their behavior, their pain points, and so many other dynamic factors. Using predictive analytics and modeling can take a lot of the "guesswork" out of creating a marketing campaign, leading to faster and more informed decision-making. Data-driven insights from predictive analytics empower marketers and decision-makers with the information they need to make informed and strategic choices.

Some benefits of predictive analytics in marketing are portrayed in Figure 4.8 [12].

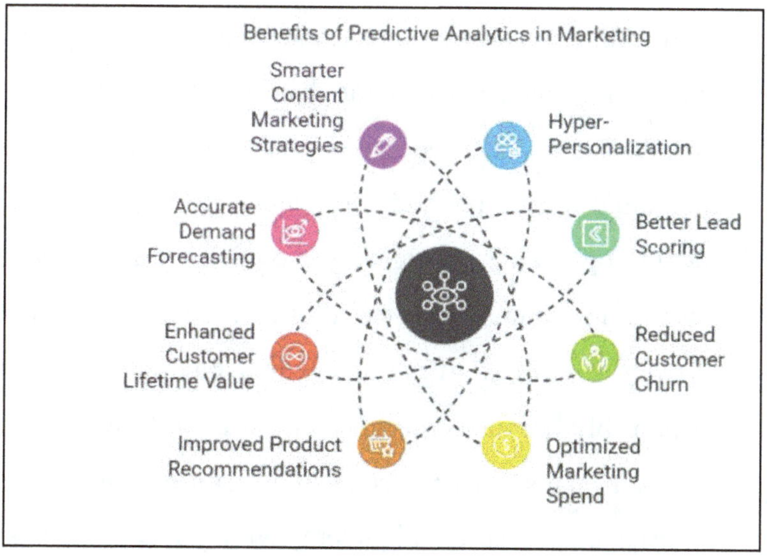

Figure 4.8 Some benefits of predictive analytics in marketing [12].

4.6 CHALLENGES

Predictive analytics can be a game-changer for marketing teams, but putting it into action is not without its challenges, which the adopter needs to know about and understand how to address in advance. Issues such as data privacy, algorithmic bias, system integration, complexities, and the potential over-reliance on automation must be addressed through responsible practices. Other challenges include the following [13,17]:

- *Data Quality:* Predictive models are only as good as the data they are trained on. Ensuring data quality and accuracy is essential for reliable predictions. Collecting and using customer data for predictive analytics must be done ethically and in compliance with data privacy regulations. Businesses must prioritize customer privacy and gain explicit consent for data usage. To ensure data quality, the dataset undergoes meticulous preprocessing, including robust methods for handling missing values, identifying and mitigating outliers, and feature engineering to maximize the informative value of the data.
- *Privacy Concerns:* It is crucial to handle customer data responsibly because consumers are wary of how their data is used. This means collecting, storing, and using information in strict alignment with privacy laws and industry regulations. Failing to do so can erode trust and

lead to significant legal consequences. Predictive analytics relies on large volumes of personal and behavioral data, which raises questions about compliance with regulations such as GDPR and the California Consumer Privacy Act (CCPA). Regulations like CCPA demand transparency, robust consent systems, and data minimization. Balancing responsibilities with the benefits of predictive analytics is essential for building trust.

- *Algorithmic Bias:* Algorithms and datasets can unintentionally reflect biases, which might result in unfair or discriminatory outcomes. When training data reflects historical biases or lacks diversity, predictive models can produce unfair or discriminatory outcomes. This can result in certain groups being excluded from campaigns or perpetuate harmful stereotypes. To address this, teams should use diverse datasets, regularly test models for fairness, and involve cross-functional teams to validate results for demographic equity.
- *Transparency:* Customers and internal teams deserve to understand how predictive models operate. Providing clear explanations and maintaining accountability ensures greater trust and confidence in the technology.
- *Interpretability:* Also, some AI algorithms can be complex and difficult to interpret. Marketers need to strike a

balance between model accuracy and interpretability to build trust in their predictions.

- *Integration:* Predictive analytics tools must seamlessly connect with existing marketing platforms, CRM systems, and data warehouses, often requiring extensive IT resources and coordination across departments. This complexity can slow implementation. Strong integration frameworks not only speed up deployment but also ensure systems communicate effectively, reducing friction down the line.
- *Skills Gap:* Predictive analytics demands expertise in data science and machine learning, skills that many marketing teams lack. Organizations can address this by investing in training, hiring specialized talent, or partnering with external experts.

4.7 FUTURE OF PREDICTIVE ANALYTICS IN MARKETING

Predictive analytics is constantly evolving. Predictive analytics and other related technologies, such as artificial intelligence (AI), will play an increasingly important role in personalizing marketing efforts. As more marketing teams begin to see the benefits of predictive analytics marketing, this trend will likely continue. With so much changing day to day in the world of predictive analytics, only time will tell what the future holds for this exciting and relatively new tool. As artificial intelligence (AI) technology continues to advance, exciting new applications are emerging, and predictive analytics will become even more sophisticated.

If you want to stay ahead of the curve, you need to keep an eye out for the latest trends. The future of predictive analytics in marketing looks promising. As technology continues to advance, predictive analytics will continue to reshape the marketing landscape. Automation will continue to play a larger role in marketing, with AI-powered systems taking over routine tasks. Predictive analytics will become more real-time, allowing marketers to make instant decisions based on the most up-to-date data. It will become more integrated across various marketing channels, providing a holistic view of customer interactions and preferences [13].

4.8 CONCLUSION

Predictive analytics is about using past data to make smart guesses about the future. In marketing, predictive analytics uses historical customer and campaign data to forecast behavior, optimize spend, reduce churn, and personalize outreach, delivering smarter and more cost-effective campaigns. This forward-looking approach empowers marketers to anticipate customer needs, optimize campaigns, and make data-driven decisions with confidence. Predictive analytics is not some futuristic trend; it is already shaping how smart marketers work today. You are missing out and leaving money on the table if you are not implementing predictive analytics in your marketing.

Although predictive analytics has been used in other industries for many years, it is still a relatively new concept in the world of marketing. Marketing professionals who want to remain relevant and competitive in their field should be prepared to apply predictive analytics in their own marketing strategies [9]. Predictive analytics in marketing is no longer a dispensable luxury; it is an indispensable necessity for businesses looking to stay ahead of the competition. It has become a powerful tool that is revolutionizing the way businesses approach their marketing strategies. More information on the use of predictive analytics in marketing is available from the books in [20-26].

REFERENCES

[1] M. Shahbandi, "AI-powered predictive analytics in marketing: Trends, challenges, and future directions," *International Business & Economics Studies,* vol. 7, no. 2, March 2025.

[2] "How predictive analytics drives smarter marketing,"

https://www.snowflake.com/en/fundamentals/predictive-analytics-marketing/

[3] M. N. O. Sadiku and J. O. Sadiku, "Predictive analytics in marketing," *International Journal of Trend in Research and Development,* vol. 13, no. 2, March-April, 2026, pp. 180-186.

[4] "Supply chain predictive analytics: What is it and who's doing it?"

https://riverlogic.com/?blog=supply-chain-predictive-analytics-what-is-it-and-whos-doing-it

[5] N. Babin, "AI and predictive analytics: Revolutionizing demand forecasting in supply chain management,"

https://www.linkedin.com/pulse/ai-predictive-analytics-revolutionizing-demand-supply-nicolas-babin-xrj2e/

[6] "From insight to innovation: Why data analysis will define industry leaders in 2025,"

https://www.inkl.com/news/from-insight-to-innovation-why-data-analysis-will-define-industry-leaders-in-2025

[7] "An overview of supply chain analytics," February 2023, Unknown Source.

[8] I. Tymchuk, "Big data and predictive analytics in supply chain: Success stories and tips," November 2020,

https://www.n-ix.com/big-data-predictive-analytics-supply-chain-case-study/

[9] "Predictive analytics: A comprehensive guide for businesses," November 2024, https://www.jobspikr.com/blog/guide-to-predictive-analytics/

[10] "How predictive analytics is shaping the future of marketing," March 2025, https://online.champlain.edu/blog/how-predictive-analytics-is-shaping-the-future-of-marketing

[11] "What is predictive marketing?" https://www.salesforce.com/marketing/predictive-marketing-guide/

[12] "Predictive analytics in marketing unlocking growth through customer insights," December 2025, https://metsertive.com/blog/predictive-analytics-in-marketing-strategy/

[13] E. Mayfield, "Predictive analytics: Leveraging AI for data-driven marketing," https://ermarketing.net/navigate-the-channel/predictive-analytics-leveraging-ai-for-data-driven-marketing/

[14] A. Kot, "Predictive analytics in marketing: Techniques, applications and success strategies," February 2025,

https://www.mgid.com/blog/predictive-analytics-in-marketing

[15] S. Jonwal, "Predictive analytics in marketing: A complete guide 2026," July 2025,

https://www.youngurbanproject.com/predictive-analytics-in-marketing/

[16] V. Boiko, "Predictive analytics in marketing: A technology & market state overview," January 2026,

https://www.itransition.com/predictive-analytics/marketing

[17] "Predictive analytics in marketing: 10 Real-world use cases driving results," April 2026,

https://www.data-mania.com/blog/predictive-analytics-in-marketing/

[18] M. K. Pratt, "Predictive analytics in marketing: Achieving success,"

https://www.techtarget.com/searchbusinessanalytics/tip/Predictive-analytics-in-marketing-Achieving-success

[19] S. Yaramionak, "Using predictive analytics in retail: Benefits, examples, and best practices,"

https://www.effectivesoft.com/blog/predictive-analytics-in-retail.html

[20] A. Q. Arnold, *Future Forecasts: Leveraging Predictive Analytics for Marketing Campaign Success.* Amazon Digital Services, 2024.

[21] E. Harfield, *The Forecaster's Edge: Mastering Predictive Analytics in Marketing: Unlocking Data-Driven Success for Modern Marketers.* Amazon Digital Services, 2025.

[22] A. Bari, M. Chaouchi, and T. Jung, *Predictive Analytics For Dummies*. For Dummies, 2nd edition, 2016.

[23] O. Artun and D. Levin, Predictive *Marketing: Easy Ways Every Marketer Can Use Customer Analytics and Big Data.* Wiley, 2015.

[24] B. P. Singh, *AI-Powered Predictive Analytics in Marketing: Driving Decisions.* Independently Published, 2024.

[25] T. W. Miller, *Marketing Data Science: Modeling Techniques In Predictive Analytics With R And Python.* Pearson India, 2018.

[26] B. Leventhal, *Predictive Analytics for Marketers: Using Data Mining for Business Advantage.* Kogan Page, 2018.

CHAPTER 5: PREDICTIVE ANALYTICS IN FINANCE

"Resentment is like drinking poison and then hoping it will kill your enemies."

– Nelson Mandela

5.1 INTRODUCTION

Finance is a broad term associated with activities in capital markets that encompasses intertemporal and portfolio decisions. Financial institutions are constantly seeking new ways to increase accuracy, minimize risk, and improve profitability. Today's financial professionals are forward-looking strategic partners to the business. This shift away from a purely retrospective perspective to proactive value creation has brought about demand for a new set of tools. Among these is predictive analytics. Predictive analytics is transforming the finance sector [1].

The term "predictive analytics" is more commonly applied when moving beyond explanatory statistical models to computational prediction. Predictive analytics is a data science discipline that utilizes predictive models to forecast future outcomes using historical data. Predictive analytics for the finance industry uses machine learning and artificial intelligence to forecast future outcomes, driving financial forecasting and risk management. It allows institutions and investors to make smarter decisions by predicting trends like stock market movements, credit events, and key economic indicators such as GDP growth, unemployment, and inflation rates. Financial institutions and companies use predictive analytics to accurately forecast revenue streams and cash flows [2].

Predictive analytics leverages statistical techniques, machine learning, and data analysis to help forecast future events by looking at historical and current data. It is widely used to predict future outcomes with better accuracy, especially in situations involving high financial risks. Predictive analytics shifts finance from reactive to proactive decision-making by using AI, machine learning, and real-time data to anticipate risks, customer behavior, and market movements. From detecting fraudulent transactions in real time to forecasting cash flows and personalizing banking experiences, predictive analytics has become crucial for modern finance. Financial institutions use predictive analytics to improve their operations and stay ahead of the competition. The integration of predictive analytics within the finance sector is not just a trend; it is a transformative force driving efficiency, accuracy, and customer satisfaction [3].

This chapter provides useful information on how predictive analytics techniques are used in the finance sector. The chapter begins by explaining predictive analytics. It describes predictive analytics in finance and provides some of its applications. It highlights some benefits and challenges of predictive analytics in finance. It predicts the future of predictive analytics in finance. The last section concludes with comments.

5.2 WHAT IS PREDICTIVE ANALYTICS?

As its name implies, predictive analytics is about predicting future trends such as sales demand and exchange rates. and other important metrics. The technique relies on the application of statistical modeling and regression analysis to historical data to determine and understand trends and formulate future predictions. Strictly speaking, predictive analytics does not predict the future, but rather uses probability theories to determine what is likely to happen based on patterns and trends revealed by analyzing historical data [4]. Predictive analytics accurately anticipates customer demand, preventing overstocking and stockouts while adapting to market changes. Figure 5.1 illustrates predictive analytics [5], while Figure 5.2 shows different components of predictive analytics [6].

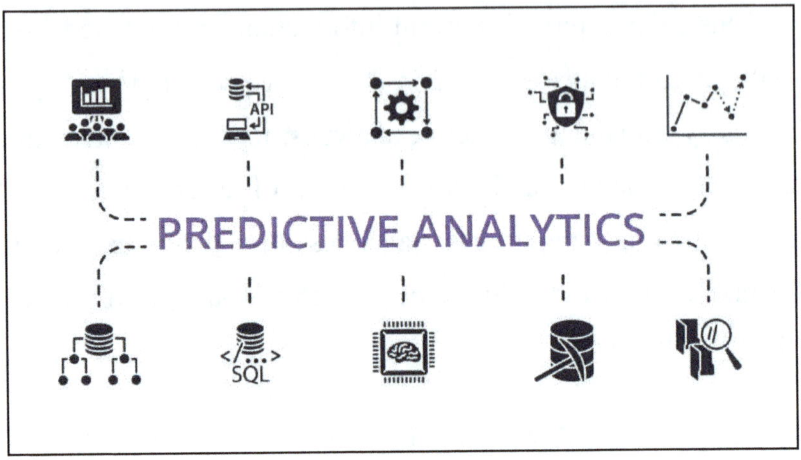

Figure 5.1 Predictive analytics [5].

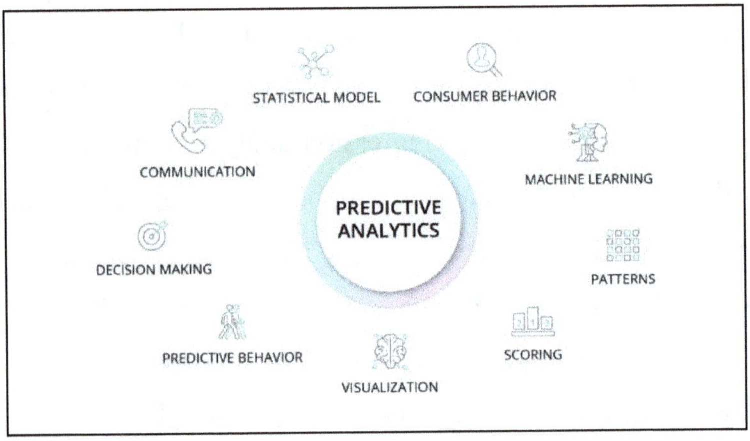

Figure 5.2 Different components of predictive analytics [6].

In general, analytics provides an efficient way to improve planning because it gives you better forecasts. There are different types of data analytics. They are briefly explained as follows [7]:

- *Descriptive Analytics:* Descriptive analytics examines what has happened over the years. They are capable of detecting trends in historical data. Analytics can uncover trends and postulate probable reasons for change by comparing the same data from various periods. It can be seen as the baseline of the industry, which basically assesses past and current data for more meaningful insights and delivers it to the people to use their own intelligence and knowledge to make decisions.

- *Predictive Analytics:* This assists businesses in predicting what might happen and the impact of various situations, such as possible supply chain bottlenecks. Managers can be proactive rather than responsive by pushing them to evaluate these prospective circumstances before they occur. Predictive analytics may be used to identify patterns and trends as well as anticipate breakdowns that may impact suppliers and, consequently, production processes. Predictive analytics for the supply chain leverages data, statistical algorithms, and machine learning techniques to identify the likelihood of future outcomes.
- *Prescriptive Analytics:* Prescriptive analytics builds on predictive analytics and dives deeper into predicting future insights on what can be done next. Prescriptive analytics uses the findings of descriptive and predictive analytics to recommend what measures a business should take to achieve its objectives. Because prescriptive analytics is increasingly complicated, they need more powerful

software capable of rapidly processing and interpreting large amounts of data.

- *Cognitive Analytics:* Cognitive analytics attempts to mimic human thought and behavior, and it can assist companies in answering challenging, complex problems. Cognitive analytics does this by utilizing artificial intelligence (AI), which allows it to improve over time. With the use of AI in the industry, answering complex questions and draw out contextual conclusions on how humans would have interacted with the situation. It helps with more meaningful data and scales experience and knowledge with better decisions.
- *Diagnostic Analytics:* This gives the ability to identify the root cause. It is characterized by techniques such as drill-down, data discovery, data mining, and correlations. It involves analyzing overall performance and figuring out why errors, mistakes, and delays occur. It lets the manager know the delays, breakdowns, and disruptions in the demand and supply processes and the reasons behind them.

Figure 5.3 shows these major types of data analytics [7]. Unlike diagnostic and descriptive analytics, which were designed to analyze situations after they happened, predictive analytics utilizes advanced data analytics techniques to forecast future outcomes. In the supply chain, the time has come to shift from mere descriptive and diagnostic analytics to predictive and prescriptive analytics. Predictive analytics is a branch of data analytics that makes predictions about future outcomes using historical data combined with statistical modeling, data mining techniques, and machine learning. Figure 5.4 shows the predictive analytics process [9].

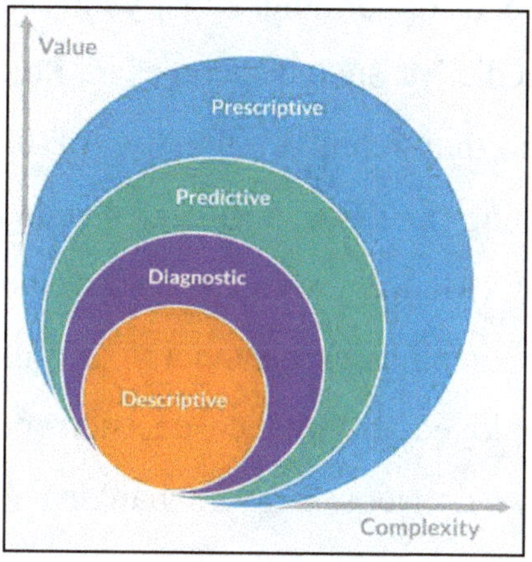

Figure 5.3 Types of data analytics [8].

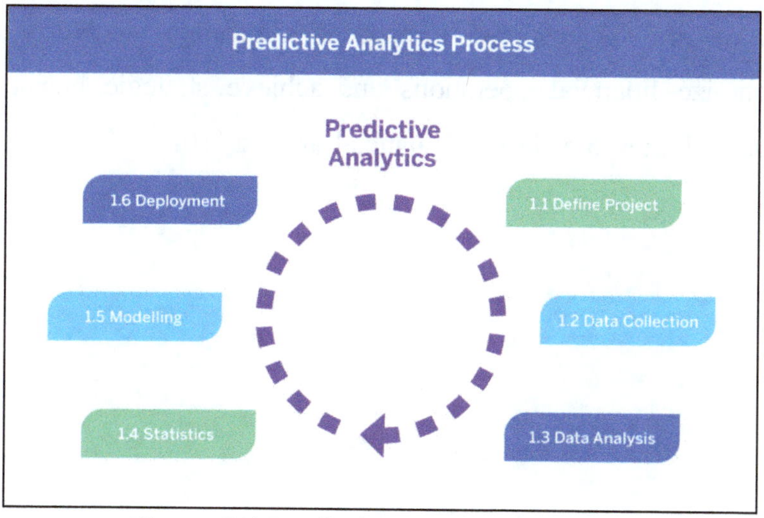

Figure 5.4 Predictive analytics process [9].

5.3 PREDICTIVE ANALYTICS IN FINANCE

Increasing digitalization and continuous shifts in customer behavior are making it difficult for finance professionals to plan. What they need is a technology that can help them navigate uncertainties and also empower them to identify potential investment opportunities that yield maximum returns. That is where predictive analytics comes in. Predictive analytics is a broad term that refers to the use of big data mining, statistics, modeling methods, artificial intelligence (AI), and machine learning (ML) algorithms to analyze huge data sets and forecast future outcomes or behaviors. In finance, predictive analytics is employed to enhance decision-making processes across various domains, from banking to investment management. It is used to predict future trends, manage risks, optimize portfolios, and even detect fraud. Corporate finance teams are increasingly turning to predictive analytics to optimize financial operations and achieve strategic business goals. Figure 5.5 shows a financial analyst [10].

Figure 5.5 A financial analyst [10].

Predictive analytics (PA) is a subset of business analytics that combines statistical analysis and machine learning (ML) to analyze datasets and make predictions about a dependent variable. It can be applied to continuous variables, such as the weight of raw materials ruined during production, or discrete variables, such as the number of unsatisfied customers during a quarter. It can be used to run sophisticated "what-if" scenarios by quickly simulating the financial impact of hundreds of potential business scenarios. As predictive analytics enhances finance processes, it also transforms the skill set required of financial professionals. Predictive analytics can enhance the accuracy of financial forecasts, enabling organizations to make informed decisions regarding budgeting, resource allocation, and investment strategies [11]. Figure 5.6 shows predictive analytics in finance [12].

Integrating PA into financial operations can lead to improved customer relationship management, targeted marketing, and enhanced decision-making. By leveraging historical data and advanced algorithms, financial institutions can forecast future needs, streamline operations, and make informed decisions that minimize costs while maximizing resource utilization. By utilizing predictive analytics, organizations can improve risk management, optimize pricing strategies, and tailor financial products to meet customer needs, thereby fostering a competitive edge in an increasingly data-driven industry [13].

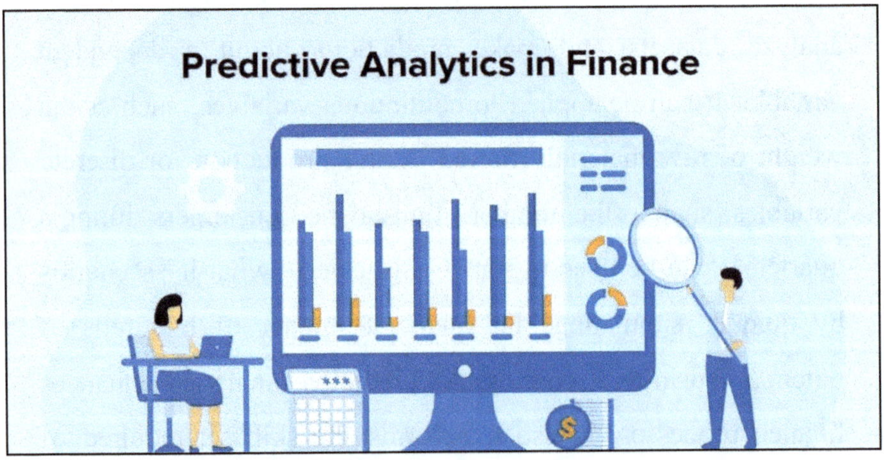

Figure 5.6 Predictive analytics in finance [12].

5.4 APPLICATIONS OF PREDICTIVE ANALYTICS IN FINANCE

Predictive analytics is widely used in the financial industry today by banks, insurance companies, credit unions, and other institutions that deal with monetary business on a daily basis. Figure 5.7 shows how predictive analytics is used in finance [14]. Key applications of predictive analytics include credit risk, fraud detection, compliance, investment optimization, credit scoring, personalized banking, investment analytics, financial forecasting, and portfolio optimization. Common applications of predictive analytics in the financial sector include the following [15-19]:

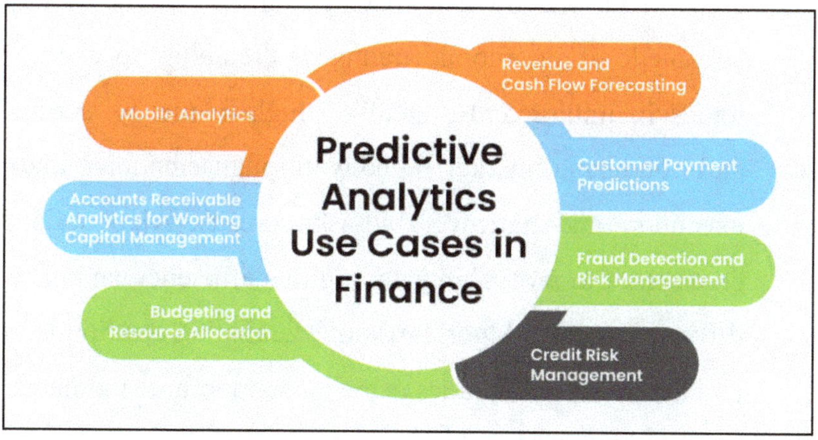

Figure 5.7 How predictive analytics is used in finance [14].

- *Algorithmic Trading:* Algorithmic trading, commonly referred to as algo trading, is the use of computer programs to automate one or more stages of the trading process. These stages include pre-trade analysis, trading signal generation, and trade execution. Trading strategies increasingly rely on predictive signals drawn from price histories, macroeconomic data, and even sentiment analysis from news or social media. Investment firms use predictive models to develop trading algorithms that predict stock performance based on historical data, social media sentiment, and economic indicators. These algorithms can execute trades at high speeds and with great precision, often outpacing human traders. A key advantage of algorithmic trading is the ability to execute trades in milliseconds, enabling high-frequency trading and optimizing market liquidity through smoother trade execution and narrower bid-ask spreads. Algo trading contributes to profitability through its efficiency and data-driven strategies. Algorithms analyze market conditions in real time to execute trades at the most opportune moments, maximizing gains and minimizing losses.
- *Fraud Detection:* Fraud detection is one of the most mature and impactful applications of PA. Predictive analytics plays an important role in detecting fraudulent activities and managing risks. It is an effective method for

detecting fraud early. Predictive analytics tools assess data and identify activities that suggest fraudulent patterns. Financial institutions use advanced analytics techniques to monitor transactional data in real-time, identifying unusual patterns and suspicious behavior that may indicate fraud or money laundering. This helps with identifying suspicious patterns and anomalies that may indicate fraud. Certainly, this proactive approach helps in thwarting fraud before it happens. Banks employ predictive analytics models to identify fraudulent transactions by detecting deviations from typical user behavior. For example, if a credit card is used for an unusually large purchase in a typical location, the model can flag the transaction as suspicious.

- *Risk Management:* One of the key applications of predictive analytics in finance is risk management. Financial institution managers must take appropriate measures to manage risk effectively in today's continuously changing environment. Predictive models help in robust risk management, enabling investors to forecast market volatility and prepare proactive strategies to mitigate risks. Financial institutions use predictive analytics to identify, measure, and manage credit, market, and liquidity risks. By analyzing historical data and stress scenarios, predictive models help estimate potential losses and assess financial stability. Predictive analytics helps identify financial risks proactively before they become serious problems. Banks and financial organizations use predictive analytics models to prevent cyberattacks, detect fraudulent transactions, and assess credit risks. Predictive models assess credit risk by analyzing a borrower's credit history, financial profile, and market conditions. Figure 5.8 illustrates predictive analytics in financial risk management [20].

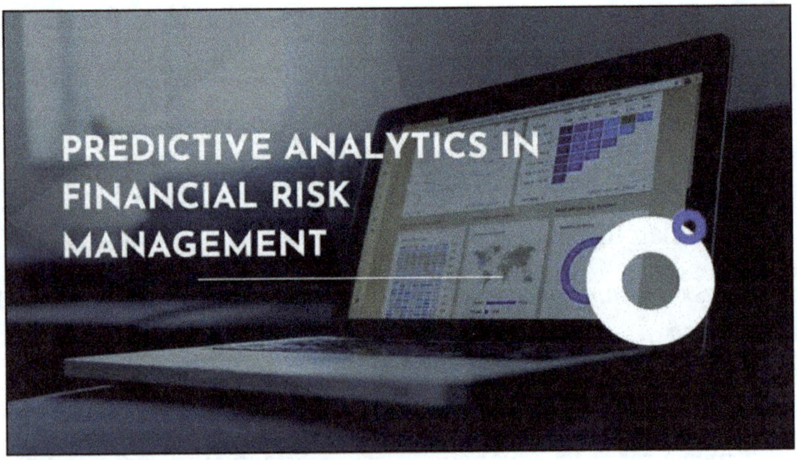

Figure 5.8 Predictive analytics in financial risk management [20].

- *Financial Forecasting:* In the finance industry, forecasting plays a vital role in helping businesses evaluate risks, predict market trends, and choose where to invest. Financial forecasting is among the most essential use cases of predictive analytics in corporate finance.

Accurate cash flow forecasting is essential for maintaining liquidity and financial stability. With predictive analytics, finance professionals can rely on data-driven insights to make proactive decisions. Predictive analytics helps banking institutions anticipate revenue trends, expense patterns, and funding requirements. Figure 5.9 displays use cases of predictive analytics in banking [21]. These insights support better budgeting, scenario planning, and decision-making, especially during periods of economic uncertainty.

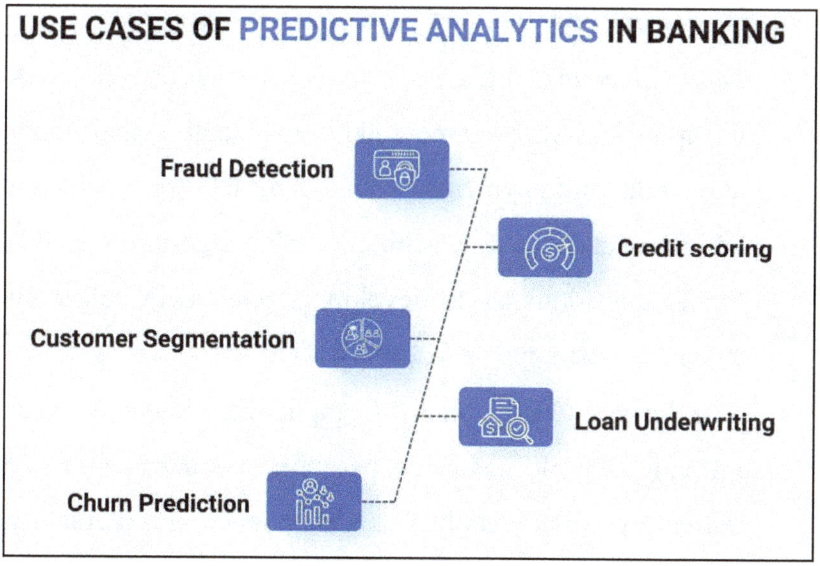

Figure 5.9 Use cases of predictive analytics in banking [21].

- *Stock Market Forecasting:* Predictive analytics (PA) is critical for stock market forecasting. Forecasting helps predict stock price movements by analyzing historical price trends, market conditions, and economic indicators, allowing investors to make calculated buy or sell decisions. Finance and investment professionals use it to estimate cash flows, mitigate risks, and make informed decisions by analyzing past trends and patterns. Moreover, PA tools can also assess the risks associated with stocks and their future movements, helping to identify potential investment opportunities.
- *Debt Collection:* Predictive analytics can easily identify the applicants who are more likely to default on their loans and credit card payments by analyzing their past behavior and transaction data. Machine learning algorithms enable financial institutions to develop targeted debt collection strategies and improve recovery rates.
- *Regulatory Compliance*: Compliance functions face growing workloads as transaction volumes rise and regulatory scrutiny tightens. Compliance and regulatory reporting are essential processes in the finance industry, but they can be time-consuming and overwhelming. These processes can be automated using predictive analytics, which analyzes historical data to forecast potential issues. This approach helps reduce costs and minimize the risks

of non-compliance. Predictive analytics supports regulatory compliance by identifying high-risk activities and potential compliance breaches before they occur.

- *Portfolio Optimization*: Portfolio optimization in financial markets serves as a cornerstone of effective investment management. Its primary objective is to strike an optimal balance between maximizing returns and minimizing risks. Predictive models are used to forecast optimal outcomes when faced with quadratic problems. Wealth managers and institutional investors are using predictive analytics to balance portfolios more effectively. They use PA to anticipate asset correlations and potential market moves to achieve stronger risk-adjusted returns and personalize client strategies. At the heart of portfolio optimization lies the principle of the risk-return trade-off. Investors aim to attain the highest possible returns for a given level of risk.
- *Earnings Prediction:* Corporate earnings are easier to forecast than the economy, although they too have a high degree of idiosyncratic complexity. As with economic variables, the data has to be sourced from an external vendor. Unlike in economics, however, regressions are not good predictive techniques.
- *Stock Volatility:* The financial markets are inherently volatile, requiring constant monitoring and adjustments to

ensure that a portfolio remains aligned with an investor's goals. Volatility forecasting plays an essential role in risk management by helping stakeholders anticipate periods of heightened market instability. The stock market, because it is considered important to the process of financial intermediation, is an area that has proved extremely challenging to predict. The stock market is therefore considered to be efficient if prices would be unaffected by revealing any available information to everyone. Predictive analytics plays a pivotal role in managing market volatility by equipping investors with real-time insights, allowing them to anticipate price swings and implement measures to hedge against downturns.

- *Insurance*: In insurance, predictive analytics enhances underwriting and pricing by estimating risk more accurately. Insurers use predictive models to forecast claim frequency, assess policyholder risk, and detect fraudulent claims, leading to more competitive pricing, reduced losses, and improved overall profitability.
- *Sentiment Analysis*: Market sentiment analysis complements traditional analysis, offering a deeper understanding of market behavior and empowering investors to navigate complexities with precision. Automated trading systems incorporate sentiment insights for real-time decision-making. Market sentiment analysis

aids in forecasting market trends, managing risks, and optimizing trading. For example, positive sentiment surges can signal potential bullish trends, guiding market entry points. Predictive models also help detect sentiment changes that may indicate increased volatility, enabling preemptive adjustments to investment strategies.

5.5 BENEFITS

Leveraging predictive analytics in the finance sector offers a wide range of measurable business benefits, ranging from proactive decision-making to higher accuracy, efficiency, better risk control, improved customer experiences, and stronger financial performance. Predictive analytics strengthens risk management by anticipating market fluctuations and mitigating uncertainties posed by economic disruptions or geopolitical changes. It assists companies in increasing productivity and profitability by spotting inefficiencies, anticipating operational bottlenecks, and optimizing workflows. Other benefits of PA in finance include the following [12,18]:

- *Automation:* Automation embedded within predictive systems streamlines resource-intensive processes across finance functions. By embedding intelligence into routine operations, organizations reduce manual intervention while maintaining precision at scale. Automated predictive models analyze large volumes of data with greater speed and consistency than manual processes. These models reduce human error, improve forecast accuracy, and streamline operations across areas such as lending, fraud detection, and financial planning, allowing teams to focus on higher-value strategic activities.

- *Lower Costs:* Efficiency gains achieved through automation, improved risk detection, and streamlined processes lead to meaningful cost reductions. Predictive analytics reduces manual intervention, minimizes fraud-related losses, and optimizes resource utilization across financial operations.
- *Increased Profitability:* By improving targeting, pricing strategies, and investment decisions, predictive analytics directly contributes to revenue growth. Better insights into customer behavior and market trends enable financial institutions to identify new opportunities, optimize margins, and enhance overall profitability.
- *Proactive Decision-making:* Decision-making benefits immensely from forecasting, as it eliminates guesswork and facilitates rational choices regarding asset acquisition, pricing strategies, and expansion plans. Powered by AI, predictive analytics enables financial institutions to move from reactive decision-making to a proactive approach. By anticipating risks, market changes, and customer behavior in advance, organizations can take timely action,

reduce uncertainty, and respond more effectively to emerging opportunities and potential threats.

- *Reduced Loss:* By identifying potential credit defaults, fraudulent transactions, and market downturns early, predictive analytics helps institutions minimize losses. These insights enable better risk mitigation strategies, stronger portfolio management, and more resilient financial operations, particularly in volatile or uncertain economic conditions.
- *Customer Satisfaction:* Predictive models analyze historical patterns and data to gain insights into current behavior and predict future trends. This helps understand your customers' needs, preferences, and areas of improvement. As a result, you can offer more personalized products or services, leading to an improved customer experience.
- *Better Resource Allocation:* Predictive analytics in finance helps optimize resource allocation strategy by detecting inefficient or underperforming functionalities, identifying areas for improvement, and recommending necessary changes to resolve the issues. This leads to more efficient use of resources, reducing waste and supporting the organization's long-term objectives.
- *Revenue Growth:* Predictive models help identify which products to invest in, leading to increased revenue.

Financial analysts and investment professionals can use these models to develop more effective and profitable strategies.

- *Personalization:* Predictive analytics allows financial institutions to understand customer needs, preferences, and behavior. It allows these organizations to offer personalized products, faster approvals, and relevant recommendations, improving customer satisfaction, strengthening loyalty, and building long-term relationships.

Some of the benefits of predictive analytics are shown in Figure 5.10 [22].

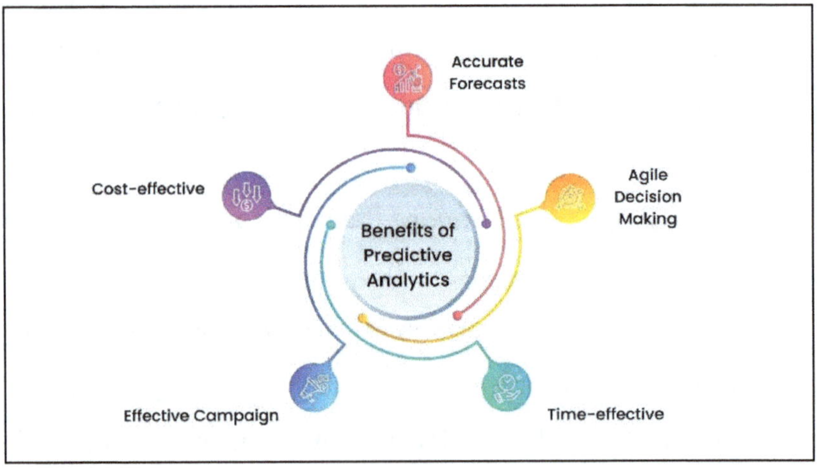

Figure 5.10 Some of the benefits of predictive analytics [22].

5.6 CHALLENGES

Though there are many advantages of using predictive analytics to streamline financial operations and improve efficiency and outcomes, adapting it is not an easy task. Predictive analytics in finance presents several challenges, including data quality, data privacy, availability issues, interpretability, regulatory and compliance concerns, problems of algorithm bias, compatibility problems with integrated large traditional systems, and problems of human resources. Other challenges of PA in finance include the following [12,18,23]:

- *Data Quality:* To implement predictive analytics technologies, finance leaders must have access to accurate data. This helps align financial plans with operational plans and improve forecast accuracy. An output is only as good as the input in predictive analytics. The PA tools make forecasts by analyzing accumulated data. If the quality of the data sets feeding the predictive models is poor, the outcomes will also be unreliable. To ensure better results and accurate predictions, financial forecasting models require high-quality data.
- *Lack of Skilled Professionals*: Lack of skilled professionals is a major challenge in implementing predictive analytics. You need a talented team that can not only perform advanced financial data analytics, but also

harness its full potential. Hire data engineers with a strong understanding of ML algorithms, statistical modeling, and data manipulation.

- *Interpretability*: Interpreting predictive models is a complex task. So, understanding how models made the prediction is difficult for finance professionals. It often takes a significant amount of time to analyze the data used by the models and extract valuable insights that explain a specific prediction.
- *Market Complexities:* The complexities of financial decision-making and risk management pose persistent challenges for practitioners. Financial markets are complex because they are influenced by numerous factors, such as geopolitical events, economic indicators, and more. Including all these variables in a predictive model is quite challenging. The skills, tools, and methods associated with predictive analytics are constantly evolving, particularly as AI continues to advance. As such, financial professionals must maintain a mindset of continuous learning to stay current.
- *Cybersecurity:* Managing large volumes of sensitive financial data increases exposure to cybersecurity threats and data privacy breaches. Implement robust cybersecurity measures, encryption standards, and access controls, while aligning data handling practices with

privacy regulations such as GDPR and similar frameworks.

- *Integration*: If predictive models cannot easily integrate with your existing finance software system, their value is significantly reduced. A seamless integration between predictive models and your financial system improves operational efficiency and productivity.
- *Training:* Predictive models use big data technologies for efficient data processing and ML algorithms for accurate predictions. Managing these models can be challenging, so you need a skilled staff to perform data analysis and maximize the value of these analytical tools. If your team does not have the required skills, then you have to arrange training sessions that would help them learn and gain a solid understanding of these models and technologies. Having solutions with predictive features alone will not help unless your employees are trained to use them effectively. Train your employees to help them understand the various scenarios in which predictive analytics helps.

5.7 FUTURE OF PREDICTIVE ANALYTICS IN FINANCE

As technology continues to advance and more data becomes available, the applications of predictive analytics in finance are only set to grow. From improving customer experience to enhancing risk management and investment decisions, predictive analytics has the potential to revolutionize the finance industry. Today, predictive analytics in finance has proven to be incredibly valuable.

Predictive analytics is the future of finance. It continues to evolve with the emergence of new technologies. As technologies mature and adoption expands, predictive analytics will continue to shape the future of finance. The future trends of predictive analytics in finance include AI-driven real-time analytics and decision-making, integration with blockchain and decentralized finance, and more. Data science and advanced technology are undergoing a revolution that will likely expand the application of predictive analytics' efficacy.

As financial markets continue to evolve, the integration of predictive models drives innovation, adaptability, and resilience, ensuring stable and profitable outcomes while advancing a data-driven approach to navigating an increasingly complex financial ecosystem. Finance is moving toward a predictive model of operation. Trends such as real-time analytics, behavioral risk modeling, ESG-integrated predictions, and regulatory compliance will soon be standard practice. Organizations that embrace predictive analytics now will not only manage risk more effectively but also position themselves to capture new opportunities faster than competitors. More advanced financial predictive analytics algorithms will even be able to predict the day or date when a customer can be expected to pay. Ultimately, the most effective use of predictive analytics in finance will involve a combination of data-driven insights and human insight and expertise [24].

5.8 CONCLUSION

The ability to predict trends and outcomes has become more and more important in the face of an abundance of data flows. Predicting the future direction of the economy is important to almost all aspects of finance. In the ever-evolving landscape of the business world, predicting the future is tough. For modern finance leaders, mastering this skill has become indispensable. In the domain of finance, predictive analytics plays a crucial role in decision-making, risk management, and fraud detection.

Predictive analytics is a powerful data analytics technique that uses big data mining, statistics, modeling, machine learning, and artificial intelligence to analyze large volumes of data and make predictions about future events or behaviors. Predictive analytics in finance refers to the use of historical and real-time data and statistical techniques to forecast future financial outcomes, like market trends, customer behavior, and risks. The use of predictive analytics in finance is transforming the industry. Financial institutions use predictive models for various purposes, such as portfolio management and fraud detection. Financial professionals can gain a significant competitive edge by leveraging historical data, machine learning algorithms, and advanced statistical techniques. Predictive analytics in finance equips finance leaders with the ability to manage risks proactively, improve accuracy in planning, optimize investments, and create better customer experiences.

Predictive analytics has redefined financial markets by harnessing the capabilities of big data, artificial intelligence, and machine learning to revolutionize investment strategies, risk management, and market efficiency. Predictive analytics in finance has moved from just being a competitive advantage to a necessity, especially in this digitally proliferating marketplace where customers' expectations continuously change. Understanding predictive analytics models is essential for finance professionals seeking to leverage data-driven insights in their decision-making processes. More information on the use of predictive analytics in finance is available from the books in [25-29] and the following related journals:

- *The Journal of Finance and Data Science*
- *Journal of Financial Risk Management*

REFERENCES

[1] A. Ahramovich, "Predictive analytics in finance: Use cases, platforms & adoption guidelines," October 2025, https://www.itransition.com/predictive-analytics/finance

[2] J. N. Okonkwo and O. Augustine, "Predictive analytics techniques for forecasting financial trends and optimizing business processes," *International Journal of Research and Innovation in Social Science,* vol. 8, no. 11, November 2024, pp. 2763-2775.

[3] M. N. O. Sadiku, P. A. Adekunte, and J. O. Sadiku, "Predictive analytics in finance," *International Journal of Trend in Scientific Research and Development*, vol. 10, no.2, March-April, 2026, pp. 1094-1104.

[4] "Supply chain predictive analytics: What is it and who's doing it?" https://riverlogic.com/?blog=supply-chain-predictive-analytics-what-is-it-and-whos-doing-it

[5] N. Babin, "AI and predictive analytics: Revolutionizing demand forecasting in supply chain management," https://www.linkedin.com/pulse/ai-predictive-analytics-revolutionizing-demand-supply-nicolas-babin-xrj2e/

[6] "From insight to innovation: Why data analysis will define industry leaders in 2025,"

https://www.inkl.com/news/from-insight-to-innovation-why-data-analysis-will-define-industry-leaders-in-2025

[7] "An overview of supply chain analytics," February 2023, Unknown Source.

[8] I. Tymchuk, "Big data and predictive analytics in supply chain: Success stories and tips," November 2020, https://www.n-ix.com/big-data-predictive-analytics-supply-chain-case-study/

[9] "Predictive analytics: A comprehensive guide for businesses," November 2024, https://www.jobspikr.com/blog/guide-to-predictive-analytics/

[10] "Predictive analytics for finance: Insights and case studies," August 2025, https://sigmatechnology.com/articles/predictive-analytics-for-finance-insights-and-case-studies/

[11] "Predictive analytics," https://www.financialprofessionals.org/glossary/predictive-analytics

[12] "A complete guide to predictive analytics in finance," https://www.tatvasoft.com/outsourcing/2025/07/predictive-analytics-in-finance.html

[13] O. E. Aro, "Predictive analytics in financial management: enhancing decision-making and risk management,"

International Journal of Research Publication and Reviews, vol. 5, no. 10, October 2024, pp. 2181-2194.

[14] "Predictive analytics in finance: Use cases and next steps," November 2023, https://www.highradius.com/resources/Blog/predictive-analytics-in-finance-guide/

[15] J. Richard, "Predictive analytics in finance," https://www.solving-finance.com/post/predictive-analytics-finance

[16] "Predictive analytics in finance: Use cases, benefits & more (2025)," September 2025, https://rtslabs.com/predictive-analytics-in-finance/

[17] D. Broby, "The use of predictive analytics in finance," *The Journal of Finance and Data Science*, vol. 8, November 2022, pp. 145-161.

[18] "Predictive analytics in finance: Use cases, benefits, examples, and future trends," https://www.mindinventory.com/blog/predictive-analytics-in-finance/

[19] S. Agarrwal, "Predictive analysis in financial markets," *IOSR Journal of Business and Management*, vol. 27, no. 4, April 2025, pp. 7-12.

[20] "Predictive analytics in financial risk management: Building models with R," October 2024, https://imarticus.org/blog/predictive-analytics-in-financial-risk-management/

[21] J. Kaur, "Reinventing predictive analytics in banking with agentic AI," October 2024, https://www.elixirclaw.ai/blog/predictive-analytics-ai-agents

[22] "AI-enabled analytics solutions for BFSI," November 2022, https://datenwissen.com/blog/ai-analytics-bfsi/

[23] M. F. Olagoke, "The role of predictive analytics in enhancing financial decision-making and risk management," *Journal of Financial Risk Management,* vol. 14, no. 1, February 2025, pp. 47-65.

[24] K. Ashwani, "How can predictive analytics be used in finance?" https://www.devopsschool.com/blog/how-can-predictive-analytics-be-used-in-finance/

[25] R. Modak, *Predictive Analytics in Finance: Machine Learning Models for Credit Scoring and Investment.* Kindle Edition, 2025.

[26] A. C. Tatto, *Predictive Analytics in Finance: Forecasting Trends and Market Movements.* Independently Published, 2025.

[27] A. Bari, M. Chaouchi, and T. Jung, *Predictive Analytics For Dummies*. For Dummies, 2nd edition, 2016.

[28] J. P. Morgan, *Python for Predictive Analytics in Finance: Anticipate Market Movements (Python for Finance: Algorithmic Trading, Automated Trading, Cryptocurrency Trading, Financial Data, Predictive Analytics).* Independently Published, 2024.

[29] A. Peak, Financial *Forecasting With R: Master Predictive Analytics, Build Accurate Models, and Drive Smarter Investment Decisions*. Independently Published, 2025.

CHAPTER 6: PREDICTIVE ANALYTICS IN MANUFACTURING

"Every time history repeats itself, the price goes up."

- James C. Maxwell

6.1 INTRODUCTION

Today's digital world requires organizations to intelligently process and leverage data to stay ahead in the market. The manufacturing industry is becoming increasingly competitive, and staying ahead requires leveraging the latest technologies. Marketing professionals and industry leaders are now adopting AI-powered business analytics for predictions and prescriptions to handle the unprecedented rate of data generation. By leveraging advanced algorithms, machine learning, and historical data, predictive analytics transforms raw information into actionable insights, driving innovation and competitiveness. From healthcare's personalized patient care plans to retail's inventory management, and from finance's risk assessment to manufacturing's maintenance scheduling, the examples of predictive analytics are as diverse as they are impactful. Predictive analytics in manufacturing can be the game-changer you need to provide this foresight and propel your business to new heights [1].

Predictive analytics is simply looking at the historic trends, conducting analysis in the present, and forecasting the future. In manufacturing, predictive analytics refers to the use of statistical techniques, machine learning algorithms, and data mining to analyze historical and real-time data. The key benefits of predictive analytics in manufacturing include minimizing downtime and maintenance costs, improving product quality, optimizing supply chain management, enhancing operational efficiency, and increasing customer satisfaction [2].

Predictive analytics is a branch of data science that uses historical data, machine learning algorithms, and statistical models to analyze potential future outcomes. It is reshaping manufacturing by enabling proactive decision-making and reducing inefficiencies. This type of advanced analytics focuses on data science, statistical modeling, machine learning (ML), big data, and data mining techniques to derive insights from vast amounts of historical data. In manufacturing, predictive analytics has been widely used for improving operational efficiency, minimizing expenses, vision inspecting system, and enhancing overall decision-making. The goal is to predict future outcomes, identify potential issues, and uncover opportunities for improvement [3].

This chapter examines how predictive analytics is transforming manufacturing processes. It begins by explaining predictive analytics. It describes predictive analytics in manufacturing and provides some of its applications. It highlights some benefits and challenges of predictive analytics in manufacturing. It predicts the future of predictive analytics in manufacturing. The last section concludes with comments.

6.2 WHAT IS PREDICTIVE ANALYTICS?

As its name implies, predictive analytics is about predicting future trends such as sales demand and exchange rates. and other important metrics. The technique relies on the application of statistical modeling and regression analysis to historical data to determine and understand trends and formulate future predictions. Strictly speaking, predictive analytics does not predict the future, but rather uses probability theories to determine what is likely to happen based on patterns and trends revealed by analyzing historical data [4]. Predictive analytics accurately anticipates customer demand, preventing overstocking and stockouts while adapting to market changes. Figure 6.1 illustrates predictive analytics [5], while Figure 6.2 shows different components of predictive analytics [6].

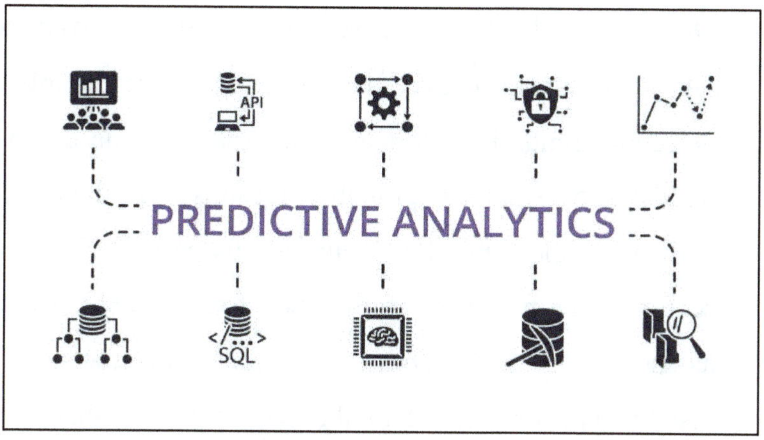

Figure 6.1 Predictive analytics [5].

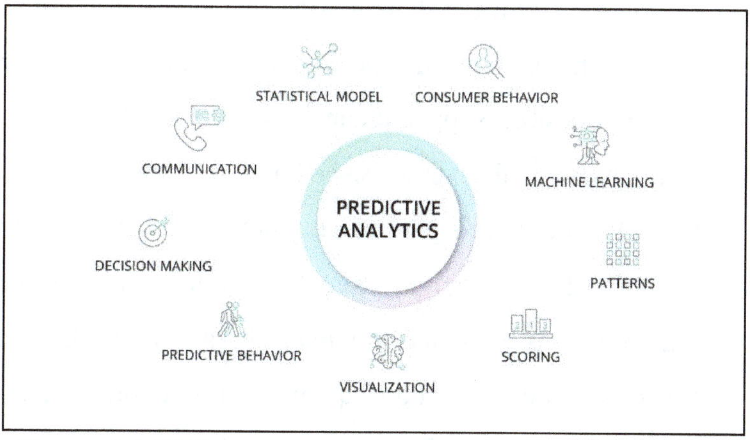

Figure 6.2 Different components of predictive analytics [6].

In general, analytics provides an efficient way to improve planning because it gives you better forecasts. There are different types of data analytics. They are briefly explained as follows [7]:

- *Descriptive Analytics:* Descriptive analytics examines what has happened over the years. They are capable of detecting trends in historical data. Analytics can uncover trends and postulate probable reasons for change by comparing the same data from various periods. It can be seen as the baseline of the industry, which basically assesses past and current data for more meaningful insights and delivers it to the people to use their own intelligence and knowledge to make decisions.
- *Predictive Analytics:* This assists businesses in predicting what might happen and the impact of various situations, such as possible supply chain bottlenecks. Managers can be proactive rather than responsive by pushing them to evaluate these prospective circumstances before they occur. Predictive analytics may be used to identify patterns and trends as well as anticipate breakdowns that may impact suppliers and, consequently, production processes. Predictive analytics for the supply chain leverages data, statistical algorithms, and machine learning techniques to identify the likelihood of future outcomes.
- *Prescriptive Analytics:* Prescriptive analytics builds on predictive analytics and dives deeper into predicting future insights on what can be done next. Prescriptive analytics uses the findings of descriptive and predictive analytics to recommend what measures a business should take to

achieve its objectives. Because prescriptive analytics is increasingly complicated, they need more powerful software capable of rapidly processing and interpreting large amounts of data.

- *Cognitive Analytics:* Cognitive analytics attempts to mimic human thought and behavior, and it can assist companies in answering challenging, complex problems. Cognitive analytics does this by utilizing artificial intelligence (AI), which allows it to improve over time. With the use of AI in the industry, answering complex questions and draw out contextual conclusions on how humans would have interacted with the situation. It helps with more meaningful data and scales experience and knowledge with better decisions.
- *Diagnostic Analytics:* This gives the ability to identify the root cause. It is characterized by techniques such as drill-down, data discovery, data mining, and correlations. It involves analyzing overall performance and figuring out why errors, mistakes, and delays occur. It lets the manager know the delays, breakdowns, and disruptions in the demand and supply processes and the reasons behind them.

Figure 6.3 shows these major types of data analytics [8]. Unlike diagnostic and descriptive analytics, which were designed to analyze situations after they happened, predictive analytics utilizes advanced data analytics techniques to forecast future outcomes. In the supply chain, the time has come to shift from mere descriptive and diagnostic analytics to predictive and prescriptive analytics. Predictive analytics is a branch of data analytics that makes predictions about future outcomes using historical data combined with statistical modeling, data mining techniques, and machine learning. Figure 6.4 shows the predictive analytics process [9].

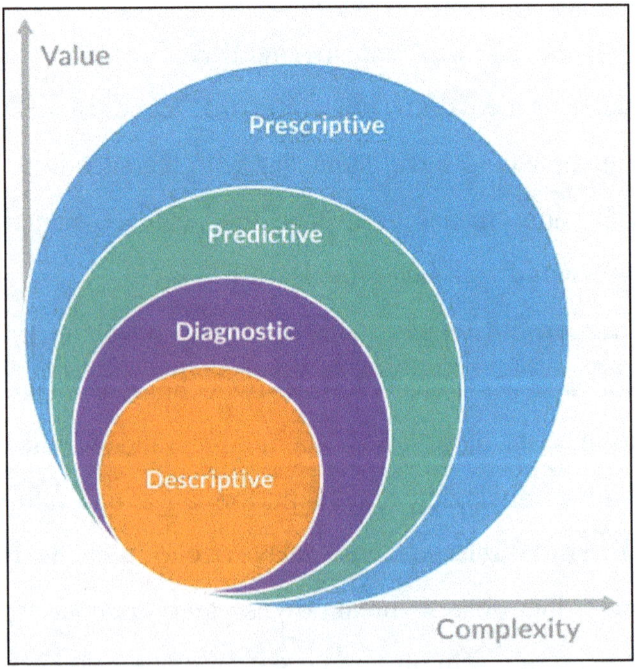

Figure 6.3 Types of data analytics [8].

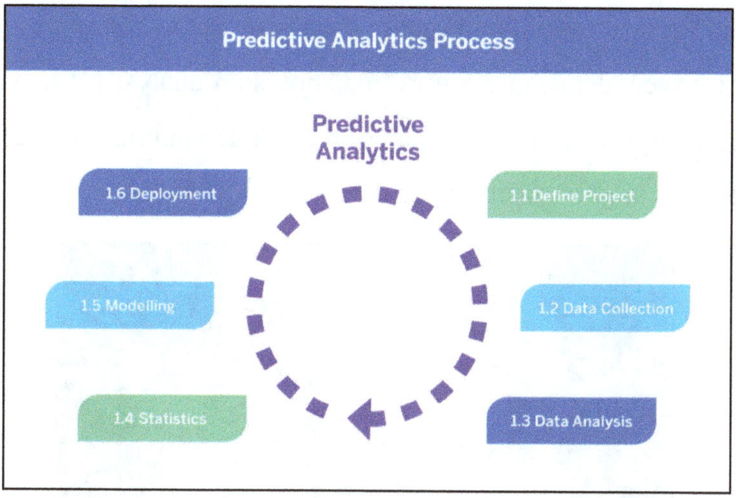

Figure 6.4 Predictive analytics process [9].

6.3 PREDICTIVE ANALYTICS IN MANUFACTURING

Today's manufacturing organizations operate in a dynamic environment characterized by increased complexity and uncertainty. Manufacturing companies are under constant pressure to improve efficiency, reduce costs, and maintain high-quality standards. Predictive analytics has emerged as a game-changing tool, enabling manufacturers to harness the power of data to anticipate challenges, optimize operations, and make informed decisions. Predictive analytics in the manufacturing industry refers to a branch of advanced analytics that makes predictions about future outcomes with the help of historical data integrated with statistical modeling, AI, data mining techniques, and machine learning, and much more. It comprises multiple processes that organizations can use to reinforce their data-driven decisions. Figure 6.5 shows an analyst [10], while Figure 6.6 displays the steps for implementing predictive analytics in manufacturing [2].

Figure 6.5 An analyst [10].

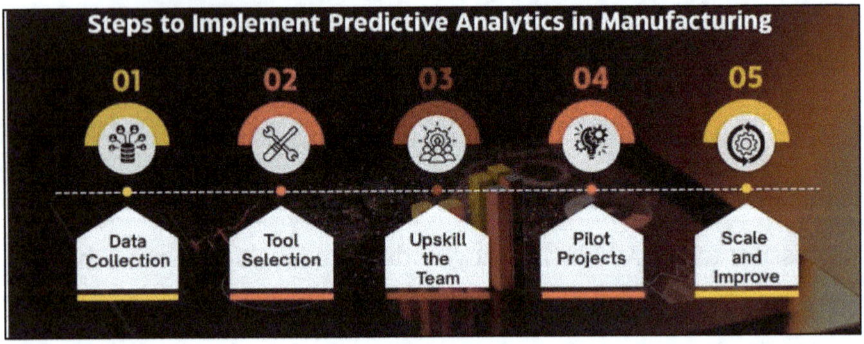

Figure 6.6 Steps for implementing predictive analytics in manufacturing [2].

For decades, manufacturers have used data as a way to gain a competitive edge. Using technology and analytics turns data into knowledge. Companies have started transitioning to digital software and connected devices to reduce labor associated with manual data collection and documentation. Connected real-time devices are able to collect more data points. This can help predict how much time or how many pieces can be produced before a failure. Predictive analytics becomes increasingly accurate as more data is collected and correlations are made [11].

6.4 APPLICATIONS OF PREDICTIVE ANALYTICS IN MANUFACTURING

Predictive analytics in manufacturing can help with manufacturing data analytics, predictive maintenance, demand forecasting, inventory optimization, price optimization, quality control, and workforce management. Figure 6.7 shows some applications of predictive analytics in manufacturing [12]. Common applications of predictive analytics in manufacturing include the following [12-16]:

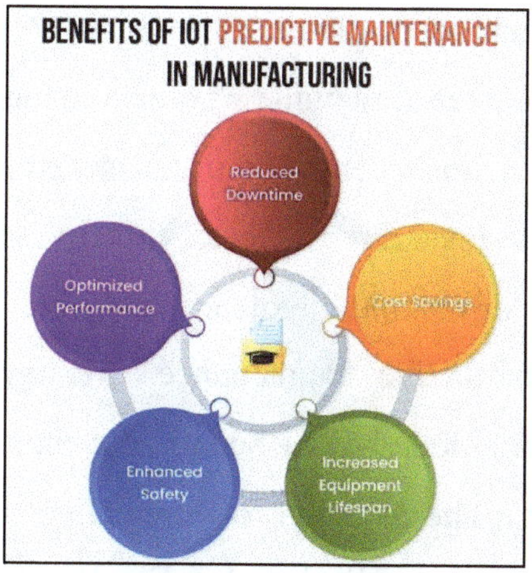

Figure 6.8 Some benefits of predictive maintenance in manufacturing [17].

- *Predictive Maintenance*: Unplanned downtime is the enemy of efficiency. In traditional manufacturing, manufacturers either perform maintenance on a fixed schedule or wait until a machine breaks down before taking action. Issues like equipment failures, quality defects, or supply chain disruptions tend to be ignored until after they cause problems. Predictive analytics flips this approach on its head. Predictive maintenance involves analyzing data from machinery to predict potential equipment failures. It makes use of real-time data connections and analytics to prevent unplanned breakdowns in manufacturing technology. Analytics obtained via IoT for predictive maintenance utilize sensor data and patterns in historical data to predict any type of failure expected in equipment before it can occur. It is used to minimize the occurrence of unplanned downtime and maintenance-related expenses. Consequently, you can schedule maintenance before any breakdown occurs, thereby saving costs and reducing downtime. Not every piece of equipment requires predictive maintenance. We have to determine which equipment would benefit the most from minimal downtime. The benefits of predictive maintenance in manufacturing are displayed in Figure 6.8 [17].

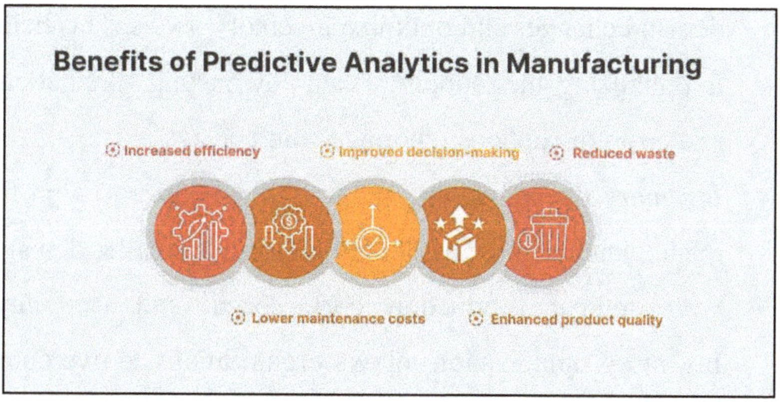

Figure 6.9 Some benefits of predictive analytics in manufacturing [13].

- *Quality Control:* Predictive manufacturing analytics can be used to anticipate defects and quality issues in products by analyzing production data. It works by identifying patterns that usually lead to product defects, therefore improving product consistency and reducing waste. Plant operators do not work blindly anymore, but can check the quality of goods as well as factory operations through ERP software. This helps in taking proactive measures to ensure product quality and reduce waste.
- *Supply Chain Optimization:* Managing a global supply chain is complex, where any misstep can cause major delays and dissatisfied customers. Predictive analytics in logistics helps build resilience by analyzing historical data on customer demand and inventory needs. By analyzing data from various points in the supply chain, manufacturers can predict and respond to supply and

demand changes and optimize inventory levels. This helps in optimizing the supply chain by making predictions related to disruptions, shortages, and delays.

- *Inventory Optimization:* To maximize profit, manufacturers must be able to respond to market demand with optimal production cost, speed, and flexibility. Inventory optimization allows organizations to overcome common challenges that might come from maintaining an inventory of various products. It works in the best possible way to maintain the correct amount of product stock to meet the demand of the customers. Predictive analytics can be used in forecasting and optimizing inventory requirements to reduce carrying costs while ensuring availability of material, thus supporting just-in-time manufacturing strategies.
- *Price Optimization:* Price optimization is a procedure of determining customer and market data to ensure the optimal cost of a product. It can include the accumulation of demographic, psychographic, and historical sales data to better understand the behavior of the customers and use the data to analyze discounted and promotional prices. The primary goal is to analyze the right price that works in the best possible ways to attract consumers, maximize sales, and increase profits.

- *Demand Forecasting:* The digital strength is powered by demand forecasting capabilities. Predictive analytics and AI take in historical sales data from a stock monitoring system and market trends to predict customer demand. Predictive analytics in supply chain helps in forecasting future customer demand, which allows companies to optimize inventory levels, reducing the risk of stockouts or excess inventory. Predictive models are designed to consider factors such as seasonality, promotional activities, economic indicators, and changes in consumer preferences to generate reliable predictions.
- *Risk Management:* By analyzing various risk factors such as geopolitical events, natural disasters, or market fluctuations, predictive analytics can help identify potential disruptions in the supply chain. This enables companies to develop contingency plans and strategies to minimize impact. This helps prevent workplace accidents, improves worker safety, and ensures compliance with safety regulations.
- *Production Planning:* Predictive modeling offers collection and analysis of historical data, risk assessment, continuous improvement, and decision support to generate products that can deliver satisfactory value to customers, ensuring their success. Predictive analytics, when powered with AI, are deemed useful in

optimizing production schedules based on demand forecasts and resource availability. This results in reduced idle time and improved utilization of machines and labor planning.

- *Fraud Detection:* This involves analyzing real-time data streams from sensors and production systems to identify anomalies and deviations from the normal operational framework. It analyzes transaction data to recognize patterns that may indicate fraud and predict potential fraudulent practices using historical data. This enhances security measures with the help of proactive fraud detection measures.
- *Order Management*: Order management is a process of capturing, tracking, and ultimately fulfilling the orders of the customers. This system works in the best possible way to automate the complete lifecycle of an order. It includes everything, i.e., inventory tracking, work order creation, and even other options like refunds and exchanges. It makes the best out of manufacturing analytics by generating consumer trends so that businesses can understand when to restock to avoid any kind of shortages.
- *Automotive Industry:* Predictive analytics helps automotive manufacturers forecast demand, optimize production schedules, and ensure timely delivery of parts. By using predictive maintenance tools, automotive

manufacturers can track the condition of key components, such as engines or assembly line machines, and predict when they are likely to fail. This allows manufacturers to schedule maintenance in advance, avoiding unexpected breakdowns that can halt production.

- *Pharmaceutical Manufacturing*: Maintaining regulatory compliance and product consistency is critical in the pharmaceutical industry. With predictive analytics, pharmaceutical manufacturers can monitor environmental variables, such as temperature, humidity, and pressure, throughout the production process. In the pharmaceutical sector, predictive models are used to monitor production conditions, ensuring compliance with stringent quality standards. Maintaining regulatory compliance and product consistency is critical in the pharmaceutical industry.

6.5 BENEFITS

A predictive analytics solution provides numerous benefits in a manufacturing company, like reduced downtime with extended equipment life, production optimization, AI-driven quality control, better quality control, reduced cost, supply chain resilience that navigates uncertainty, energy efficiency cuts costs, and boosts sustainability. Forecasting helps the business to timely anticipate potential issues and take corrective and informed decisions. Predictive analytics helps improve energy efficiency by uncovering usage patterns and optimizing energy loads in real time. Other benefits of predictive analytics in manufacturing include the following [2,13,16]:

- *Improved Decision-making:* Intelligent prediction models empower leaders and supervisors with a 360-degree view of manufacturing processes. It provides foresight into inventory levels, market trends, supply chain dynamics, and changing customer demands. These insights help the decision makers to make strategic choices in their business and optimize their production workflows. Time-sensitive decisions can be easily accomplished using AI-based data analysis in real-time for crucial insights. Demand forecasts inform long-term planning and strategic decisions, such as capacity expansion, new product introductions, and market entry strategies.
- *Enhanced Customer Satisfaction*: Understanding your customers' needs and preferences is vital for delivering products that meet their expectations. Predictive analytics use cases in manufacturing can analyze customer data to identify trends and anticipate demand. They enable the manufacturing company to deliver better customer service and on-time delivery without delays. This allows you to tailor your products and services to meet market needs, improving customer satisfaction and loyalty.

- *Reduced Waste:* Predictive maintenance and balanced workflow sustained from manufacturing analytics solutions deprive businesses of any kind of resource wastage or redundant workflows. Producers can overview the entire production process and identify patterns indicating material overuse or energy inefficiency, channeling the improvements to the required parts. Targeted refinements of the manufacturing processes remove scrap building, power misuse, and chances of rework, resulting in cost savings as well as fulfilling environmental responsibility.
- *Increased Efficiency:* Predictive analytics in manufacturing has been playing an important role in minimizing inefficiencies and increasing revenue. The time and costs previously utilized for manual data analysis are automated using predictive AI, thus resulting in cost savings and efficient operations. Predictive maintenance significantly eliminates unplanned downtime, ensuring higher productivity of equipment by increasing its lifespan through timely repairs and servicing. Predictive software delivers actionable solutions by spotting inefficiencies, strengthening product development strategy, and optimally employing available resources. Organizations that effectively utilize predictive analytics for demand forecasting are better positioned to enhance operational

efficiency, respond to market changes, and achieve competitive advantages.

- *Lower Maintenance Costs*: Timely detection of potential machinery failure with the help of predictive analytics in manufacturing saves the production unit from big blunders. Shift from reactive to predictive maintenance: fewer emergency callouts, reduced overtime, less emergency parts procurement, and lower repair costs from earlier intervention. Early fault detection enables targeted component repair at stage 2 degradation, costing one-third to one-fifth of full asset replacement required at catastrophic failure stage.
- *Accuracy*: Analytics powered by AI algorithms and machine learning have proved to be useful in increasing the accuracy of prediction-making. These processes process complex and huge datasets more precisely as compared to statistical processes. Analytical techniques can detect correlation within the data and subtle patterns that may not be recognized by analysts at times.

Figure 6.9 shows some benefits of predictive analytics in manufacturing [2].

6.6 CHALLENGES

Manufacturing companies face numerous challenges that can impact their efficiency, profitability, and competitiveness. Common challenges include data privacy and security, data quality, integration, reliability, risks, and the need for skilled personnel. Many small and medium manufacturing enterprises lack the infrastructure and technical know-how to collect, store, process, and analyze their data and translate them to productivity gains. Other challenges of predictive analytics in manufacturing include the following [1,13,14,16]:

- *Data Privacy*: The increasing cases of data breaches and hacking have turned the attention of business owners toward data security and privacy. Predictive analytics is expected to be a part of this trend that helps businesses add an extra security layer. The new technology will implement advanced encryption, privacy-preserving machine learning techniques, and multi-layer computations to protect information related to inventory, business, or clients.
- *Data Quality*: Inaccurate, incomplete, or inconsistent data can lead to unreliable predictions. AI video analytics models are heavily dependent on data, which at times may be incomplete or inaccurate in nature. This data may have been collected from legacy machines with limited sensors

or stored in silos across departments. When these models are trained on low-quality data, it leads to unreliable predictions and insights.

- *Integration:* Integrating predictive analytics tools with existing systems can be technically challenging. Legacy systems and older technologies often struggle to communicate with newer platforms, which means valuable data collected from various sources (e.g., machinery, sensors, inventory management systems) is stored in isolated systems. Integrating modern AI tools with these systems is time-consuming, expensive, and technically complex to execute. To overcome this, manufacturers must develop effective integration strategies.
- *High Initial Costs*: Manufacturing processes involve significant costs related to labor, materials, energy, and equipment maintenance. Implementing predictive analytics requires investment in software, hardware, and skilled personnel. The initial investment is significantly high for setting a sturdy framework of predictive analytics in manufacturing. Small and mid-sized manufacturers may face investment barriers as predictive analytics tools require high implementation costs. This is mainly because it involves sensors, IoT devices, data

infrastructure over the cloud or on-premises, and skilled personnel.

- *Skills Gap*: Implementing predictive analytics requires specialized knowledge, and many manufacturers face a shortage of skilled professionals who can build, manage, and refine predictive models. Also, existing workers may resist change and require retraining, leading to issues in workforce readiness. Manufacturers can tackle this challenge by upskilling their workforce and partnering with external experts. Educate employees on the benefits of predictive analytics and provide training to build confidence and skills.
- *Reliability:* There is a possibility of the production of false positives and negatives by AI models, thus creating uncertainty around model accuracy and reliability. These models require continuous tuning and retraining, the absence of which may lead to struggles with rare or unexpected events, errors, downtime, and even safety risks.
- *Scalability:* Scalability, cost-effectiveness, and flexibility are the new foundation stones for any business that aims to sustain itself in the competitive market. A major issue in predictive analytics in manufacturing is related to the shift from pilot projects to full-scale deployments. This may be due to limitations in

infrastructure, variability across production lines, or high maintenance requirements.

- *Resistance:* Manufacturing analytics solutions are still novel concepts in the technological world, and thus, the limited exposure makes it challenging for businesses to efficiently implement the models and leverage the benefits. Employees may resist adopting new technologies, fearing job displacement or increased workload. Trust issues over automated systems may be raised internally related to change management and cultural resistance. Major shifts in decision-making processes and organizational culture are inevitable during the adoption of AI, as employees and managers may hesitate to rely completely on AI-based outputs.
- *Change Management:* Adopting predictive analytics requires more than just implementing new technologies; it requires a shift in mindset. Employees across all levels must be on board with the change. In many cases, resistance can arise due to fear of job displacement or a lack of understanding of how new technologies will fit into existing workflows. Addressing these concerns head-on and providing consistent support throughout the implementation process will increase the likelihood of a successful transition.

- *Complexity:* Manufacturing is a complex and daunting task that involves machines, materials, and workers. With the help of predictive analytics in manufacturing, businesses get a smarter way to manage these complexities by analyzing the production data to identify inefficiencies and enhance workflows.
- *Supply Chain Disruptions:* Supply chain disruptions, such as delays in raw material deliveries, transportation issues, and supplier performance problems, can impact production schedules and increase operational costs. By using predictive analytics in manufacturing, companies can anticipate these disruptions and optimize supply chain management to ensure timely deliveries and reduce risks.

6.7 FUTURE OF PREDICTIVE ANALYTICS IN MANUFACTURING

Manufacturing operations have come a long way. The manufacturing sector is moving fast and is completely driven by tech and data science. As manufacturing companies continuously evolve and become more data-driven, predictive analytics can help drive innovation and competitiveness. With the advancements in cloud computing and data analytics, manufacturers are now able to make informed decisions and predict potential problems before they occur. Predictive analytics in manufacturing has become a powerful tool for manufacturing businesses that are looking forward to improving their operations and optimizing their processes. The future trends of predictive analytics include artificial intelligence (AI) and machine learning (ML), real-time analytics, and predictive maintenance in IoT. AI and ML in place allow predictive models to learn from new data over time without human intervention and become more accurate and efficient. As these technologies improve, predictive analytics is expected to become more intuitive and dynamic, producing reliable and faster forecasts [15].

The future of predictive analytics in manufacturing depends on the different trends and predictive analytics tools for manufacturing that are taking the lead in this niche. The trend of artificial intelligence and machine learning empowers predictive analytics in manufacturing by analyzing massive datasets to forecast equipment failures, enhancing production, ensuring quality control, streamlining the supply chain, reducing costs, and enhancing decision-making. There is no doubt that IoT brings convenience with control. These changes are just the beginning, and there is a lot to witness with the use of predictive analytics in manufacturing in the future.

When people talk about the future of manufacturing, Industry 4.0 is often mentioned as a key driver of change. Industry 4.0 became a global trend that started in Germany as a high-tech manufacturing concept. It builds on previous industrial revolutions by integrating modern technologies like artificial intelligence (AI), machine learning (ML), and the Internet of Things (IoT) directly into manufacturing processes. Its goal is to incorporate vertical and horizontal integrations of all core functions, from manufacturing, procurement, and warehousing, all the way to sales of the final product [18].

6.8 CONCLUSION

Predictive analytics uses statistical techniques, machine learning, and data mining to discover facts in order to make predictions about unknown future events. In the manufacturing sector, predictive analytics refers to the application of sophisticated data analysis techniques and machine learning models to predict future events and trends based on historical data. It helps manufacturing businesses to enhance processes, increase efficiency, and improve their decision-making. For this reason, manufacturers are making the best of predictive analytics in manufacturing.

Predictive analytics offers a powerful solution to the common challenges faced by manufacturing companies. By leveraging data, statistical algorithms, and machine learning techniques, you can enhance operational efficiency, reduce downtime, improve product quality, optimize supply chain management, and increase customer satisfaction. Adopting predictive analytics in manufacturing is no longer an option but a necessity to stay competitive in the market. More information on the use of predictive analytics in manufacturing is available from the books in [19-21].

REFERENCES

[1] "Predictive analytics in manufacturing: Key benefits, use cases, and implementation strategies," June 2024,https://www.matellio.com/blog/predictive-analytics-in-manufacturing/

[2] "Predictive analytics in manufacturing – Use cases, benefits, and implementation guide," June 2025, https://www.a3logics.com/blog/predictive-analytics-in-manufacturing/

[3] M. N. O. Sadiku, P. A. Adekunte, and J. O. Sadiku, "Predictive analytics in manufacturing," International Journal of Trend in Scientific Research and Development, vol. 10, no.2, March-April, 2026, pp. 1221-1231.

[4] "Supply chain predictive analytics: What is it and who's doing it?" https://riverlogic.com/?blog=supply-chain-predictive-analytics-what-is-it-and-whos-doing-it

[5] N. Babin, "AI and predictive analytics: Revolutionizing demand forecasting in supply chain management," https://www.linkedin.com/pulse/ai-predictive-analytics-revolutionizing-demand-supply-nicolas-babin-xrj2e/

[6] "From insight to innovation: Why data analysis will define industry leaders in 2025,"

https://www.inkl.com/news/from-insight-to-innovation-why-data-analysis-will-define-industry-leaders-in-2025

[7] "An overview of supply chain analytics," February 2023, Unknown Source.

[8] I. Tymchuk, "Big data and predictive analytics in supply chain: Success stories and tips," November 2020, https://www.n-ix.com/big-data-predictive-analytics-supply-chain-case-study/

[9] "Predictive analytics: A comprehensive guide for businesses," November 2024, https://www.jobspikr.com/blog/guide-to-predictive-analytics/

[10] "Exploring predictive quality analytics in manufacturing," February 2024, https://cerexio.com/blog/exploring-predictive-quality-analytics-manufacturing

[11] "Predictive analytics in manufacturing: Use cases and benefits," https://www.machinemetrics.com/blog/predictive-analytics-in-manufacturing

[12] "7 Predictive analytics examples across industries: From sports and marketing to finance and healthcare," November 2023, https://pixelplex.io/blog/predictive-analytics-examples/

[13] "Predictive analytics and AI in manufacturing: Use cases, benefits, and challenges," April 2026,

https://kritikalsolutions.com/predictive-analytics-and-ai-in-manufacturing/

[14] “Predictive analytics in manufacturing processes,” https://www.meegle.com/en_us/topics/predictive-analytics/predictive-analytics-in-manufacturing-processes

[15] “Comprehensive guide to predictive analytics in manufacturing,” April 2026, https://www.mindinventory.com/blog/predictive-analytics-in-manufacturing/

[16] T. Czaban, “Predictive analytics in manufacturing: What it means for the future of production,” March 2025, https://www.gooddata.com/blog/predictive-analytics-in-manufacturing-what-it-means-for-the-future-of-production/

[17] D. Pandey, “Benefits of IoT predictive maintenance in manufacturing,” July 2024, https://www.aeologic.com/blog/benefits-of-iot-predictive-maintenance-in-manufacturing/

[18] B. Nikolic et al., “Predictive manufacturing systems in Industry 4.0: Trends, benefits and challenges,” Proceedings of the 28th DAAAM International Symposium, Vienna, Austria, 2017, pp. 796-802.

[19] A. Bari, M. Chaouchi, and T. Jung, Predictive Analytics For Dummies. For Dummies, 2nd edition, 2016.

[20] H. Jeong, Predictive Analytics for Smart Manufacturing: Use and Impact from a Systems Thinking Perspective. MIT, 2016.

[21] M. Salehi, Bayesian-Based Predictive Analytics for Manufacturing Performance Metrics in the Era of Industry 4.0. KIT Scientific Publishing, 2019.

CHAPTER 7: PREDICTIVE ANALYTICS IN SUPPLY CHAIN

"You have the power to make the world a better place by being kind to someone today."

– Joyce Meyer

7.1 INTRODUCTION

The global supply chain landscape is undergoing a profound transformation, driven by an increasing need for resilience, efficiency, and responsiveness. At the forefront of this evolution is predictive analytics, a powerful capability that leverages data, statistical algorithms, and machine learning techniques to identify the likelihood of future outcomes based on historical data. Predictive analytics, when combined with artificial intelligence (AI), is set to redefine how supply chains operate, shifting them from reactive to proactive and even prescriptive models.

In the modern global economy, the supply chain is no longer a back-office function but a primary driver of competitive advantage and corporate resilience. The transition from reactive to proactive management has been accelerated by the integration of predictive analytics. Predictive analytics has emerged as a key success factor in supply chain management, using historical data and machine learning to turn uncertainty into actionable insights. This forward-looking capability allows businesses to make proactive, data-driven decisions rather than reactive ones [1].

Predictive analytics in supply chain works by collecting and analyzing large amounts of historical data from various sources such as sales, inventory levels, weather patterns, and supplier performance. By using predictive analytics in the supply chain, organizations can optimize their supply chain operations, reduce costs, improve efficiency, and enhance overall decision-making, ultimately leading to a more agile and responsive supply chain [2].

Predictive analytics is a sophisticated branch of advanced analytics that leverages historical data, statistical algorithms, and machine learning techniques to forecast future outcomes. Predictive analytics in the supply chain refers to the use of data, statistical algorithms, and machine learning techniques to forecast future events and trends within the supply chain. It uses data to forecast what will happen so you can make smarter decisions about inventory, shipping, and risk. It analyzes historical data and then predicts inventory levels, demand, supplier performance, transportation logistics, and other critical factors. Using predictive analytics in supply chain can indeed increase profits and provide several compelling reasons to do so [3].

This chapter aims to explore the role of predictive analytics in supply chain management. It begins by explaining predictive analytics. It describes predictive analytics in supply chain and provides some of its applications. It highlights some benefits and challenges of predictive analytics in supply chain. It predicts the future of predictive analytics in supply chain. The last section concludes with comments.

7.2 WHAT IS PREDICTIVE ANALYTICS?

As its name implies, predictive analytics is about predicting future trends such as sales demand and exchange rates. and other important metrics. The technique relies on the application of statistical modeling and regression analysis to historical data to determine and understand trends and formulate future predictions. Strictly speaking, predictive analytics does not predict the future, but rather uses probability theories to determine what is likely to happen based on patterns and trends revealed by analyzing historical data [4]. Predictive analytics accurately anticipates customer demand, preventing overstocking and stockouts while adapting to market changes. Figure 7.1 illustrates predictive analytics [5], while Figure 7.2 shows different components of predictive analytics [6].

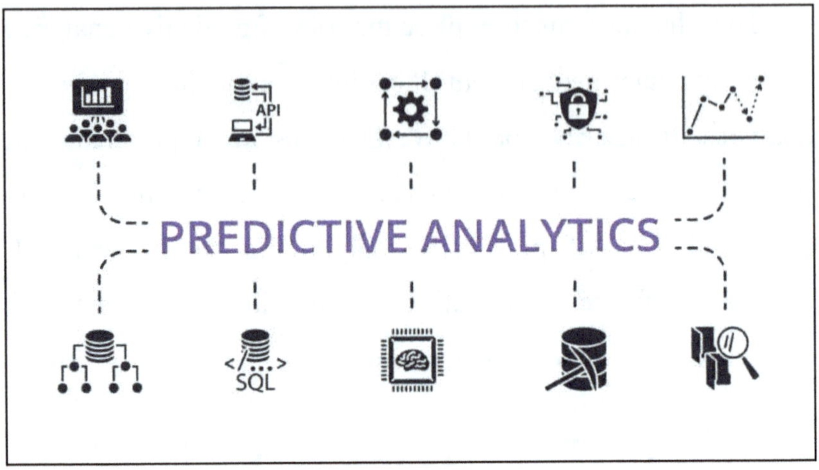

Figure 7.1 Predictive analytics [5].

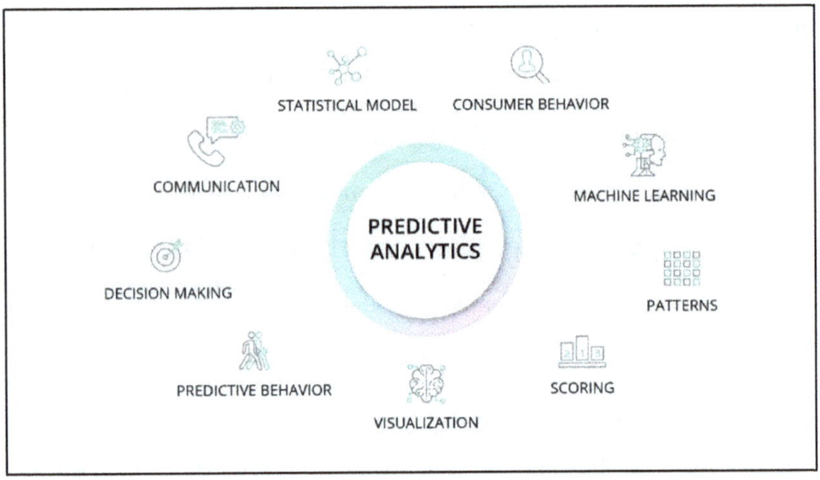

Figure 7.2 Different components of predictive analytics [6].

In general, analytics provides an efficient way to improve planning because it gives you better forecasts. There are different types of data analytics. They are briefly explained as follows [7]:

- *Descriptive Analytics:* Descriptive analytics examines what has happened over the years. They are capable of detecting trends in historical data. Analytics can uncover trends and postulate probable reasons for change by comparing the same data from various periods. It can be seen as the baseline of the industry, which basically assesses past and current data for more meaningful insights and delivers it to the people to use their own intelligence and knowledge to make decisions.
- *Predictive Analytics:* This assists businesses in predicting what might happen and the impact of various situations, such as possible supply chain bottlenecks. Managers can be proactive rather than responsive by pushing them to evaluate these prospective circumstances before they occur. Predictive analytics may be used to identify patterns and trends as well as anticipate breakdowns that may impact suppliers and, consequently, production processes. Predictive analytics for the supply chain leverages data, statistical algorithms, and machine learning techniques to identify the likelihood of future outcomes.
- *Prescriptive Analytics:* Prescriptive analytics builds on predictive analytics and dives deeper into predicting future insights on what can be done next. Prescriptive analytics uses the findings of descriptive and predictive analytics to recommend what measures a business should take to

achieve its objectives. Because prescriptive analytics is increasingly complicated, they need more powerful software capable of rapidly processing and interpreting large amounts of data.

- *Cognitive Analytics:* Cognitive analytics attempts to mimic human thought and behavior, and it can assist companies in answering challenging, complex problems. Cognitive analytics does this by utilizing artificial intelligence (AI), which allows it to improve over time. With the use of AI in the industry, answering complex questions and draw out contextual conclusions on how humans would have interacted with the situation. It helps with more meaningful data and scales experience and knowledge with better decisions.
- *Diagnostic Analytics:* This gives the ability to identify the root cause. It is characterized by techniques such as drill-down, data discovery, data mining, and correlations. It involves analyzing overall performance and figuring out why errors, mistakes, and delays occur. It lets the manager know the delays, breakdowns, and disruptions in the demand and supply processes and the reasons behind them.

Figure 7.3 shows these major types of data analytics [8]. Unlike diagnostic and descriptive analytics, which were designed to analyze situations after they happened, predictive analytics utilizes advanced data analytics techniques to forecast future outcomes. In the supply chain, the time has come to shift from mere descriptive and diagnostic analytics to predictive and prescriptive analytics. Predictive analytics is a branch of data analytics that makes predictions about future outcomes using historical data combined with statistical modeling, data mining techniques, and machine learning. Figure 7.4 shows the predictive analytics process [9].

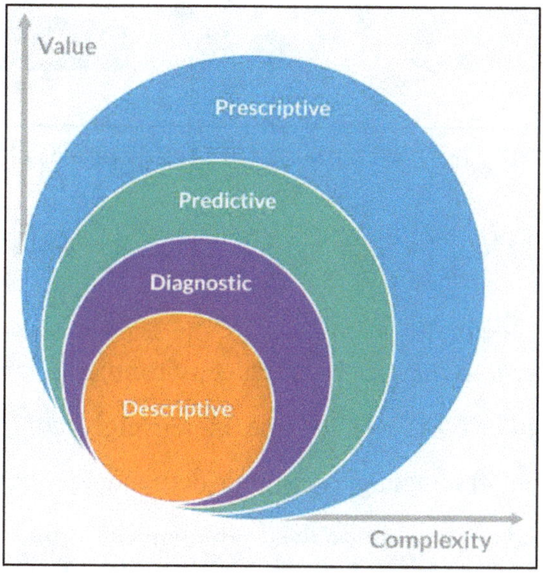

Figure 7.3 Types of data analytics [8].

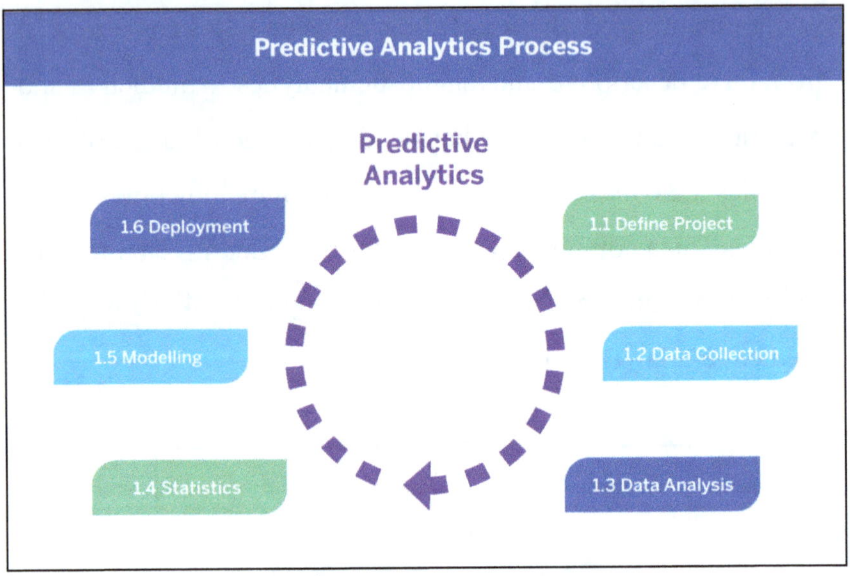

Figure 7.4 Predictive analytics process [9].

7.3 PREDICTIVE ANALYTICS IN SUPPLY CHAIN

In today's dynamic business environment, supply chain management (SCM) has become increasingly complex due to globalization, fluctuating consumer demand, and unpredictable market trends. To address these challenges, organizations are turning to predictive analytics powered by artificial intelligence (AI) and machine learning (ML) to enhance demand forecasting. Predictive analytics is a process that connects your existing systems, cleans up your data, and uses statistical models to help you make better decisions. Predictive analytics in supply chain helps you move from reactive to proactive. By leveraging historical data, machine learning (ML), and real-time market signals, organizations aim to anticipate demand shifts, optimize inventory, and mitigate risks before they manifest. The integration of AI-driven predictive analytics in SCM enables businesses to make data-informed decisions, mitigating risks associated with demand variability [10].

For decades, supply chain planning has been a backward-looking exercise, heavily reliant on spreadsheets and periodic updates. These traditional methods are reactive, often struggling to keep pace with the fast-moving, data-driven supply chains. Globalization, e-commerce, and increased customer expectations have introduced new levels of complexity. The limitations of traditional planning are evident: static forecasts, typically updated monthly or quarterly, simply cannot keep up with the rapid pace of change. Predictive analytics is changing how organizations plan, operate, and compete in real time. It is fundamentally different because it is forward-looking and continuous [11]. AI-driven predictive analytics helps supply chain managers spot early warning signals from global news, weather, trade, and supplier performance, which is not possible with traditional ways of managing supply chains.

Supply chain predictive analytics uses historical data, real-time inputs, and predictive models to help companies plan better and act faster. It allows teams to analyze historical data, track current activity, and respond quickly to changing supply chain challenges. It helps supply chain managers spot problems before they happen and make informed choices backed by data. It also helps companies navigate uncertainty, reduce waste, and make better decisions using real-time data and intelligent forecasting. By applying predictive analytics in supply chain management, teams improve supply chain management, cut delays, and align with future trends [12]. Figure 7.5 shows some supply chain workers [11], while Figure 7.6 shows a representation of the supply chain [13].

Figure 7.5 Some supply chain workers [11].

Figure 7.6 A representation of the supply chain [13].

7.4 APPLICATIONS OF PREDICTIVE ANALYTICS IN SUPPLY CHAIN

Predictive analytics enables supply chain professionals to improve several aspects such as logistics, predictive maintenance, demand forecasting, pricing strategies, and inventory management. By leveraging predictive analytics, organizations can anticipate disruptions, optimize resources, and enhance their overall supply chain performance. Figure 7.7 shows some use cases of predictive analytics in supply chains [14]. Common applications include the following [1,14-18]:

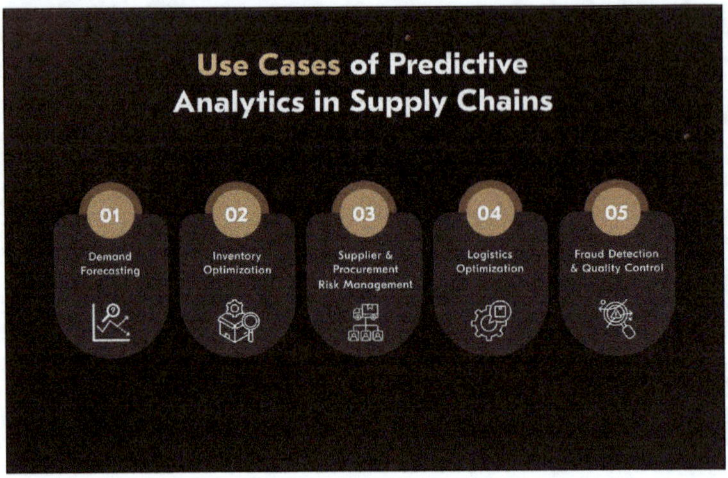

Figure 7.7 Some use cases of predictive analytics in supply chains [14].

- *Demand Forecasting:* One of the most impactful applications is in demand forecasting. Accurate demand forecasting is a key component of an efficient supply chain. Traditional forecasting methods often struggle with the inherent complexities and external variables influencing customer demand. Predictive analytics, however, can integrate a vast array of data points, including historical sales, promotional activities, economic indicators, weather patterns, and even social media sentiment, to generate highly accurate demand predictions. By forecasting demand more accurately, you avoid tying up cash in excess stock. Accurate demand forecasting relies on strong predictive models and clean supply chain data. These tools help companies track customer demand shifts and seasonal cycles. Each company forecasts requirements differently, with different time horizons, but the ones that use predictive analytics are one step ahead.

- *Inventory Management:* Supply chain managers, by using predictive analytics, can determine the optimal level of inventory to meet the demand at reduced costs for each location. Building on accurate demand forecasts, predictive analytics allows for dynamic inventory management. Instead of static safety stock levels, businesses can use predictive models to determine optimal inventory quantities, anticipate potential obsolescence, and prepare for periods of high demand. This optimization reduces carrying costs, minimizes waste, and ensures product availability when and where it is needed. Figure 7.8 shows a typical warehouse [18].

Figure 7.8 A typical warehouse [18].

- *Inventory Optimization:* One of the biggest challenges for businesses is maintaining optimal inventory levels. Predictive analytics algorithms use AI to analyze historical sales, seasonal trends, supplier lead times, and disruption signals, which helps real-time adjustment of reorder points and stock allocations. For example, Walmart uses predictive analytics to optimize store-level inventory, which cuts excess stock and reduces stockouts.
- *Price Optimization:* Manufacturers can use advanced analytics to adjust pricing as per market demand. Machine learning algorithms go through a myriad of data points ranging from location to product attributes to make accurate price predictions.
- *Risk Management:* The ability to foresee potential disruptions is a game-changer for supply chain resilience. Predictive analytics can help you identify and mitigate supply chain risks, such as disruptions or fluctuations in demand. By minimizing the impact of unexpected events, you can maintain consistent profitability. By analyzing historical data on supplier performance, transportation routes, geopolitical events, and even natural disaster patterns, predictive analytics can identify high-risk areas and potential points of failure before they materialize. This allows organizations to proactively implement mitigation strategies, such as diversifying their supplier base or

rerouting shipments, thereby minimizing the impact of unforeseen events.

- *Predictive Maintenance*: Businesses are using predictive maintenance to improve supply chain efficiency and maximize equipment uptime. Beyond the flow of goods, predictive analytics extends to the maintenance of critical assets. Machine learning and AI-based predictive analytics process IoT sensor readings, usage patterns, and historical maintenance data to forecast equipment wear. By analyzing sensor data from machinery in warehouses, manufacturing plants, or transport fleets, predictive models can forecast equipment failures before they occur. This enables proactive maintenance, reducing costly downtime, extending asset lifespan, and ensuring continuous operational flow. For example, General Motors uses predictive maintenance in its factories by analyzing IoT sensor data, which helps them reduce unplanned downtime by up to 20% while extending the lifespan of assembly-line equipment.
- *Market Volatility:* In an era of increasing volatility, traditional supply chain planning methods are increasingly being outpaced by the complexities and speed of modern predictive logistics. Predictive analytics relies on the assumption that the future will, in some way, resemble the past. However, we live in an era of unprecedented volatility.

Geopolitical shifts, climate-related disasters, and global health crises, often termed “Black Swan” events, do not follow historical patterns. Geopolitical events, raw material shortages, climate volatility, and demand swings that used to happen once a decade now happen every year. Predictive supply chain analytics is the only way to manage today’s extreme volatility and global risks.

- *Disruption Management:* Predictive analytics in supply chain helps managers by detecting disruptions earlier, tightening forecasts, and making proactive decisions. It enables you to identify and address potential disruptions in your supply chain proactively. This minimizes downtime, delays, and unexpected costs, ensuring smoother operations and ultimately higher profits.
- *Last-mile Delivery:* The last-mile delivery option is a key area in supply chain where predictive analytics can have a huge impact. Carbon dioxide emissions from freight transportation account for 30% of carbon emissions from fuel combustion. Using predictive analytics in supply chain areas like route optimization, anticipatory shipping, robotics, and quantifiable improvements can be made in last-mile delivery.
- *Supply Chain Visibility:* Service providers can use predictive analytics in the supply chain process to avoid late shipments by monitoring devices. It will improve the

visibility of shipment status and location and eliminate costs related to late or off-schedule shipments. For example, Apple is using forecasting capabilities to establish real-time visibility into demand patterns and anticipate online orders of products like iPhones and Apple Watches to prevent delayed shipments.

- *Logistics:* Efficient transportation is the cornerstone of any successful supply chain. As transport costs represent a significant portion of the final product price, predictive analytics enable us to know the frequency and quantity of transport needed to meet demand while minimizing costs. The fastest routes according to traffic, distance, weather, and delivery point can be known. One of the prominent examples of predictive analytics in supply chains is Walmart, which uses data-driven route planning to cut down on unnecessary mileage and lower its carbon footprint. Figure 7.9 is a representation of logistics [19].

Figure 7.9 A representation of logistics [19].

- *Fraud Detection:* Fraud detection and quality monitoring are critical to maintaining trust and efficiency in the supply chain. Predictive supply chain instruments monitor various data points, from sensor readings on shipments to supplier performance metrics, to identify unusual patterns that may indicate fraud or performance issues. By catching these anomalies early, companies can address potential problems before they escalate into expensive errors.
- *Capacity Planning:* Capacity planning is a critical aspect of supply chain management. It involves determining the optimal level of resources required to meet future demand. With the ability to analyze historical data and identify patterns, predictive analytics can help with accurate demand forecasts, allowing supply chain professionals to make informed decisions about production levels, staffing, and resource allocation.

7.5 BENEFITS

The adoption of predictive analytics in supply chain management translates into several benefits. Supply chain predictive analytics helps companies navigate uncertainty, reduce waste, and make better decisions. By applying predictive analytics in supply chain, teams improve supply chain management, cut delays, and align with future trends. For organizations that bridge the gap between data and decision-making, the benefits are substantial: a more resilient, efficient, and sustainable supply chain capable of thriving in an increasingly unpredictable world. Other benefits of predictive analytics in supply chain include the following [2,17]:

- *Cost Reduction:* Predictive analytics can help optimize inventory levels, reduce transportation costs, and minimize production downtime. You can lower operating expenses and increase overall profitability. Predictive tools eliminate guesswork in day-to-day planning. Fewer delays, faster routing, and better data availability lower transportation costs and streamline workflows. By minimizing costs, companies can reallocate savings toward strategic improvements and meet budget goals more consistently. In procurement, warehousing, and transport, manual reviews often overlook hidden costs like excess safety stock, underutilized fleet capacity, or inefficient supplier contracts, which drain resources over time.
- *Waste Reduction:* Enhanced quality control and production process optimization can reduce waste and product defects. This not only lowers production costs but also enhances your reputation for quality, potentially attracting more customers and increasing profits.
- *Lower Inventory Costs:* Predictive analytics helps you order only what you will actually sell. By predicting what you will actually sell, you avoid tying up cash in excess

stock. You need reliable supplier lead times and up-to-date inventory counts, or you will still end up with too much or too little. By forecasting demand more accurately, you avoid tying up cash in excess stock. This works if your sales and inventory data are updated at least weekly and your team trusts the forecasts enough to act on them.

- *Proactive Decision-making:* Proactive decision-making is essential in today's and tomorrow's fast-paced supply chain planning environment. By identifying potential risks early, organizations can take preventive measures to mitigate their impact. Predictive analytics empowers planners with the tools and insights needed to make smarter decisions, faster. It gives your planners and buyers data-driven recommendations. This speeds up planning cycles and reduces second-guessing. However, this only works if your team is trained to interpret and trust the model's output.
- *Better Risk Management:* Risk prediction models look for signs of trouble like supplier delays, transport bottlenecks, or quality issues. They use historical incident data, supplier performance, and sometimes external data like weather or geopolitical events. By spotting likely disruptions, like supplier delays or demand spikes, you can act before problems hit. This only works if you have

real-time or near-real-time data from your suppliers and logistics partners.

- *Improved Customer Service*: Better demand forecasting and inventory management result in improved product availability and on-time deliveries. This enhances customer satisfaction, potentially leading to increased sales, customer loyalty, and positive word-of-mouth, which can boost profits. Stronger predictions lead to faster deliveries, accurate order fulfillment, and fewer delays. With fewer stockouts and better order fill rates, customers get what they want more often. But if your logistics partners cannot deliver reliably, even the best forecast cannot fix service gaps.
- *Enhanced Customer Satisfaction:* Faster, more reliable deliveries make customers happier. Predictive analytics in transportation aims to determine demand spikes, manage delays, and maintain optimal inventory levels. Improved last-mile delivery routes contribute to minimized disruptions, which, in turn, will help you meet tight service-level agreements and provide a seamless customer experience.
- *Efficient Operations:* Predictive analytics can help you schedule labor and shipments more precisely, cutting overtime and rush shipping. This requires close

coordination between planning, operations, and logistics teams, which is not always easy.

- *Smooth Supply Chain:* Predictive analytics enables you to identify and address potential disruptions in your supply chain proactively. By doing so, you minimize production downtime, avoid unexpected costs, and ensure a consistent flow of materials for your manufacturing process. This results in smoother operations and higher profitability for your company.
- *Adaptability:* Predictive analytics allows you to adapt quickly to emerging trends and market shifts. This adaptability can lead to seizing new opportunities and optimizing profitability.
- *Personalization:* Predictive analytics enables continuous analysis of customer data, enabling advanced personalization capabilities. In today's increasingly competitive e-commerce environment, personalization is one of the key differentiators. Consumers are more likely to make a purchase when brands offer a personalized experience.

7.6 CHALLENGES

While the benefits are clear, implementing predictive analytics is not without its challenges, which can limit success without the right strategies in place. In an increasingly complex and volatile global economy, supply chain management faces unprecedented challenges. Challenges such as data quality, model interpretability, and implementation costs remain critical considerations. Other challenges of predictive analytics in supply chain include the following [1,12,19]:

- *Data Quality:* The efficacy of any predictive model is inextricably linked to the quality of the data it consumes. If your data is not accurate, your forecasts will be wrong and so will your decisions. In supply chain management, data is often generated across a disparate ecosystem of systems, warehouse management tools, and external logistics providers. Many organizations struggle with fragmented, incomplete, or inaccurate historical data, which can compromise the reliability of predictive models. The biggest risk is trusting predictions built on bad or incomplete data. Costs rise quickly when your data is messy, you have lots of systems, or you need custom integrations. Clean data and fewer platforms keep costs down.
- *Data Privacy*: Protecting sensitive data and ensuring compliance with data governance policies and regulations can become a significant challenge when implementing predictive analytics in supply chain management. For example, you often need to encrypt data to safeguard it from unauthorized access.

- *Skills Gap:* Implementing predictive analytics requires a unique intersection of skills: deep domain expertise in supply chain operations and advanced proficiency in data science. There is a significant demand for skilled data scientists, machine learning engineers, and domain experts who can develop, deploy, and manage these sophisticated systems. The scarcity of professionals who can "speak both languages" remains one of the most significant barriers to successful adoption.
- *Integration:* Integrating predictive analytics into any existing supply chain involves several challenges and considerations. Old, legacy systems do not always connect well with modern analytics tools. Many global supply chains are still anchored by legacy systems designed decades ago for record-keeping, not for high-velocity data analytics. These systems often lack the connectivity and processing power required to support real-time predictive engines. Successfully integrating predictive insights into daily operational workflows and ensuring adoption by business teams requires careful planning and change management.
- *Resistance:* Overcoming resistance to change within the organization and gaining buy-in from stakeholders is challenging for any significant system upgrade. And the implementation of predictive analytics is no exception. As

a company, you must push for effective communication, training, and education to ensure employees understand the value and use of predictive analytics.

- *Interpretability*: Supply chain managers must understand why a model recommends specific reorder points, shipment schedules, or supplier selections. Modern machine learning models, particularly deep learning architectures, are often criticized for being “black boxes.” While they may provide highly accurate predictions, they rarely explain the why behind them. For a supply chain executive responsible for millions of dollars in inventory, following a recommendation without understanding the underlying logic is a high-risk proposition. This lack of interpretability leads to a "trust deficit," where human planners revert to manual overrides or ignore the model's suggestions entirely, rendering the investment in analytics moot. Favor interpretable algorithms and provide contextual insights to support informed decision-making and stakeholder trust.
- *Over-reliance on Technology*: Data can guide decisions, but human oversight remains essential. Teams must use experience, context, and logic to verify results. Blind trust in algorithms without checks can lead to mistakes. Supply chain managers should validate model outputs using real-world experience and operational input.

Figure 7.10 shows some challenges of predictive analytics in supply chains [14].

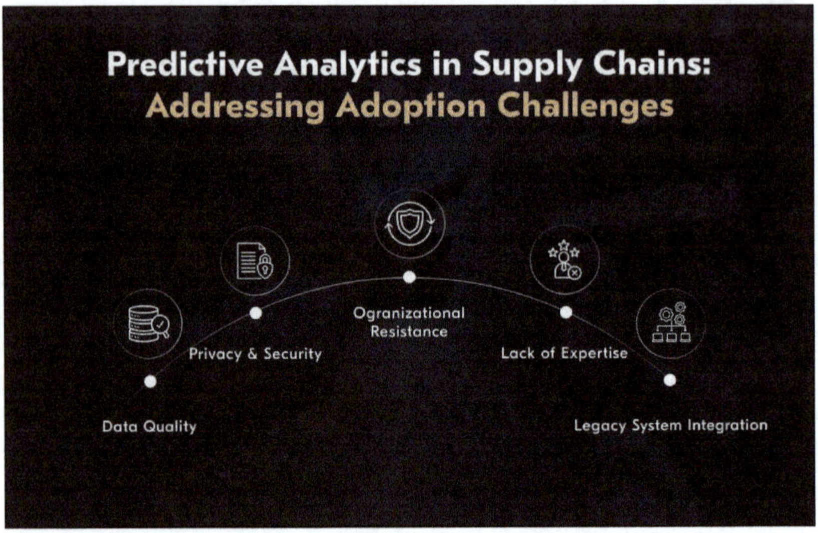

Figure 7.10 Some challenges of predictive analytics in supply chains [14].

7.7 FUTURE OF PREDICTIVE ANALYTICS IN SUPPLY CHAIN

Predictive analytics is improving the efficiency of supply chain processes by collecting and analyzing data for better decision-making. Predictive models are not static. You need to retrain them as business conditions change, or as you get more data. The landscape of predictive analytics continues to shift toward even greater integration and autonomy. AI has become a necessity for predictive analytics in the logistics industry. As organizations increasingly embrace AI-driven solutions, understanding their impact on supply chain performance becomes crucial for sustaining competitive advantage.

The future of predictive analytics in supply chain management is bright, promising a landscape of unprecedented efficiency, resilience, and strategic advantage. By embracing AI-driven forecasting, unified data models, and autonomous decision-making, organizations can move beyond merely reacting to disruptions and instead proactively shape their future. The journey requires a clear vision, robust data strategies, and a commitment to change, but the rewards, in terms of optimized operations, reduced costs, and enhanced customer satisfaction, are substantial [1].

7.8 CONCLUSION

Predictive analytics is no longer a futuristic concept but a present-day imperative for competitive supply chain management. In the contemporary global economy, predictive analytics has transitioned from a competitive advantage to a fundamental necessity for supply chain resilience. Predictive analytics holds the key to a more agile and responsive supply chain, but it is not a "plug-and-play" solution. Predictive analytics is reshaping the landscape of supply chain management. Organizations that continue to rely on traditional, static planning methods will struggle to keep pace with the demands of modern logistics analytics.

There is a strong belief among companies that predictive analytics has the potential to completely transform the supply chain. Its introduction is helping logistics and supply chain companies meet increasing demands. Investing in a predictive analytics solution might no longer be an option; it has become a necessity to maintain competitiveness with other players that have still embraced this solution. More information on the use of predictive analytics in supply chain is available from the books in [20-24].

REFERENCES

[1] https://manus.im

[2] "Predictive analytics in supply chain: Examples and use cases," February 2026, https://www.latentview.com/blog/predictive-analytics-in-supply-chain/

[3] M. N. O. Sadiku, S. A. Ajayi, and J. O. Sadiku, "Predictive Analytics for Supply Chain," International Journal of Trend in Research and Development, vol. 2, no. 2, March-April 2025, pp. 250-256.

[4] "Supply chain predictive analytics: What is it and who's doing it?" https://riverlogic.com/?blog=supply-chain-predictive-analytics-what-is-it-and-whos-doing-it

[5] N. Babin, "AI and predictive analytics: Revolutionizing demand forecasting in supply chain management," https://www.linkedin.com/pulse/ai-predictive-analytics-revolutionizing-demand-supply-nicolas-babin-xrj2e/

[6] "From insight to innovation: Why data analysis will define industry leaders in 2025," https://www.inkl.com/news/from-insight-to-innovation-why-data-analysis-will-define-industry-leaders-in-2025

[7] "An overview of supply chain analytics," February 2023, Unknown Source.

[8] I. Tymchuk, “Big data and predictive analytics in supply chain: Success stories and tips,” November 2020, https://www.n-ix.com/big-data-predictive-analytics-supply-chain-case-study/

[9] “Predictive analytics: A comprehensive guide for businesses,” November 2024, https://www.jobspikr.com/blog/guide-to-predictive-analytics/

[10] H. Kagalwala et al., “Predictive analytics in supply chain management: The role of AI and machine learning in demand forecasting,” *Advances in Consumer Research*, vol. 2, no.1, January-February 2025, pp. 142-149.

[11] M. Dill, “How predictive analytics in supply chain revolutionizes operations,” March 2026, https://www.ryder.com/en-us/insights/blogs/logistics/predictive-analytics-in-supply-chain

[12] “Supply chain predictive analytics: What it is, key components, and benefits,” August 2025, https://www.inboundlogistics.com/articles/supply-chain-predictive-analytics-what-it-is-key-components-and-benefits/

[13] “From data to action: Leveraging predictive analytics to improve supply chain performance,” April 2025, https://mltechsoft.com/blog/predictive-analytics-to-improve-supply-chain-performance/

[14] "Why use predictive analytics in supply chains? Advantages, use cases & solutions," March 2025, https://acropolium.com/blog/why-use-predictive-analytics-in-supply-chains-advantages-use-cases-solutions/

[15] "Predictive analytics in supply chain: What, why, benefits, use cases," September 2025, https://rtslabs.com/predictive-analytics-in-supply-chain/

[16] A. Dutt, "Using predictive analytics for an efficient supply chain," January, 2020, https://erpsolutions.oodles.io/blog/predictive-analytics-in-supply-chain/

[17] "Supply chain predictive analytics," https://solutyics.com/supply-chain-predictive-analytics/

[18] P. Benaddi, "Impact of predictive analytics on supply chain," August 2020, https://www.daacap.com/impact-of-predictive-analytics-on-supply-chain/

[19] A. Raj, "Predictive analytics in supply chain: Enterprise guide to ROI, use cases & implementation (2026)," December 2023, https://throughput.world/blog/predictive-analytics-in-supply-chain/

[20] N. Tipi, *Supply Chain Analytics and Modelling: Quantitative Tools and Applications*. Kogan Page, 2nd edition, 2025.

[21] K. Deep, M. Jain, and S. Salhi (eds.), *Logistics, Supply Chain and Financial: Predictive Analytics*. Springer Nature Singapore, 2018.

[22] A. Bari, M. Chaouchi, and T. Jung, *Predictive Analytics For Dummies*. For Dummies, 2nd edition, 2016.

[23] M. C. Cohen et al., Demand *Prediction in Retail: A Practical Guide to Leverage Data and Predictive Analytics (Springer Series in Supply Chain Management).* Springer 2022.

[24] J. San, *AI Implementation in Supply Chain Management: A Comprehensive Guide to AI Integration, Predictive Analytics, Machine Learning, IoT, Blockchain, and Sustainable Innovations for Future-Ready Operations.* Independently Published, 2024.

CHAPTER 8: PREDICTIVE ANALYTICS IN INSURANCE

"The strongest among you is the one who controls his anger."

- Muhammad

8.1 INTRODUCTION

The insurance industry, traditionally reliant on historical data and actuarial science, is currently undergoing a profound transformation, moving away from traditional, reactive business models toward a proactive, data-centric approach. At the heart of this evolution is predictive analytics, which is the use of historical data, statistical algorithms, and machine learning techniques to identify the likelihood of future outcomes. Predictive analytics acts as helpful, competent assistance for insurance companies. It replaces old, cumbersome methods that insurers usually used in the past to calculate risks, premiums, and policies. It aids companies in understanding customer behavior, and they can spot customers who are not happy with their insurance or are planning to shift [1].

Data is becoming one of the most valuable assets for any organization. It has become the bread and butter of insurers. Insurers are generating and collecting more data than ever before. With so much data available, the biggest challenge facing insurers is turning data into insights. Insurance companies need to make data-driven decisions and stay ahead of the competition. Predictive analytics in insurance is reshaping how insurers operate by turning vast data into actionable insights to forecast risks, improve customer experiences, and more. It lets you work smarter, not harder, by guiding every choice with real, actionable data. It looks at past data to find patterns to forecast the future. Training a predictive model means feeding it with clean data, so it learns patterns and can spot issues before they cause trouble [2].

At its heart, the insurance industry depends on the ability to predict outcomes and behavior changes. Predictive analytics is all about forecasting the likelihood of future events. This technology, leveraging advanced statistical algorithms, machine learning, and artificial intelligence, enables insurers to forecast future events and behaviors with unprecedented accuracy. Predictive analytics in insurance is the use of statistical models, machine learning techniques, and historical data to forecast future outcomes such as claims frequency, customer churn, or fraud likelihood. It uses historical and real-time insurance data to forecast risks, optimize underwriting, detect fraud, and enhance customer satisfaction. By analyzing patterns in vast datasets, insurers gain actionable insights for smarter decision-making. Predictive analytics in insurance is a way to increase profit and mitigate risks. It is a data-centric approach to predicting the future and making smarter insurance product and service decisions [3].

This chapter delves into how predictive analytics is revolutionizing the insurance sector. It begins by explaining predictive analytics. It describes predictive analytics in insurance and provides some of its applications. It highlights some benefits and challenges of predictive analytics in insurance. It predicts the future of predictive analytics in insurance. The last section concludes with comments.

8.2 WHAT IS PREDICTIVE ANALYTICS?

As its name implies, predictive analytics is about predicting future trends such as sales demand and exchange rates. and other important metrics. The technique relies on the application of statistical modeling and regression analysis to historical data to determine and understand trends and formulate future predictions. Strictly speaking, predictive analytics does not predict the future, but rather uses probability theories to determine what is likely to happen based on patterns and trends revealed by analyzing historical data [4]. Predictive analytics accurately anticipates customer demand, preventing overstocking and stockouts while adapting to market changes. Figure 8.1 illustrates predictive analytics [5], while Figure 8.2 shows different components of predictive analytics [6].

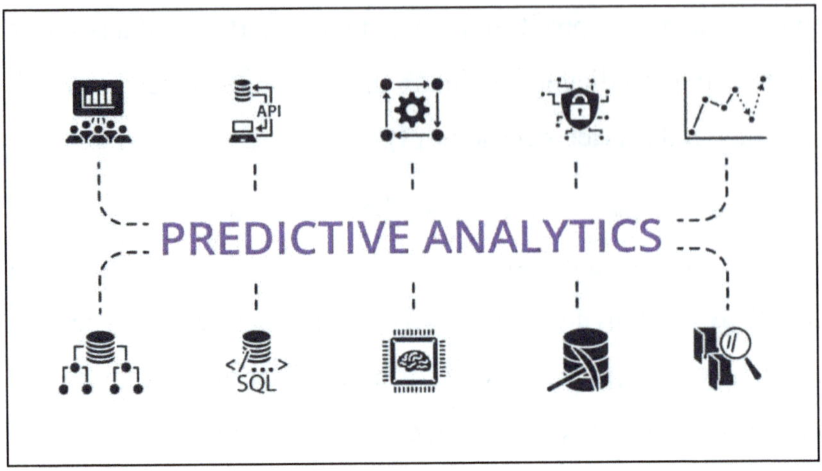

Figure 8.1 Predictive analytics [5].

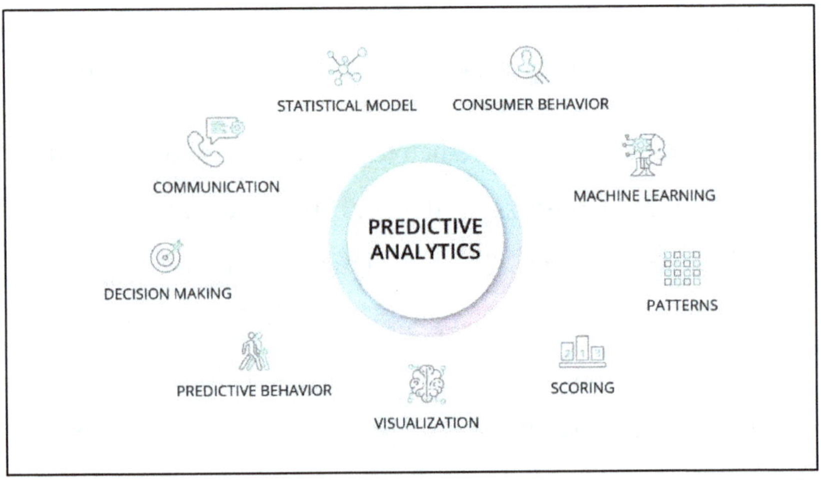

Figure 8.2 Different components of predictive analytics [6].

In general, analytics provides an efficient way to improve planning because it gives you better forecasts. There are different types of data analytics. They are briefly explained as follows [7]:

- *Descriptive Analytics:* Descriptive analytics examines what has happened over the years. They are capable of detecting trends in historical data. Analytics can uncover trends and postulate probable reasons for change by comparing the same data from various periods. It can be seen as the baseline of the industry, which basically assesses past and current data for more meaningful insights and delivers it to the people to use their own intelligence and knowledge to make decisions.
- *Predictive Analytics:* This assists businesses in predicting what might happen and the impact of various situations, such as possible supply chain bottlenecks. Managers can be proactive rather than responsive by pushing them to evaluate these prospective circumstances before they occur. Predictive analytics may be used to identify patterns and trends as well as anticipate breakdowns that may impact suppliers and, consequently, production processes. Predictive analytics for the supply chain leverages data, statistical algorithms, and machine learning techniques to identify the likelihood of future outcomes.
- *Prescriptive Analytics:* Prescriptive analytics builds on predictive analytics and dives deeper into predicting future insights on what can be done next. Prescriptive analytics uses the findings of descriptive and predictive analytics to recommend what measures a business should take to

achieve its objectives. Because prescriptive analytics is increasingly complicated, they need more powerful software capable of rapidly processing and interpreting large amounts of data.

- *Cognitive Analytics:* Cognitive analytics attempts to mimic human thought and behavior, and it can assist companies in answering challenging, complex problems. Cognitive analytics does this by utilizing artificial intelligence (AI), which allows it to improve over time. With the use of AI in the industry, answering complex questions and draw out contextual conclusions on how humans would have interacted with the situation. It helps with more meaningful data and scales experience and knowledge with better decisions.
- *Diagnostic Analytics:* This gives the ability to identify the root cause. It is characterized by techniques such as drill-down, data discovery, data mining, and correlations. It involves analyzing overall performance and figuring out why errors, mistakes, and delays occur. It lets the manager know the delays, breakdowns, and disruptions in the demand and supply processes and the reasons behind them.

Figure 8.3 shows these major types of data analytics [8]. Unlike diagnostic and descriptive analytics, which were designed to analyze situations after they happened, predictive analytics utilizes advanced data analytics techniques to forecast future outcomes. In the supply chain, the time has come to shift from mere descriptive and diagnostic analytics to predictive and prescriptive analytics. Predictive analytics is a branch of data analytics that makes predictions about future outcomes using historical data combined with statistical modeling, data mining techniques, and machine learning. Figure 8.4 shows how predictive analytics works [9].

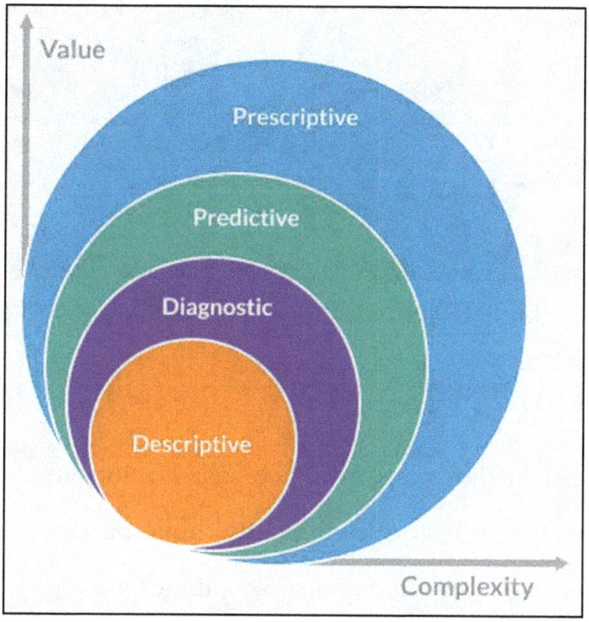

Figure 8.3 Types of data analytics [8].

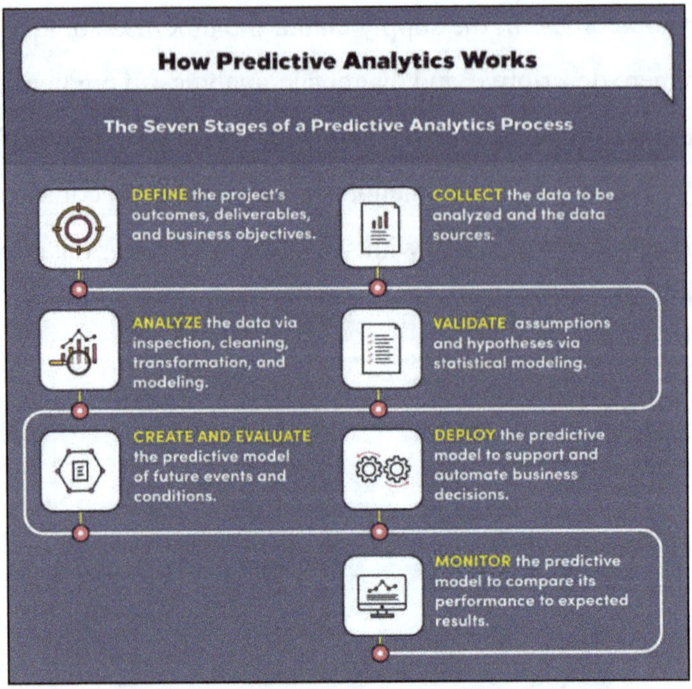

Figure 8.4 Predictive analytics process [9].

8.3 PREDICTIVE ANALYTICS IN INSURANCE

The old methods of insurance just do not cut it anymore. The insurance industry, traditionally built on risk assessment and actuarial calculations, is undergoing a seismic transformation driven by AI and data scraping technologies. As global insurers face rising customer expectations and complex risk landscapes, the strategic adoption of advanced analytics has become a critical driver of growth, efficiency, and competitive advantage. Predictive analytics transforms raw insurance data into valuable insights, helping insurers reduce risks, streamline operations, and stay competitive in a dynamic market. Across various domains, predictive analytics is reshaping insurance models, empowering insurers to operate with greater precision, transparency, and customer-centricity. AI-driven predictive analytics is transforming the insurance industry by delivering numerous competitive advantages. Figure 8.5 shows an insurance professional [2], while Figure 8.6 shows a representation of predictive analytics in insurance [10].

Figure 8.5 An insurance professional [2].

Figure 8.6 A representation of predictive analytics in insurance [10].

In today's insurance market, predictive analytics enables carriers to move beyond "what happened" to "what will happen," delivering granular accuracy that legacy tables simply cannot match. While traditional methods rely heavily on demographic buckets (such as age, zip code, or credit score), predictive modeling in insurance takes a "high-definition" approach. The traditional thirty-day waiting period for a policy is now a relic. Underwriting analytics allows for risk assessment in insurance that goes far beyond basic demographics [11]. Predictive analytics allows insurers to anticipate claims, optimize pricing, detect fraud, and manage risk more accurately. It transforms historical and real-time data into actionable insights that improve both operational efficiency and profitability. The insurance industry is based on a simple equation [9]:

Better data = more accurate risk calculations = higher profits

The reliance on data analysis makes insurance uniquely suited to predictive analytics.

8.4 APPLICATIONS OF PREDICTIVE ANALYTICS IN INSURANCE

Predictive analytics (PA) has emerged as a powerful force reshaping the insurance industry, promising enhanced accuracy in underwriting, more precise fraud detection, streamlined claims processing, and improved customer retention. Its applications span from enhancing risk assessment and underwriting to revolutionizing fraud detection, claims management, customer retention, and market expansion. Figure 8.7 shows some top applications of PA in insurance [12]. Common applications of predictive analytics in insurance include the following [1,13-17]:

Figure 8.7 Some top applications of PA in insurance [12].

- *Health Insurance:* The health insurance industry is experiencing a significant transformation driven by technological advancements and data-driven decision-making. Health insurers manage enormous claim volumes while balancing member care, risk pools, and reserves. The integration of predictive analytics in health insurance has revolutionized risk assessment and policy customization, leading to improved efficiency, cost reduction, and personalized coverage plans. Predictive analytics adds precision to this balancing act by surfacing high-risk members before their conditions escalate into costly claims. This insight allows insurers to design proactive intervention strategies, encouraging preventive healthcare measures and reducing the frequency of high-cost claims. By leveraging advanced AI models, insurers can predict potential health risks and suggest wellness programs, ultimately improving both customer health outcomes and cost efficiency. Figure 8.8 shows the key applications of predictive analytics in healthcare [18].

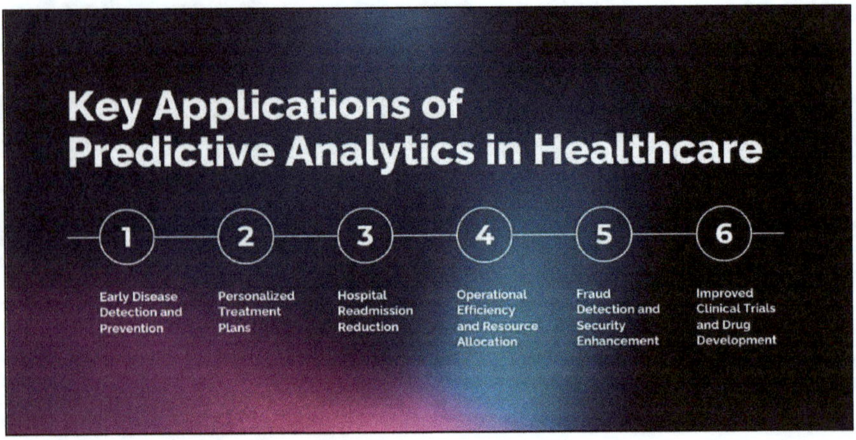

Figure 8.8 Key applications of predictive analytics in healthcare [18].

- *Auto Insurance:* In auto insurance, predictive analytics has revolutionized the way insurers evaluate risk and set premiums. Telematics data, gathered from connected devices in vehicles, allows insurers to monitor driving behavior, including speed, braking habits, and mileage.

These insights enable the creation of usage-based insurance policies tailored to individual driving habits. Additionally, predictive models analyze geographic and behavioral data to forecast accident-prone zones, allowing insurers to adjust risk models dynamically and improve claim predictability.

- *Life Insurance:* Mortality risk is the foundation of life insurance pricing, but traditional actuarial methods rely heavily on static data sets. For life insurance, predictive analytics enhances traditional actuarial models by introducing AI-powered mortality models. These systems analyze vast datasets, including lifestyle habits, medical records, and demographic information, to calculate life expectancy with greater accuracy. Intensifying competition and raising customer expectations are driving investment in predictive analytics in life insurance. Companies offering individual life insurance and group life insurance are expected to lead adoption of predictive analytics in the industry. Furthermore, insurers can offer personalized policy recommendations based on individual risk profiles, ensuring that customers receive coverage plans aligned with their specific needs.
- *Property Insurance:* In property insurance, predictive analytics is used to assess and mitigate risks associated with natural disasters, theft, and other property-related

incidents. By analyzing geographic, weather, and historical claims data, insurers can predict disaster-prone areas and adjust premiums accordingly. AI-driven image recognition tools further streamline the claims process by assessing property damage from photos and videos, enabling faster claim settlements and reducing fraud risks. ML models can predict property insurance risk by applying AI to climate data, geographic information, and claims history. Beyond catastrophe modeling, the property and casualty insurance industry is moving toward IoT integration.

- *Risk Assessment*: One key benefit of predictive analytics is accurate risk assessment, where data from customer demographics, claim histories, and IoT devices refine pricing models and prevent over- or under-insurance. The fundamental core of the insurance industry has always been the evaluation and pricing of risk. Insurers are moving beyond traditional demographic and historical claims data to incorporate richer, real-time information from diverse sources such as telematics, smart home devices, and even social media interactions. This allows for more granular risk profiling and dynamic pricing models that accurately reflect individual policyholder behavior and potential risks. The ultimate goal of insurance risk assessment analytics is to enable more sophisticated and dynamic pricing strategies. In a competitive market, the ability to accurately differentiate risk is the primary driver of profitability.

- *Fraud Detection*: Fraud detection represents another critical area where predictive analytics delivers substantial value. Insurance fraud is a persistent challenge that imposes a significant financial burden on the industry and its customers. It is a pervasive and costly problem, with an estimated $80 billion lost annually to fraudulent claims in the United States alone. Fraud detection would diminish the chances of data exploits, and they would proactively manage vulnerabilities. Using old-school methods to catch red flags and detect insurance fraud is not working anymore. Predictive models analyze vast datasets to identify suspicious patterns, anomalies, and connections that human investigators might miss. By monitoring social media activity post-claim or cross-referencing data from third-party vendors, insurers can detect and prevent fraudulent activities more effectively, leading to significant cost savings and improved claims integrity.
- *Claims Management:* In claims management, predictive analytics revolutionizes the process from initial reporting to final settlement. It enables claims triage and prioritization, allowing insurers to identify high-cost or outlier claims early in the process. This early detection

allows for proactive intervention, reducing the likelihood of escalating costs and accelerating resolution times. This leads to more efficient resource allocation and improved customer satisfaction through faster processing.

- *Customer Retention:* Customer retention and experience are profoundly enhanced by predictive analytics. By analyzing customer interactions, feedback, and behavioral patterns, insurers can identify policyholders at risk of churn and proactively address their concerns. This allows for personalized communication, tailored product offerings, and proactive problem-solving, fostering stronger customer loyalty.
- *Market Expansion:* Predictive analytics plays a crucial role in market expansion and product development. By analyzing demographic trends, behavioral patterns, and emerging risks, insurers can identify underserved markets and develop innovative products that cater to evolving customer needs. This data-driven approach allows for strategic marketing efforts and the creation of highly targeted insurance solutions, fostering growth and competitive differentiation.
- *Underwriting Processes*: It is pretty easy to see how insurers make money; the premiums they get comprise the revenue, and processing the claims incurs them a cost. Underwriters are tasked with assessing the associated risks

with onboarding any clients. Evaluating risk and determining the right pricing for each client is something insurance companies constantly face. The underwriting process works as a ripe opportunity for insurance companies when looking for AI and machine learning use cases. AI and ML systems are underwritten based on risk predictions, third-party data, and publicly available datasets. With increased automated underwriting, the manual process is slashed, and the companies can gain maximum benefits. Figure 8.9 shows how predictive analytics enhanced underwriting [9].

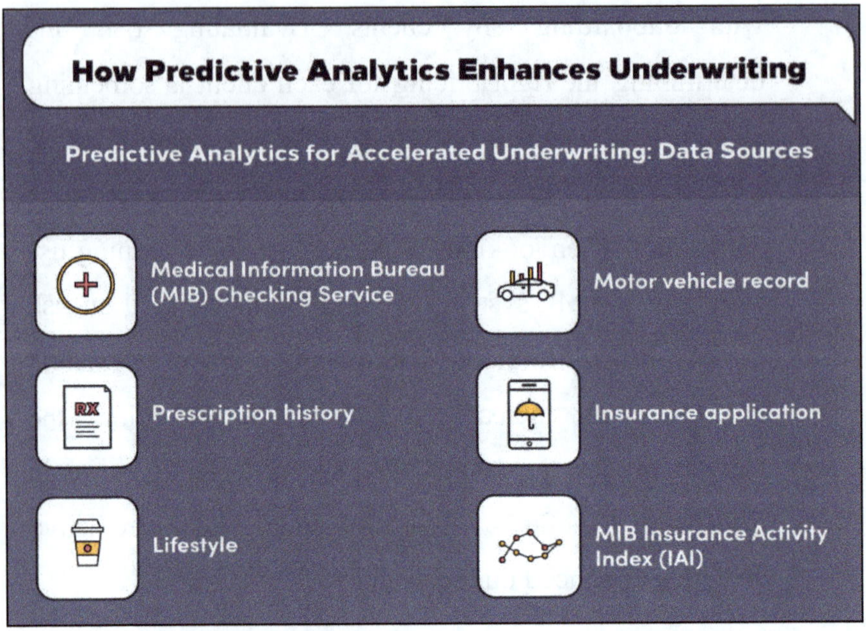

Figure 8.9 How predictive analytics enhanced underwriting [9].

- *Pricing Optimization:* Most of the pricing and premium optimization for insurance is done based on their claims' history. Predictive analytics enables insurers to develop sophisticated pricing models that consider multiple variables, such as customer demographics, claims history, policy coverage, and external factors like weather patterns or economic indicators. It can help to optimize insurance pricing and premiums even more accurately without excessive manual intervention. It does that by undertaking assessments of market trends, customer behavior, associated risk factors, claims data, and more to create dynamic pricing strategies while ensuring profitability and customer satisfaction.
- *Churn Prediction:* The insurance industry is highly competitive, where the majority of customers prefer to switch to another insurance provider that offers them competitive pricing and benefits. This is particularly the case for auto insurance companies. Hence, it becomes essential to identify customers who are at risk of discontinuing their policies. Predictive analytics provide insurers with data about churn rate by analyzing engagement metrics and satisfaction levels. These insights allow insurers to implement targeted retention strategies to retain valuable customers.

- *Predictive Intelligence:* Predictive intelligence is shifting how Insurance companies assess and predict risk. The future of Insurance is not about analyzing what happened yesterday; it is about predicting what is likely to happen tomorrow. Modernizing risk assessment requires technology partners with industry knowledge and a scalable platform.

Humans + AI = Intelligence

Humans are not being replaced by AI. Instead, AI tools augment risk underwriters' knowledge and intelligence. In the age of big data and artificial intelligence (AI), insurance companies compete to have the highest-quality data and analytics tools to convert the data into business intelligence.

8.5 BENEFITS

The widespread adoption of predictive analytics yields numerous benefits for the insurance industry, encompassing operational, financial, and customer-centric advantages. The benefits include increased profitability, improved customer satisfaction, and operational efficiency. Other benefits of predictive analytics in insurance include the following [13,16,19]:

- *Automation:* Not every claim requires the same level of human intervention. Automation reduces manual, repetitive tasks for underwriters and adjusters, allowing skilled professionals to focus on high-value, complex cases. It reduces manual effort, frees skilled staff for high-value work, and improves speed-to-decision. Automated decisioning accelerates underwriting and claims workflows, improving consistency and lowering operational overhead. This reduces manual effort, mitigates creeping costs, and ensures claims are routed to the appropriate adjusters.

- *Improved Risk Management:* The integration of predictive analytics within insurance platforms helps insurers assess historical claims, behaviors, and external variables. This data analysis provides them access to quantify risk at an individual and portfolio level. More accurate risk assessment leads to a healthier portfolio and reduced exposure to unforeseen losses. By anticipating potential risks and mitigating them proactively, insurers can maintain financial stability and ensure long-term sustainability.
- *Smarter Claims Processing*: Modern predictive models integrated with AI capabilities enable insurers to assess claim severity, authenticity, and settlement potential immediately after submission. Based on this analysis, insurers can make decisions quickly, minimize manual interventions, and accelerate straight-through processing

for low-risk claims. This enablement then improves turnaround times and customer satisfaction.

- *Personalization*: Predictive analytics enhances customer personalization by analyzing behavioral patterns to create tailored insurance plans, improving satisfaction and loyalty. With data-driven insights, insurers can design customized insurance policies aligned with individual customer needs, creating better customer retention rates. When you integrate predictive analytics into your insurance platform, you can also give it access to every customer interaction with your platform. This enables it to assess customer behavior, interactions, and thus preferences to predict their future needs.
- *Customer Retention:* Retention is critical in insurance, where customer acquisition costs are high. Customer retention improves when churn signals are identified early, allowing proactive outreach before policyholders switch providers. Predictive models flag policyholders likely to churn, allowing insurers to intervene with personalized offers or service outreach. The use of predictive analytics in insurance platforms enables insurance companies to monitor behavioral patterns, payment history, and engagement trends to identify a high risk of churn. This data-driven information helps insurance executives to

proactively engage with at-risk customers by targeting personalized retention campaigns.

- *Decision-making:* Business decision-making and action take place in the form of underwriting rules to adjust policy pricing, escalating flagged claims for deeper investigation, and boosting marketing and retention campaigns for at-risk customers. This data-driven decision-making helps insurers to improve customer loyalty towards their insurance company and, thus, customer lifetime value.
- *Enhanced Operational Efficiency:* As predictive analytics does the groundwork for insurers, like identifying potential customers, at-risk customers, fraudulent claims, and more, they get to focus on higher-value tasks. This enablement helps them improve productivity and get free from unnecessary operational overhead, which ultimately leads them to enhanced operational efficiency.
- *Competitive Advantage:* Predictive analytics in insurance platforms enables insurers to stay ahead of the curve with faster innovation cycles, sharper risk insights, and more agile customer strategies. This fosters differentiation in crowded markets, enhances brand trust, and enables quicker adaptation to emerging risks and regulatory changes.

8.6 CHALLENGES

In spite of its transformative potential, the application of predictive analytics in insurance is not without its challenges. The ethical and regulatory challenges, particularly concerning transparency, data quality and availability, legacy IT infrastructure, model bias, lack of skilled talent, resistance to change, and data privacy, demand careful consideration and proactive solutions. Other challenges of predictive analytics in insurance include the following [13,16,20]:

- *Ethical Concerns*: The deployment of AI in sensitive areas like claims processing and risk assessment raises profound regulatory and ethical questions. Issues of transparency, accountability, and privacy are paramount. Regulators increasingly demand that organizations be able to explain AI-driven decisions, which can be particularly challenging for complex, black-box models like deep neural networks. Pricing and underwriting decisions must adhere to ethical guidelines and avoid discriminatory practices. Furthermore, the handling of vast amounts of personal and sensitive customer data necessitates strict adherence to data privacy regulations such as GDPR.
- *Data Privacy*: Data privacy is another paramount concern. The collection of granular personal data, while beneficial for risk assessment, carries a significant responsibility for

stewardship. The extensive collection and analysis of personal data from various sources raise significant data privacy and security concerns. Insurers must navigate complex regulations like GDPR and CCPA, ensuring that customer data is collected, stored, and used responsibly and securely. Data privacy regulations such as GDPR force companies to be responsible with customer data.

- *Data Quality:* The efficacy of any predictive model hinges critically on the quality and quantity of the data it consumes. In the insurance context, this often translates into a complex landscape of incomplete, outdated, or inconsistent data spread across disparate systems. Biased or insufficient historical data can lead to inaccurate predictions and potentially unfair outcomes. Insurers must invest heavily in robust data governance frameworks to ensure the reliability and integrity of their data inputs.
- *Bias:* One of the most significant ethical concerns is the potential for bias and fairness issues. Predictive models, trained on historical data, can inadvertently perpetuate or even amplify existing societal biases. The use of proxy variables, data attributes that correlate with protected characteristics like race or gender, can lead to discriminatory outcomes, even if unintentional. Ensuring that models are fair, equitable, and do not lead to disparate impact on certain groups is a paramount challenge for

insurers and regulators alike. Regular audits, fairness checks, and the development of ethical AI frameworks are crucial to mitigate this risk and ensure equitable outcomes for all policyholders.

- *Digital Divide:* As insurance risk assessment analytics become more sophisticated, there is a risk that certain segments of the population those who lack a digital footprint or who are deemed high-risk by algorithms could find it more difficult or expensive to obtain coverage. Balancing the pursuit of mathematical precision with the social mission of insurance to provide a safety net for all is one of the most significant challenges facing industry leaders today.
- *Integration:* Many established insurance companies operate with legacy IT systems that were not designed to accommodate modern AI tools and large-scale data processing. Integrating sophisticated predictive analytics solutions into these older, often siloed, infrastructures present a significant technical and financial hurdle. This requires substantial investment in infrastructure upgrades, data migration, and the development of interoperable systems, alongside comprehensive personnel training.
- *Resistance to Change*: Human factors play a significant role in the successful adoption of new technologies. Resistance to change from employees and stakeholders

can impede the implementation of predictive analytics initiatives. Concerns about job displacement, distrust in automated systems, or a lack of understanding of the technology's benefits can create internal barriers. Effective change management strategies, including clear communication, comprehensive training programs, and demonstrating the value proposition of AI, are essential to foster acceptance and collaboration.

- *Skills Gaps:* Implementing AI and predictive analytics requires skilled professionals. The insurance industry is full of sales agents, legal teams, and underwriters. This makes it very obvious that they have a shortage of skilled professionals who possess both domain knowledge of insurance and technical expertise in data science, machine learning, and AI.
- *Regulation:* The insurance industry is highly regulated. There is a slew of regulations governing the insurance pricing and underwriting industry. One of them is the Affordable Care Act (ACA), which introduced norms in the health insurance market, requiring insurers to adhere to community rating rules. When you opt for AI integration services to enable smart capabilities for decision-making, especially in underwriting or claims, it is a must to comply with strict fairness, transparency, and

auditability standards. That is a big hurdle for the insurance industry to comply with.

- *Human Element:* Despite the rise of algorithms, the human element remains a critical component of insurance risk assessment analytics. The most effective systems are those that combine the processing power of machines with the judgment and intuition of experienced professionals. This collaboration between man and machine requires a new set of skills for the insurance workforce. Tomorrow's risk professionals will need to be as comfortable with data science as they are with traditional insurance principles. They must be able to interpret algorithmic outputs, identify potential biases, and communicate complex technical concepts to non-technical stakeholders. Human-in-the-loop processes provide additional oversight for high-stakes decisions, ensuring critical judgments remain accountable.

8.7 FUTURE OF PREDICTIVE ANALYTICS IN INSURANCE

Predictive analytics holds immense promise for revolutionizing the insurance industry, offering pathways to greater efficiency, accuracy, and customer satisfaction. Insurers are now shifting from reactive analysis to proactive prediction with data and artificial intelligence (AI)-powered insurance technology. Predictive analytics combined with AI chatbots will offer hyper-personalized customer service experiences.

The evolution in predictive analytics for insurance operations is working in favor of insurers. As technology evolves, insurance companies that invest in robust data strategies will emerge as industry leaders. The rise of generative AI introduces concerns around data security, privacy, and the potential for generating synthetic data that, if not carefully managed, could introduce new biases or vulnerabilities. IoT devices will continue to provide insurers with granular insurance data, especially in health and auto insurance.

Predictive analytics in insurance holds tremendous promise for the future. It can potentially not only transform the business of insurers but also improve customer acquisition and retention. The future of insurance belongs to those who act today. With AI becoming a necessity today, predictive analytics has evolved into more than just a tool for forecasting risks. Powered by the rapid convergence of ML, AI, and IoT, predictive analytics is unlocking a level of intelligence that was previously impossible. By embracing big data, predictive modeling, and real-time insights, the insurance industry is becoming more precise, efficient, and customer-centric. As these technologies mature, they grant insurers a high-definition view of customer behavior and life patterns. The future belongs to insurers who can thread this needle by using data to drive financial performance while maintaining the ethical governance necessary to maintain their customers' trust [11]. In the future, the only way to outperform the competition is by taking advantage of predictive analytics tools and other AI products.

8.8 CONCLUSION

Predictive analytics has a strong foothold in myriad industries, empowering them to serve their customer 10x better. It has already boomed the insurance industry. The strategic adoption of predictive analytics is no longer a competitive advantage but a fundamental necessity for growth, efficiency, and sustained relevance in a rapidly evolving market. For insurers, adopting predictive analytics is not just about staying competitive; it is about future-proofing their business. Modern insurers use predictive models to improve underwriting precision, reduce fraud, accelerate claims handling, and strengthen regulatory oversight.

Insurance is moving from hindsight to foresight. With rising claims volumes, fraud risks, and customer demands, predictive analytics is no longer a "nice-to-have" but a core capability. Predictive analytics has become foundational for insurers facing climate volatility, margin pressure, and increasing risk complexity. It enables insurers to move from reactive decisions to forward-looking risk, pricing, and claims management across the insurance value chain. Insurers that align predictive analytics with clear business use cases achieve measurable improvements in loss ratios, operational efficiency, and customer experience [18]. More information on the use of predictive analytics in insurance is available from the books in [20-24].

REFERENCES

[1] M. Mistry, "9+ Effective use cases of predictive analytics in insurance," December 2023, https://kodytechnolab.com/blog/top-10-use-cases-for-predictive-analytics-in-insurance/

[2] "Predictive analytics for insurance: Enterprise applications and ROI optimization," February 2026, https://binariks.com/blog/predictive-analytics-in-insurance/

[3] M. N. O. Sadiku, D. Padi, and J. O. SSadiku, "Predictive analytics in insurance," *International Journal of Management and Organizational Research*, vol. 5, no. 3, May-June, 2026, pp. 54-63.

[4] "Supply chain predictive analytics: What is it and who's doing it?" https://riverlogic.com/?blog=supply-chain-predictive-analytics-what-is-it-and-whos-doing-it

[5] N. Babin, "AI and predictive analytics: Revolutionizing demand forecasting in supply chain management," https://www.linkedin.com/pulse/ai-predictive-analytics-revolutionizing-demand-supply-nicolas-babin-xrj2e/

[6] "From insight to innovation: Why data analysis will define industry leaders in 2025," https://www.inkl.com/news/from-insight-to-innovation-why-data-analysis-will-define-industry-leaders-in-2025

[7] "An overview of supply chain analytics," February 2023, Unknown Source.

[8] I. Tymchuk, "Big data and predictive analytics in supply chain: Success stories and tips," November 2020, https://www.n-ix.com/big-data-predictive-analytics-supply-chain-case-study/

[9] "Predictive analytics in insurance: Types, tools, and the future," October 2020, https://online.maryville.edu/blog/predictive-analytics-in-insurance/

[10] "AI-driven predictive analytics in insurance," October 2024, https://defouranalytics.com/ai-driven-predictive-analytics-insurance/

[11] "AI and predictive analytics in insurance: Use cases, examples & AI applications," February 2026, https://www.latentview.com/blog/predictive-analytics-in-insurance/

[12] H. Evans, "Predictive analytics in insurance: An industry game-changer," March 2026, https://velvetech.com/blog/predictive-analytics-in-insurance/

[13] https://manus.im

[14] Bhagyashree, "Predictive analytics in insurance: The role of AI and data scraping," January 2025,

https://www.promptcloud.com/blog/predictive-analytics-in-insurance-data/

[15] "Predictive analytics in insurance: Benefits, use cases & more (2026)," September 2025, https://rtslabs.com/predictive-analytics-in-insurance/

[16] P. Pandya, "Predictive analytics in insurance: Top benefits, use cases, real-world examples," April 2026, https://www.mindinventory.com/blog/predictive-analytics-in-insurance/

[17] "Data and AI in insurance risk assessment: From static models to predictive intelligence," April 2026, https://hexaware.com/blogs/data-and-ai-in-insurance-risk-assessment-from-static-models-to-predictive-intelligence/

[18] T. Trantor, "Predictive analytics in healthcare: Transforming patient outcomes and operational efficiency," April 2025, https://www.trantorinc.com/blog/predictive-analytics-healthcare

[19] "Predictive analytics in insurance: The complete guide for modern insurers," https://data-sleek.com/industry-solutions/insurance/predictive-analytics-in-insurance-guide/

[20] "Data analytics transforming insurance risk assessment," https://www.worldfinanceinforms.com/insurance/data-analytics-transforming-insurance-risk-assessment/

[21] S. Sumanth, H. S. Nagamani, and P. Zanke, *Insurance Analytics: Driving Profitability through Data-Driven Decision.* LAP LAMBERT Academic Publishing, 2024.

[22] A. Bari, M. Chaouchi, and T. Jung, *Predictive Analytics For Dummies*. For Dummies, 2nd edition, 2016.

[23] B. Sikka, P. Yadav, and P. Verma, *Practical Data Analytics for BFSI: Leveraging Data Science for Driving Decisions in Banking, Financial Services, and Insurance Operations (English ... Analytics Specialist — Industry Path).* Orange Education Pvt Ltd, 2023.

[24] S. Castillo, *Predictive Analytics & Risk Modeling: For Insurance and Actuarial Science.* Kindle Edition, 2025.

[25] R. K. Ravi, *Transforming Insurance and Healthcare With Cloud Intelligence: The New Era of Predictive Analytics and Data Engineering.* Kindle Edition, 2025.

CHAPTER 9: PREDICTIVE ANALYTICS FOR CUSTOMER SERVICE

"A life not lived for others is not a life."

– Mother Teresa

9.1 INTRODUCTION

The best businesses do not wait for problems to appear; they detect early signs and take action that smooths the customer's journey. With that kind of proactive posture, it becomes easier to prepare, prioritize, and stay ahead of service demands. Predictive analytics in customer service makes this possible by uncovering patterns in existing data to anticipate customer needs before they turn into problems. By identifying patterns and spotting trends, it forecasts potential customer behaviors, issues, and needs. Instead of reacting to issues after they happen, support teams can now use data to anticipate what is coming next [1].

Traditional analytics tell you what happened. Predictive analytics tells you what is going to happen. Predictive analytics analyzes historical customer data to identify patterns and trends. In various industries, including customer service, predictive analytics plays a crucial role in anticipating and understanding patterns, enabling businesses to make informed decisions and take proactive measures. Integrating predictive analytics into customer service can significantly enhance a company's ability to anticipate customer needs, leading to a more efficient and effective customer service strategy. Predictive customer analytics is important because it helps businesses forecast customer behaviors, anticipate needs, and take proactive actions to improve satisfaction and retention [2].

Every business leader would love to be able to predict the future. While there is no encompassing business "crystal ball," there is predictive analytics. Predictive analytics is a transformative tool that enables businesses to anticipate future trends and make informed decisions based on historical data. Businesses can use predictive analytics to improve the customer experience by analyzing customer behavior patterns. Predictive analytics in customer service refers to the use of historical data, artificial intelligence, statistical algorithms, and machine learning to anticipate future customer behaviors, potential issues, and service needs. It helps you anticipate what customers need – before they ask. It is about using data to personalize support, resolve issues early, and boost customer satisfaction [3].

In this chapter, we will explore the transformative impact of predictive analytics on customer service. It begins by explaining the concept of predictive analytics. It describes predictive analytics in customer service and provides some of its applications. It highlights the benefits and challenges of predictive analytics in customer service. It predicts the future of predictive analytics in customer service. The last section concludes with comments.

9.2 WHAT IS PREDICTIVE ANALYTICS?

As its name implies, predictive analytics is about predicting future trends such as sales demand and exchange rates. and other important metrics. The technique relies on the application of statistical modeling and regression analysis to historical data to determine and understand trends and formulate future predictions. Strictly speaking, predictive analytics does not predict the future, but rather uses probability theories to determine what is likely to happen based on patterns and trends revealed by analyzing historical data [4]. Predictive analytics accurately anticipates customer demand, preventing overstocking and stockouts while adapting to market changes. Figure 9.1 illustrates predictive analytics [5], while Figure 9.2 shows different components of predictive analytics [6].

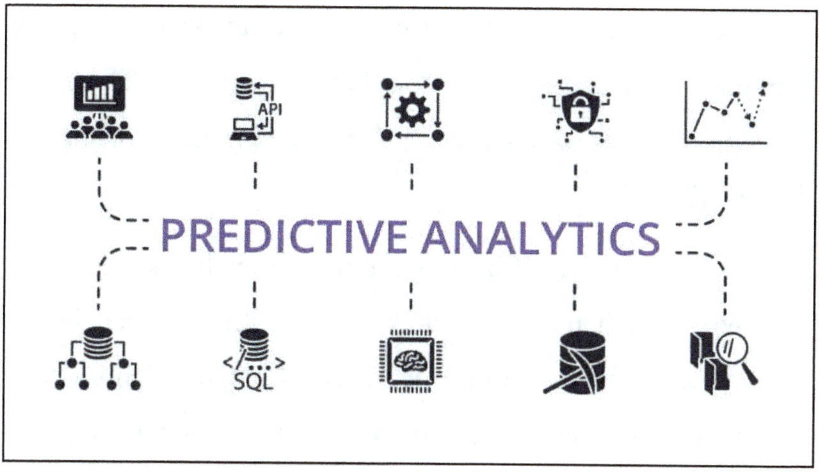

Figure 9.1 Predictive analytics [4].

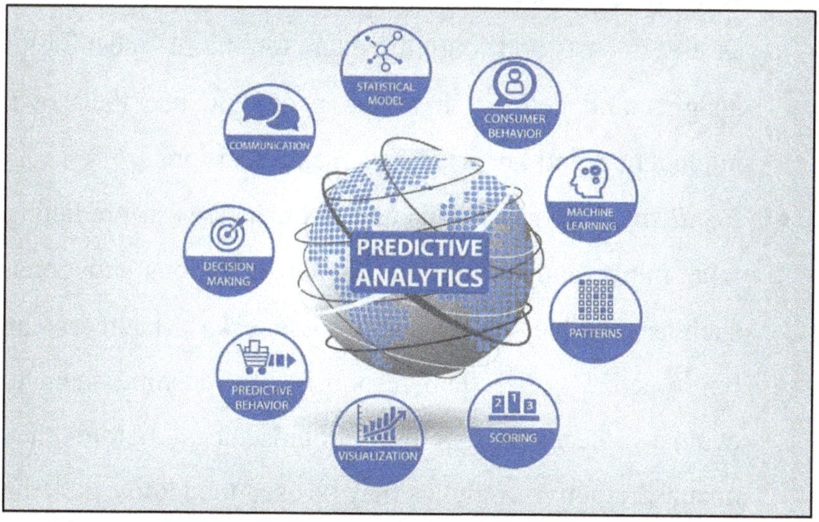

Figure 9.2 Different components of predictive analytics [5].

In general, analytics provides an efficient way to improve planning because it gives you better forecasts. There are different types of data analytics. They are briefly explained as follows [7]:

- *Descriptive Analytics:* Descriptive analytics examines what has happened over the years. They are capable of detecting trends in historical data. Analytics can uncover trends and postulate probable reasons for change by comparing the same data from various periods. It can be seen as the baseline of the industry, which basically assesses past and current data for more meaningful insights and delivers it to the people to use their own intelligence and knowledge to make decisions.
- *Predictive Analytics:* This assists businesses in predicting what might happen and the impact of various situations, such as possible supply chain bottlenecks. Managers can be proactive rather than responsive by pushing them to evaluate these prospective circumstances before they occur. Predictive analytics may be used to identify patterns and trends as well as anticipate breakdowns that may impact suppliers and, consequently, production processes. Predictive analytics for the supply chain leverages data, statistical algorithms, and machine learning techniques to identify the likelihood of future outcomes.

- *Prescriptive Analytics:* Prescriptive analytics builds on predictive analytics and dives deeper into predicting future insights on what can be done next. Prescriptive analytics uses the findings of descriptive and predictive analytics to recommend what measures a business should take to achieve its objectives. Because prescriptive analytics is increasingly complicated, they need more powerful software capable of rapidly processing and interpreting large amounts of data.
- *Cognitive Analytics:* Cognitive analytics attempts to mimic human thought and behavior, and it can assist companies in answering challenging, complex problems. Cognitive analytics does this by utilizing artificial intelligence (AI), which allows it to improve over time. With the use of AI in the industry, answering complex questions and draw out contextual conclusions on how humans would have interacted with the situation. It helps with more meaningful data and scales experience and knowledge for better decisions.
- *Diagnostic Analytics:* This gives the ability to identify the root cause. It is characterized by techniques such as drill-down, data discovery, data mining, and correlations. It involves analyzing overall performance and figuring out why errors, mistakes, and delays occur. It lets the manager know the delays, breakdowns, and disruptions in the

demand and supply processes and the reasons behind them.

Figure 9.3 shows these major types of data analytics [8]. Placing them together,

Descriptive → Diagnostic → Predictive → Prescriptive

Every step of ascending adds another level of depth, which is part of making that fugue out of just the mere frame of reference of past to bottom of dreaming about the future with certainty [8]. Unlike diagnostic and descriptive analytics, which were designed to analyze situations after they happened, predictive analytics utilizes advanced data analytics techniques to forecast future outcomes. In the supply chain, the time has come to shift from mere descriptive and diagnostic analytics to predictive and prescriptive analytics. Predictive analytics is a branch of data analytics that makes predictions about future outcomes using historical data combined with statistical modeling, data mining techniques, and machine learning. Figure 9.4 shows the evolution of predictive analytics [2].

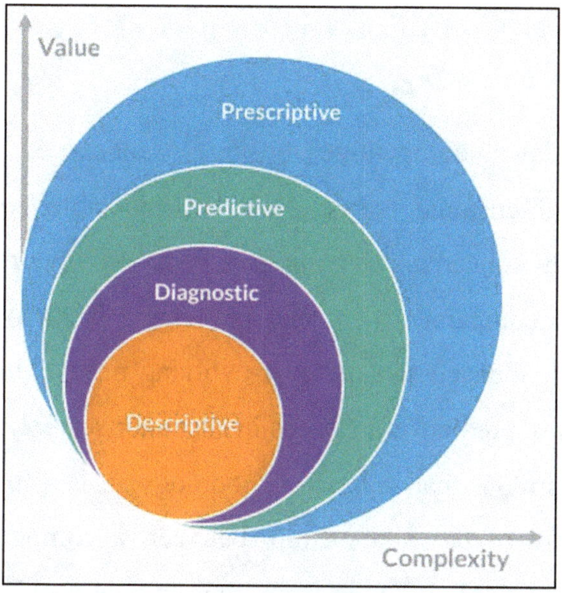

Figure 9.3 Types of data analytics [7].

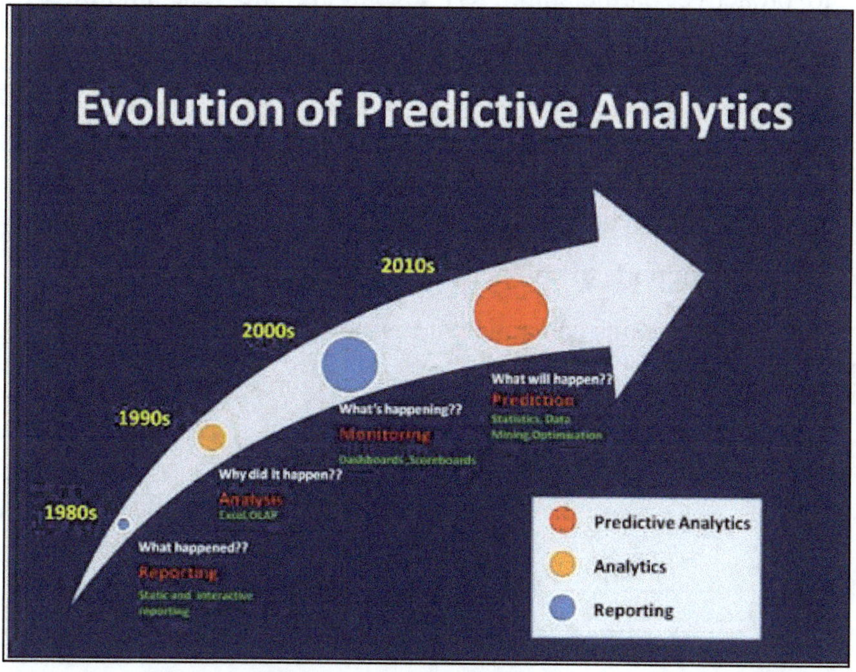

Figure 9.4 Evolution of predictive analytics [2].

9.3 PREDICTIVE ANALYTICS IN CUSTOMER SERVICE

In today's competitive business landscape, delivering exceptional customer service has become more crucial than ever. With consumers having a myriad of options at their fingertips, companies must find innovative ways to stand out and cater to their customers' ever-evolving needs. This is where the power of predictive analytics in customer service comes into play. It is more than a new methodology; it is a fundamental redefinition of the relationship between a company and its customers, a final evolution from transactional problem-solving to proactive partnership. By leveraging the vast amount of available data, businesses can gain valuable insights into customer behavior, preferences, and potential issues, enabling them to predict and proactively address customer needs. Predictive analytics is helping customer service move from reactive support to proactive solutions. By analyzing past interactions, teams can anticipate issues, reduce resolution time, and improve customer satisfaction. Figure 9.5 shows some customer service professionals [10].

Figure 9.5 Some customer service professionals [9].

Predictive analytics in customer service is an advanced data analysis technique that involves extracting meaningful insights from past data to predict what is likely to happen in the future. Predictive service models rely on behavioral preferences rather than marketing ones, like how quickly a customer expects a reply, how often they escalate, or whether they prefer human or digital help. They empower businesses to anticipate customer needs, enhance personalization, and streamline operations, ultimately improving customer satisfaction and loyalty. Embracing predictive analytics for customer retention and predictive customer satisfaction analysis is not just a competitive advantage; it is a necessity for businesses focused on shaping the future of predictive customer analytics experiences [11].

9.4 APPLICATIONS OF PREDICTIVE ANALYTICS IN CUSTOMER SERVICE

Predictive analytics is the process of using historical data, statistical models, and machine learning to forecast future events, behaviors, or trends. It is already making waves in customer service, offering innovative ways to enhance customer experience and streamline operations. Common applications include the following [1,12-15]:

- *Healthcare:* Healthcare customer support teams deal with appointment scheduling, claims processing, eligibility checks, and coverage questions. Predictive analytics helps anticipate peak inquiry periods and common patient concerns, enabling faster access to accurate, approved information while reducing operational strain. It also helps forecast ticket volume, optimize self-service content, and proactively address common issues during peak shopping periods, improving customer experience while controlling costs.
- *Ecommerce:* When a customer browses or purchases items on an online platform, predictive analytics collects valuable data such as past purchases, browsing history, items frequently bought together, product reviews and ratings, cart additions, and wish lists.
- *Telecommunication:* Telecom providers manage high volumes of service requests related to network outages,

billing issues, and plan changes. Predictive analytics helps forecast service disruptions and customer inquiries, enabling support teams to prepare knowledge and responses in advance. When a customer uses a telecom service, the predictive models collect valuable data such as call and data usage patterns, customer service interactions, payment history and billing issues, network performance in the user's location, feedback from surveys or social media.

- *Marketing:* Predictive analysis on market trends and typical business struggles allows for targeted messaging and marketing of your business to the right prospects, at the right time. Nothing is more important than sales to a business. Empowering sales efforts through trending and predictive metrics means you will end up with hot leads and interesting offerings.
- *Financial services:* When a customer interacts with a financial institution, predictive analytics collects valuable data such as transaction history and spending patterns, login behavior and device usage, location data and travel activity, past fraud alerts and resolution outcomes, customer support queries and feedback.
- *Demand Prediction:* Predictive models can forecast future demand based on historical sales data, seasonal trends, and market conditions. This helps businesses plan inventory

levels, optimize supply chains, and reduce stockouts or overstock situations.

- *Customer Support:* Customers expect instant, accurate answers across channels, while support teams struggle with rising ticket volumes, complex queries, and limited time to respond. For decades, customer support has been treated as a defensive necessity, a cost center designed solely to resolve issues after they arise. To drive growth, companies should transform customer support from reactive to predictive and proactive. Predictive analytics helps customer support teams anticipate customer issues, reduce resolution time, and deliver more consistent service. Predictive models identify early warning signals such as repeated contacts, unresolved searches, or rising ticket frequency. This allows support teams to act before issues escalate, helping prevent complaints, negative reviews, or customer churn.
- *Customer Education*: Customer education can be regarded as a strategic initiative that aims to provide customers with the knowledge and skills they need to be able to use a service or product effectively. Customer education also has traditionally been viewed as a way to generate value for customers; it plays an important role in enhancing customer satisfaction and developing customer expertise. It has proven to be an effective method for retention in organizations.

- *Customer Retention:* Predictive analytics is a powerful tool for customer retention. By analyzing historical data and customer behavior patterns, businesses can identify customers who are at risk of leaving and take proactive actions to reduce customer attrition. Predictive analysis provides all the essential details about your customers. With an extensive customer base and a lack of combined customer data, it can be difficult to understand which customers provide the most value to your brand. Using predictive analytics, you can predict the lifetime value of specific customer segments. Figure 9.6 shows different ways predictive analytics improves customer retention [16].

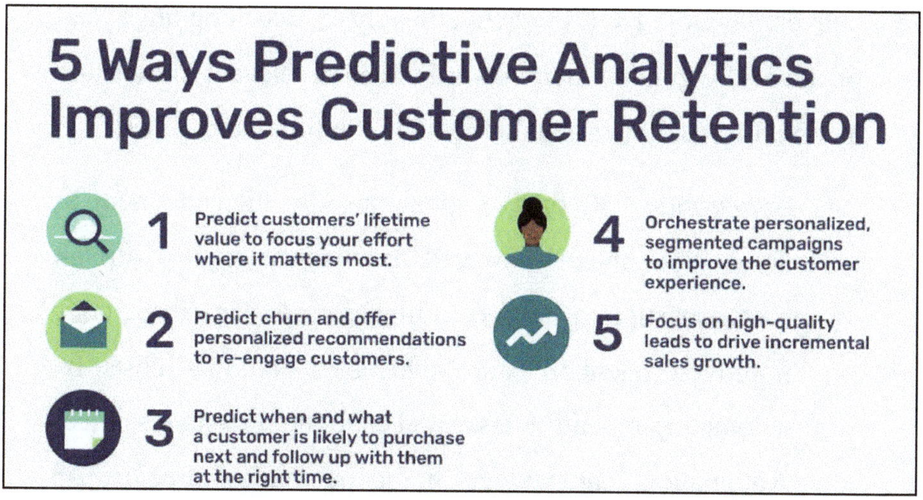

Figure 9.6 Different ways predictive analytics improves customer retention [15].

- *Customer Sentiment:* Sentiment analysis uses predictive analytics to analyze customer feedback and sentiment from social media, reviews, and surveys. By understanding customer sentiment, businesses can identify areas for improvement and promptly address any issues or concerns.

9.5 BENEFITS

Customer service predictive analytics is transforming how businesses approach customer service. Predictive analytics in customer service is a transformative tool that brings a multitude of benefits, positively impacting both businesses and their clientele. Besides operational efficiency, predictive analytics delivers tangible ROI. Predictive insights reduce cognitive load on agents by guiding them toward the most relevant knowledge and next steps. Other benefits include the following [2,17]:

- *Automation:* Predictive analytics is the entrance to automation and AI-powered decision-making. AI-driven customer support has led to higher customer satisfaction, improved retention, and reduced operational costs by automating repetitive tasks and enabling proactive service. Automation can reduce mundane duties, freeing up support professionals for more complex client issues.
- *Cost Savings*: Operational efficiency and cost-effectiveness are crucial aspects of any business.

Predictive analytics achieves this by optimizing resource allocation.

- *Decision-making:* Predictive analytics furnishes marketers with insights rooted in data, facilitating well-informed decision-making. Instead of relying on intuition or lagging metrics, customer experience leaders gain forward-looking insights. Predictive analytics helps prioritize initiatives, measure risk, and make informed decisions that align with customer expectations and business goals.
- *Customer Satisfaction:* Customer satisfaction is the cornerstone of any successful business. Predictive analytics plays a pivotal role in elevating satisfaction levels by anticipating customer needs.
- *Personalized Support:* Personalization constitutes the pinnacle of contemporary marketing, and predictive analytics is instrumental in its realization. It is the key to creating meaningful and lasting customer relationships. Predictive analytics can be used to personalize the customer experience. By analyzing a customer's past behavior and preferences, businesses can anticipate the customer's needs and provide personalized recommendations. Customer expectations have permanently changed. The new standard set by digital leaders has created a powerful demand for proactive

personalization. Predictive customer analytics enables businesses to create highly personalized customer experiences. It helps support teams quickly identify customer needs and suggest the most relevant solutions based on past behavior and interactions. Businesses must adopt customer-first approaches that use data-driven insights to deliver tailored experiences.

- *Continuous Improvement:* The integration of predictive analytics into customer service is an iterative process. Regularly updating and refining predictive models ensures that businesses stay attuned to evolving customer preferences and market dynamics. This continuous improvement loop is crucial for maintaining the effectiveness of predictive analytics in customer service.
- *Customer Feedback:* Feedback from customers, whether collected through surveys or online reviews, serves as a rich source of data for understanding customer sentiment and identifying areas for improvement, enhancing predictive analytics customer experience.
- *Enhanced Communication:* Predictive analytics in customer service allows for targeted and personalized communication, ensuring that customers receive relevant information, promotions, and support, thereby fostering a stronger emotional connection with the brand. Businesses can craft targeted marketing messages and communication

strategies, ensuring that customers receive information that resonates with their specific needs and interests, enhancing predictive customer service.

9.6 CHALLENGES

Despite the benefits, implementing predictive analytics in customer service comes with challenges. The more data a business collects, the greater the risk of a data breach. Predictive analytics systems must have robust security measures in place to safeguard against unauthorized access. Data quality, data privacy, model interpretability, ethical concerns, and transparency remain key challenges. Other challenges include the following [2,17]:

- *Costs:* The integration of predictive analytics systems often involves substantial upfront costs. Additionally, ongoing maintenance and updates require dedicated resources. Businesses need to carefully assess the financial implications and allocate resources effectively to ensure a smooth integration process into their predictive analytics customer experience strategies.
- *Information Overload*: The Internet has flooded consumers with information. They now research extensively before making decisions, from choosing a restaurant for dinner to investing in high-value products.

This translates to a more informed and discerning customer base.

- *Data Privacy:* Predictive analytics customer experience relies heavily on customer data. Ensuring the privacy and security of this information is paramount. Customers are increasingly concerned about how their data is being used. Businesses must implement robust data protection measures to build and maintain trust in their predictive customer service efforts. They must prioritize the security and privacy of customer data. They should implement robust cybersecurity measures and adhere to data protection regulations to build trust with customers and ensure compliance in their predictive customer service initiatives.
- *Data Quality:* Raw data is often incomplete, inconsistent, or noisy. Data cleaning involves removing errors and inconsistencies, while data preparation ensures that the data is structured and formatted correctly for analysis. The effectiveness of predictive analytics customer service relies heavily on the quality and diversity of the data it analyzes. Predictive models are only as good as the data they can access, so ensuring your data is clean and unified is the non-negotiable first step. Maintain data accuracy by implementing rigorous quality control measures.

- *Data Bias:* Predictive customer analytics models are only as good as the data they are trained on. If historical data contains biases, the predictive models may perpetuate those biases. This can result in unfair treatment of certain customer segments. Regular audits are necessary to identify and rectify any biases in the models to ensure fair predictive analytics in customer service.
- *Ethical Concerns:* The ethical implications of using predictive analytics in customer service cannot be overlooked. Businesses must prioritize fairness and transparency in their algorithms. Clear communication with customers about how their data is used and ensuring that predictive models do not discriminate are essential ethical considerations in predictive analytics customer experience.
- *Integration:* Many businesses have legacy systems in place, and integrating predictive analytics with these systems can be challenging. Compatibility issues may arise, leading to delays in implementation. Businesses need a well-thought-out integration strategy to overcome these challenges in their predictive customer service frameworks. Integrating predictive systems with existing IT infrastructure and customer relationship management platforms can be complex and costly.

- *Regulatory Compliance:* Various data protection regulations, such as GDPR and CCPA, impose strict guidelines on how customer data is collected, processed, and stored. Adhering to these regulations is not only a legal requirement but also essential for maintaining ethical standards in predictive analytics customer service practices.

9.7 FUTURE OF PREDICTIVE ANALYTICS IN CUSTOMER SERVICE

In an era where one step ahead can mean everything, such foresight is not just good – it is necessary. Predictive analytics is a powerful technology that makes it possible for organizations to use big data to predict future events, trends, and behaviors. It uses statistical algorithms and machine learning approaches to predict likely future patterns, events, and behaviors based on historical data. It is used by an increasing variety of industries, including marketing, finance, retail, and healthcare, to better understand customer behavior and preferences. Analytics based on the prediction of customer behavior is an approach that aims to predict future customer behavior using businesses' customer data. This approach enables a better understanding of customer needs, optimizing marketing and sales strategies and increasing customer satisfaction [18].

The future of customer service is not reactive; it is predictive. Predictive analytics empowers businesses to anticipate needs before they arise, using data-driven insights for timely, personalized support. Emerging trends, such as AI and hyper-personalization, are poised to further enhance the capabilities of predictive analytics and AI in customer service, driving more responsive, responsible, and human-like interactions. The integration of predictive analytics and AI in customer service is no longer just a technological innovation but a strategic imperative. The beauty of future analytics is that it gives leaders the right to make clever, fast decisions before the problem arises.

9.8 CONCLUSION

In an increasingly data-driven world, predictive analytics has emerged as a powerful tool that enables businesses to anticipate future trends and behaviors. Customer service has long been a reactive function: resolving tickets, handling escalations, and managing peak loads only after they occur. Predictive analytics changes that equation. It uses time-series and machine learning models to analyze historical ticket volumes and forecast future demand. It does not just forecast demand; it ensures the right resources are in the right place at the right time.

Predictive analytics is a game-changer for customer service. Predictive analytics in customer service uses data from past support interactions, including tickets, chat logs, call transcripts, feedback, and agent actions, to identify trends and customer behaviors. Rather than waiting for tickets to pile up, predictive systems alert teams early, allowing better resource planning, faster resolution, and more informed decision-making. Predictive analytics helps your brand to anticipate customer needs, personalize interactions, and boost satisfaction. More information on the integration of predictive analytics into customer service is available from the books in [19-22].

REFERENCES

[1] L. A. Okello, "Unlock the future with predictive analytics in customer service," March 2026, https://www.bolddesk.com/blogs/predictive-analytics-in-customer-service

[2] "The power of predictive analytics in customer service [2025 guide]," January 2024, https://wizr.ai/blog/the-power-of-predictive-analytics-in-customer-service/

[3] M. N. O. Sadiku, D. Padi, and J. O. Sadiku, "Predictive analytics for customer service," International Journal of Management and Organizational Research, vol. 5, no. 2, March-April, 2026, pp. 131-138.

[4] "Supply chain predictive analytics: What is it and who's doing it?" https://riverlogic.com/?blog=supply-chain-predictive-analytics-what-is-it-and-whos-doing-it

[5] N. Babin, "AI and predictive analytics: Revolutionizing demand forecasting in supply chain management," https://www.linkedin.com/pulse/ai-predictive-analytics-revolutionizing-demand-supply-nicolas-babin-xrj2e/

[6] "The role of analytics in marketing: Types of analytics, marketing analytics process and tools," February 2024, https://www.sprinkledata.com/blogs/the-role-of-analytics-in-

marketing-types-of-analytics-marketing-analytics-process-and-tools

[7] "An overview of supply chain analytics," February 2023, Unknown Source.

[8] I. Tymchuk, "Big data and predictive analytics in supply chain: Success stories and tips," November 2020, https://www.n-ix.com/big-data-predictive-analytics-supply-chain-case-study/

[9] M. Mistry, "Predictive analytics vs traditional analytics: How modern businesses make smarter decisions," April 2025, https://kodytechnolab.com/blog/predictive-analytics-vs-traditional-analytics/

[10] D. Ritchie, "How AI is helping customer service teams stay efficient and productive," June 2023, https://www.calendar.com/blog/how-ai-is-helping-customer-service-teams-stay-efficient-and-productive/

[11] "How predictive analytics improves customer service," https://www.clootrack.com/knowledge/customer-service-analytics/how-predictive-analytics-improves-customer-service

[12] "15 Ways predictive analytics can help businesses boost their CX," https://www.forbes.com/councils/forbestechcouncil/2023/08/2

4/15-ways-predictive-analytics-can-help-businesses-boost-their-cx/

[13] "What are predictive analytics in customer service?" March 2026, https://knowmax.ai/blog/predictive-analytics-in-customer-service/

[14] N. Ibrahim, "Enhancing customer retention through predictive analytics," November 2024, https://www.theseus.fi/bitstream/handle/10024/869850/Ibrahim_Nada.pdf?sequence=2

[15] B. Stanley, "Predictive analytics and customer engagement," March 2024, https://www.engageinsure.com/predictive-analytics-customer-engagement/

[16] E. Burnam, "5 Ways predictive analytics improves customer retention," February 2026, https://www.lexer.io/blog/5-ways-predictive-analytics-improves-customer-retention

[17] B. Elly, I. Luxs, and B. Nous, "Transforming customer experience with predictive analytics: Leveraging AI for personalized support," November 2024,

https://www.researchgate.net/publication/386139462_Transforming_Customer_Experience_with_Predictive_Analytics_Leveraging_AI_for_Personalized_Support/link/674600d8a7fbc259 f19021ff/download?_tp=eyJjb250ZXh0Ijp7ImZpcnN0UGFnZSI6InB1YmxpY2F0aW9uIiwicGFnZSI6InB1YmxpY2F0aW9uIn19

[18] M. Basal, K. Moulai, and A. Cetin, "Predictive analytics for customer behavior prediction in artificial intelligence," Economics World, vol. 12, no. 2, April-June 2025, pp. 142-154

[19] Q. Cortex, Predictive Analytics for Customer Service: A Business Owner's Guide. Kindle edition, 2024.

[20] E. Siegel, Predictive Analytics: The Power to Predict Who Will Click, Buy, Lie, or Die. Wiley, 2016.

[21] Innovative PJP, Predictive Customer Analytics in the Financial Sector: Leveraging AI and Predictive Analytics for Enhanced Customer Insights. Kindle edition, 2024.

[22] H. E. Parkins, Predictive Analytics for Customer Behavior: Using AI to Predict Customer Behavior Trends Helps in Making Data-Driven Marketing Decisions. Independently Published, 2024.

CHAPTER 10: PREDICTIVE ANALYTICS FOR HUMAN RESOURCES

"The greatest tragedy in life is not death but a life without purpose."

– Myles Munroe

10.1 INTRODUCTION

Businesses use different types of analytics to work well. Predictive analytics is one of them. Others are descriptive, real-time, diagnostic, and prescriptive analytics. Predictive HR analytics, also known as predictive people analytics or workforce analytics, refers to the use of data, statistical algorithms, and machine learning techniques to identify the likelihood of future outcomes based on historical data. It uses artificial intelligence to forecast future outcomes and enables more informed decisions about recruiting, staffing, employee development, and other HR functions. By leveraging predictive analytics, HR professionals can move beyond traditional methods and gain insights from historical data on hiring outcomes, employee turnover, and performance. Figure 10.1 shows some HR professionals [1].

Figure 10.1 Some HR professionals [1].

New technological tools such as predictive analytics are changing the way companies look at their human resources today. Predictive analytics is an operational analytics method that employs historical information and statistical tools, as well as algorithms, to make forecasts of future events. The integration of predictive analytics into HR practices marks a significant shift from traditional methods that often rely on intuition and anecdotal evidence. HR departments are now equipped to harness vast amounts of information to gain insights into employee behavior, engagement levels, and turnover rates [2].

Predictive modeling is a way to guess what will happen in the future. It looks for patterns from past data and uses those patterns to make predictions. Predictive analytics has become a valuable asset in many industries. It has emerged as a transformative force in the realm of human resources (HR), enabling organizations to make data-driven decisions. It is an important tool for companies that want to stay in the lead. It helps them make smart decisions about the future. Businesses use predictive analytics to manage their products and set good prices. Predictive analytics in HR leverages data and AI to enhance decision-making, identifying at-risk employees and optimizing retention strategies. Through predictive analytics, HR professionals can identify patterns and predict future outcomes based on historical data, allowing for the development of more effective employee retention strategies [3].

This chapter explores the role of predictive analytics in human resources. It begins by explaining predictive analytics. It describes predictive analytics in HR and provides some of its applications. It highlights some benefits and challenges of predictive analytics in HR. The last section concludes with comments.

10.2 WHAT IS PREDICTIVE ANALYTICS?

As its name implies, predictive analytics is about predicting future trends such as sales demand and exchange rates. and other important metrics. The technique relies on the application of statistical modeling and regression analysis to historical data to determine and understand trends and formulate future predictions. Strictly speaking, predictive analytics does not predict the future, but rather uses probability theories to determine what is likely to happen based on patterns and trends revealed by analyzing historical data [4]. Predictive analytics accurately anticipates customer demand, preventing overstocking and stockouts while adapting to market changes. Figure 10.2 illustrates predictive analytics [5], while Figure 10.3 shows different components of predictive analytics [6].

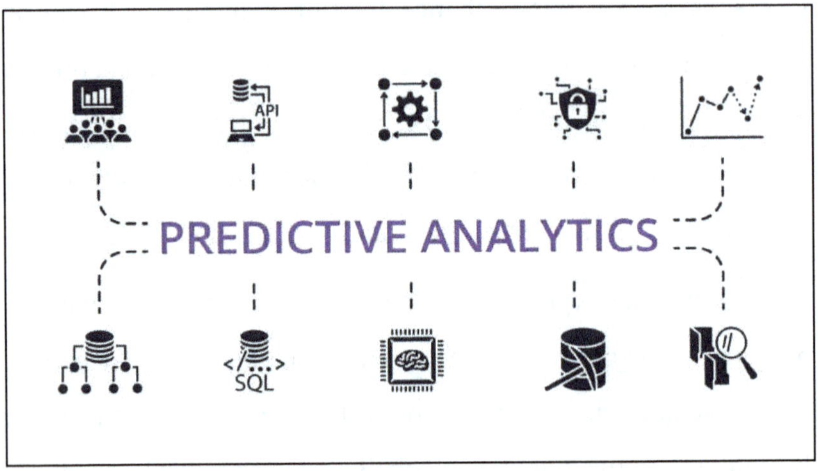

Figure 10.2 Predictive analytics [5].

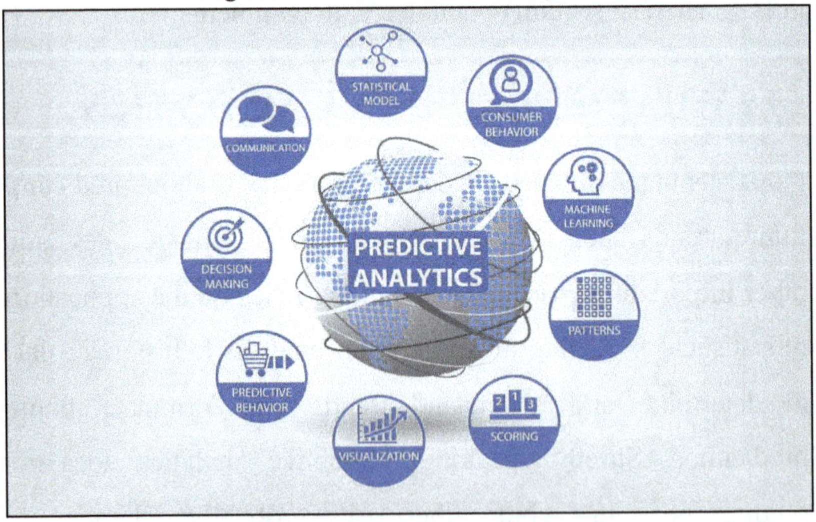

Figure 10.3 Different components of predictive analytics [6].

In general, analytics provides an efficient way to improve planning because it gives you better forecasts. There are different types of data analytics. They are briefly explained as follows [7]:

- *Descriptive Analytics:* Descriptive analytics examines what has happened over the years. They are capable of detecting trends in historical data. Analytics can uncover trends and postulate probable reasons for change by comparing the same data from various periods. It can be seen as the baseline of the industry, which basically assesses past and current data for more meaningful insights and delivers it to the people to use their own intelligence and knowledge to make decisions.
- *Predictive Analytics:* This assists businesses in predicting what might happen and the impact of various situations, such as possible supply chain bottlenecks. Managers can be proactive rather than responsive by pushing them to evaluate these prospective circumstances before they occur. Predictive analytics may be used to identify patterns and trends as well as anticipate breakdowns that may impact suppliers and, consequently, production processes. Predictive analytics for the supply chain leverages data, statistical algorithms, and machine learning techniques to identify the likelihood of future outcomes.

- *Prescriptive Analytics:* Prescriptive analytics builds on predictive analytics and dives deeper into predicting future insights on what can be done next. Prescriptive analytics uses the findings of descriptive and predictive analytics to recommend what measures a business should take to achieve its objectives. Because prescriptive analytics is increasingly complicated, they need more powerful software capable of rapidly processing and interpreting large amounts of data.
- *Cognitive Analytics:* Cognitive analytics attempts to mimic human thought and behavior, and it can assist companies in answering challenging, complex problems. Cognitive analytics does this by utilizing artificial intelligence (AI), which allows it to improve over time. With the use of AI in the industry, answering complex questions and draw out contextual conclusions on how humans would have interacted with the situation. It helps with more meaningful data and scales experience and knowledge for better decisions.
- *Diagnostics Analytics:* This gives the ability to identify the root cause. It is characterized by techniques such as drill-down, data discovery, data mining, and correlations. It involves analyzing overall performance and figuring out why errors, mistakes, and delays occur. It lets the manager

know the delays, breakdowns, and disruptions in the demand and supply processes and the reasons behind them.

Figure 10.4 shows these major types of data analytics [8]. Unlike diagnostic and descriptive analytics, which were designed to analyze situations after they happened, predictive analytics utilizes advanced data analytics techniques to forecast future outcomes. In the supply chain, the time has come to shift from mere descriptive and diagnostic analytics to predictive and prescriptive analytics. Predictive analytics is a branch of data analytics that makes predictions about future outcomes using historical data combined with statistical modeling, data mining techniques, and machine learning.

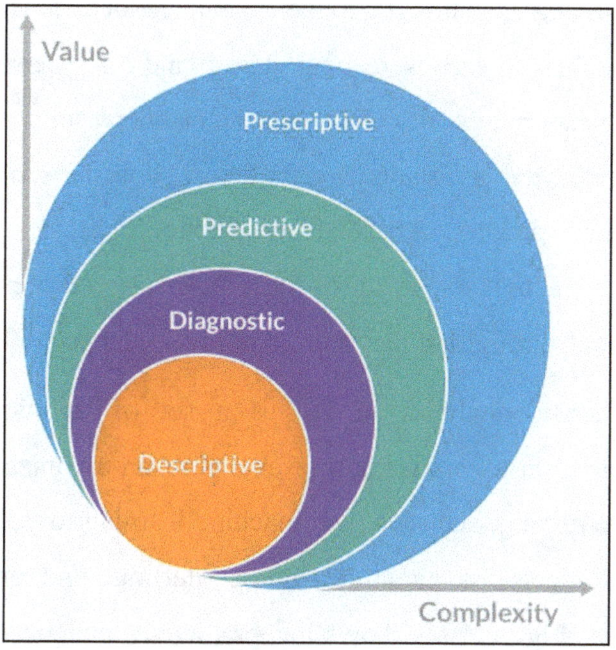

Figure 10.4 Types of data analytics [8].

10.3 PREDICTIVE ANALYTICS IN HUMAN RESOURCES

Human resource management (HRM) plays a strategic role in enhancing organizational effectiveness, innovation, and competitiveness. Among its core functions, recruitment, employee retention, and performance optimization are critical for maintaining a productive and motivated workforce. Artificial intelligence (AI) and machine learning (ML) have emerged as transformative tools in HRM, offering predictive analytics and automation for critical HR tasks. Artificial intelligence is playing an increasingly strategic role in modern recruitment processes. Organizations that successfully integrate AI technologies into recruitment can reduce time-to-hire, eliminate bias in early screening stages, and offer personalized communication at scale. HR departments increasingly use AI-powered virtual assistants and software bots to support the onboarding process. Artificial intelligence will significantly influence activities within the human resources (HR) department throughout the entire employee lifecycle [9].

Predictive analytics in HR is a set of techniques for analyzing data to predict future events in an organization. It uses data mining, statistics, and machine learning to make more informed decisions about recruiting, staffing, and other HR functions. Figure 10.5 shows the predictive analytics process [10]. By applying predictive analysis to HR data, HR is able to become a strategic partner that relies on proven and data-driven predictive models, instead of relying on gut feeling and soft science. HR predictive analytics enable HR to forecast the impact of people policies on well-being, happiness, and bottom-line performance. For example, Google estimates the probability of people leaving the company by applying HR predictive analysis. One of Google's findings is that new salespeople, who do not get a promotion within four years, are much more likely to leave the company [11].

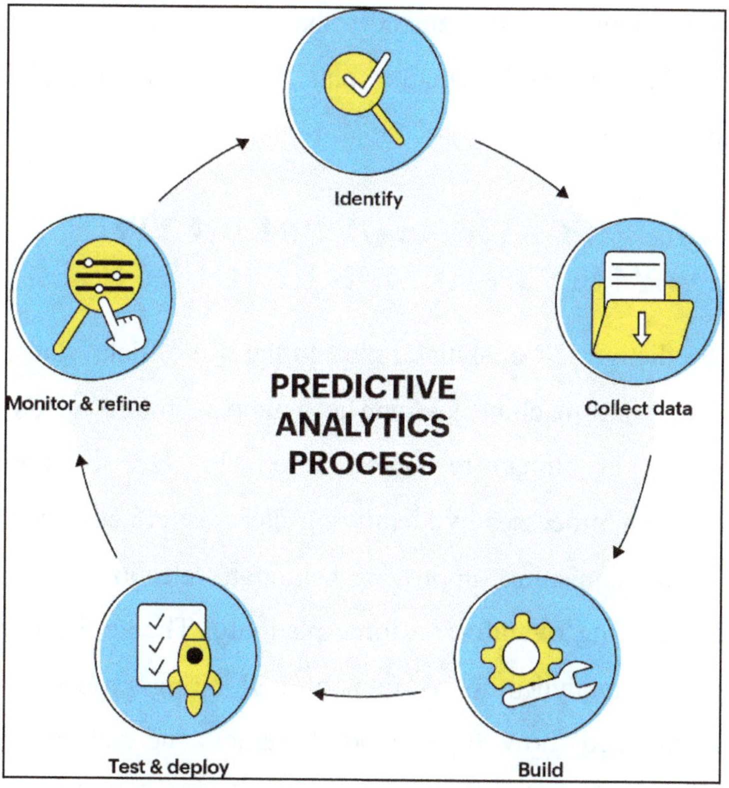

Figure 10.5 Predictive analytics process [10].

To effectively utilize predictive analytics in human resources, it is essential to identify the key metrics that will drive meaningful insights. Commonly analyzed metrics include employee turnover rates, recruitment efficiency, employee engagement scores, and performance ratings. By focusing on these indicators, HR professionals can uncover patterns that reveal underlying issues or opportunities for improvement. The success of predictive analytics in HR hinges on the quality and organization of the data being analyzed. Organizations must ensure that they are capturing comprehensive and accurate data to facilitate meaningful analysis [12].

10.4 APPLICATIONS OF PREDICTIVE ANALYTICS IN HUMAN RESOURCES

Predictive HR analytics refers to the use of data, statistical methods, and machine learning to anticipate future trends and outcomes in human resources. It enables HR to optimize recruitment processes by identifying the most effective sources for talent acquisition, improving candidate selection processes, and enhancing overall workforce planning. The application of predictive analytics in recruitment and hiring processes has revolutionized how organizations attract and select talent. Common applications include the following [1,9,12-14]:

- *Healthcare:* Healthcare roles, especially in high-stress environments like emergency and intensive care units, have high rates of burnout and turnover. Predictive analytics can assess risk factors for burnout by monitoring work hours, patient load, and staff wellness reports. Healthcare facilities can use these insights to implement preventative measures, such as adjusting workloads, offering more support, and creating wellness programs tailored to the needs identified through the data. Figure 10.6 shows the use of predictive analytics in healthcare [15].

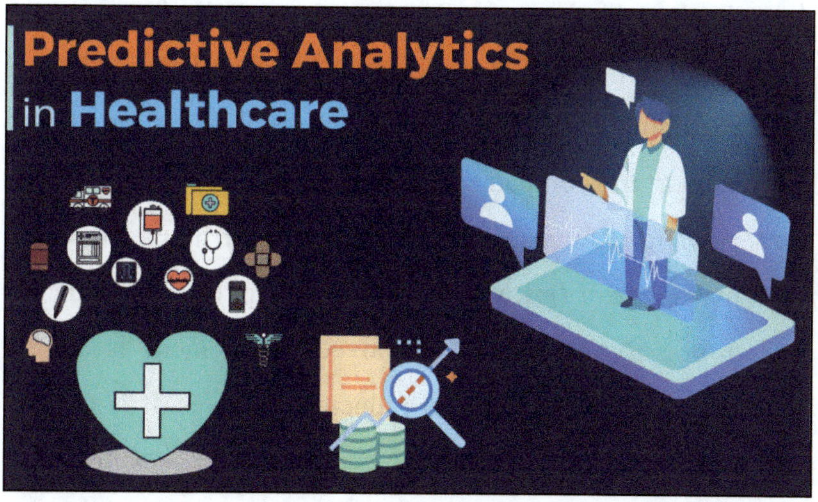

Figure 10.6 Use of predictive analytics in healthcare [15].

- *Restaurants:* In the restaurant industry, staff turnover can peak during high seasons such as holidays and summer months. Predictive analytics can help manage and reduce this turnover. By analyzing historical data on employee shifts, customer volume, and staff feedback, predictive models can identify patterns that lead to high turnover.
- *Talent Acquisition Planning*: HRs are responsible for maintaining an organization's workforce, preventing employee shortages or overstaffing. Predictive analytics can help HR specialists forecast an organization's talent requirements and workforce needs well in advance to timely address them. This enables HR leaders to make better hiring decisions, ensuring the availability of skilled personnel exactly when and where they are needed to support the company's business outcomes.
- *Employee Engagement:* In the field of human resource management (HRM), successful employee engagement is a primary objective. Employee engagement is key to retaining employees and reducing turnover. It is directly linked to productivity and business success. Employees who are engaged work harder, deliver better quality, are less absent, and are less likely to quit. Companies that invest in engagement strategies see higher employee satisfaction and increased performance. Approaches include ensuring workers are actively engaged in their

tasks, aligning personal goals with those of the organization and the project, and facilitating quality work while maintaining a healthy work–life balance. Predictive analytics can significantly boost employee engagement. By analyzing data on employee behavior, feedback, and engagement survey results, HR teams can identify trends that lead to disengagement.

- *Employee Performance:* Predictive analytics helps HR professionals identify factors that influence employee performance. It helps employees meet their performance goals and overall corporate objectives. For example, HR specialists can leverage predictive models to understand how different factors, such as employee incentive schemes, will positively or negatively impact different team members' performance.
- *Employee Retention:* Employee retention is a major issue for many companies today. It is a critical concern for organizations seeking to maintain a stable workforce and minimize turnover costs. Numerous organizations are exploring various methods to retain their employees, including generating annual reports through surveys to understand their concerns and needs. HR teams aim to identify company-specific turnover reasons and intervene early to retain employees before it is too late. Predictive analytics plays a vital role in identifying at-risk employees

who may be considering leaving the organization. An employee may decide to leave an organization for many reasons. Research shows that the probability of leaving a company varies and can be calculated based on different characteristics.

- *Performance Management:* Performance management is another area where predictive analytics can yield significant benefits. By analyzing performance data over time, organizations can identify trends that inform talent development strategies and succession planning efforts. Predictive models can help HR professionals forecast future performance outcomes based on historical data, enabling them to make informed decisions about promotions, training needs, and resource allocation.
- *Workforce Planning:* One of the key areas where predictive analytics is making a significant impact is workforce planning. Effective workforce planning is crucial for ensuring an organization has the right number of employees with the right skills and time to meet its operational needs. Predictive analytics enables HR teams to forecast future workforce requirements by analyzing patterns in employee data, such as hiring trends, turnover rates, and productivity metrics. This ability to predict future needs allows organizations to plan more effectively. By using predictive analytics to anticipate customer

service challenges and proactively address them through workforce adjustments, organizations can improve the overall customer experience. Predictive analytics has fundamentally transformed the landscape of workforce planning by enabling organizations to forecast future workforce requirements with unprecedented accuracy.

1-0.5 BENEFITS

Predictive analytics can forecast customer behavior, identify potential risks and opportunities, optimize marketing campaigns, and improve operational efficiency. This technology not only forecasts potential employee turnover but also provides actionable insights, enabling companies to proactively address retention challenges. Other benefits include the following [16,17]:

- *Improved Decision-making:* Data-driven decisions are more accurate than those made based on intuition alone. The predictive analytics framework helps HR professionals make better and wiser decisions. Using predictive HR analytics to make better decisions allows businesses to save money, increase productivity, and improve customer satisfaction. Decision-making is a complex task. Using predictive analytics in business intelligence helps ensure the best decision is made. For example, Amazon uses predictive analytics to help customers make better online shopping decisions. Amazon's recommendations are so good that many people say they are getting personal advice from the site. When decision-making becomes more efficient, productivity increases, and when people are not figuring out what to do, they can spend more time doing the tasks.

- *Fewer Disasters:* Disaster prevention is another reason why the predictive analytics framework is so valuable. It helps prevent disasters by identifying risks early enough to avoid them altogether. Risk reduction is one of any business's primary goals. Data-driven decisions reduce risk by allowing companies to identify potential problems before they occur.
- *Data Acquisition:* The foundation of effective predictive HR analytics lies in establishing a comprehensive data architecture that can seamlessly integrate diverse information sources while maintaining data quality, security, and accessibility standards. This architectural approach addresses the challenges of handling structured and unstructured data from various sources, including human resource information systems, performance management platforms, learning management systems, employee surveys, and external market data.
- *Global Adaptation:* The successful deployment of predictive HR analytics models across global

organizations requires sophisticated strategies that accommodate diverse cultural contexts, regulatory environments, and business practices while maintaining analytical consistency and accuracy. Workforce behavior and management practices vary significantly across cultures. Cultural adaptation strategies begin with a comprehensive assessment of local workforce characteristics, management practices, and regulatory requirements that may impact analytical model performance. Training programs are adapted to local learning preferences and communication styles while maintaining consistent competency standards for analytics usage across global implementations.

- *Scalability:* Scalability mechanisms ensure that implementations can grow with local organizational needs without requiring major system changes. Capacity planning and scalability assessment identify potential system limitations and guide infrastructure improvements to support growing analytical demands. Scalability planning ensures that analytical capabilities can grow and evolve to meet expanding organizational needs and opportunities. Organizations that plan for scalability from the beginning achieve more cost-effective implementations and better long-term sustainability compared to those that must rebuild capabilities as requirements grow. Scalability best practices include designing flexible architectures that accommodate growth without major redesign.

- *Change Management*: Change management integration ensures that analytical initiatives are effectively incorporated into broader organizational transformation efforts. Organizations that integrate analytics with comprehensive change management programs achieve higher adoption rates and better business outcomes compared to those that treat analytics as purely technical initiatives. Change management best practices include developing comprehensive communication strategies that address employee concerns and expectations.
- *Knowledge Management:* Organizations with strong knowledge management capabilities achieve better consistency and continuity in their analytical programs compared to those that lack systematic knowledge preservation approaches. Knowledge management best practices include documenting analytical models and decision-making processes comprehensively, creating training materials and user guides that facilitate knowledge transfer.
- *Performance Monitoring:* Organizations that establish comprehensive performance monitoring achieve better long-term outcomes and higher return on investment

compared to those that lack systematic monitoring capabilities. Performance monitoring best practices include establishing baseline measurements and clear success metrics, and implementing automated monitoring systems that track key performance indicators.

Figure 10.7 shows some benefits of predictive analytics [18].

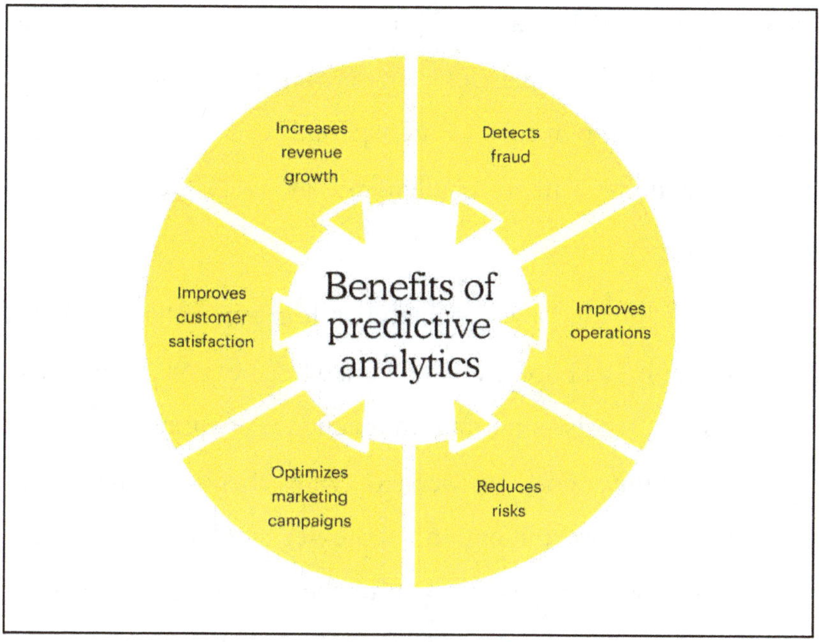

Figure 10.7 Some benefits of predictive analytics [18].

10.6 CHALLENGES

Despite its potential benefits, implementing predictive analytics in human resources is not without challenges, such as data quality issues, the need for specialized skills, and ethical considerations related to privacy and bias. While AI offers transformative opportunities for HRM, its success depends on responsible implementation, guided by theory, supported by transparent models, and aligned with ethical values. To overcome these challenges, organizations must focus on educating employees, transparency, and gradual implementation. Other challenges include the following [9,14,16]:

- *Cost:* The total cost of analytics implementation includes not only technology and consulting expenses but also training costs, ongoing maintenance requirements, and opportunity costs associated with change management efforts. Cost mitigation strategies include developing phased implementation approaches that spread costs over time, focusing initial efforts on high-value use cases that demonstrate clear return on investment, and establishing shared services approaches that spread costs across multiple organizational units.
- *Data Privacy:* Employee data must be handled with care. Implement robust data security measures and comply with

regulations such as GDPR and CCPA to protect sensitive information. Employee privacy expectations, legal restrictions on data usage, cross-border data transfer limitations, and evolving regulatory requirements can significantly constrain analytical capabilities while increasing implementation complexity and costs.

- *Data Quality*: One of the most significant challenges is data quality. Data governance excellence forms the foundation of effective predictive analytics, requiring comprehensive policies and procedures that ensure data quality, security, and appropriate usage across the organization. Organizations with mature data governance capabilities achieve higher model accuracy, better regulatory compliance, and more effective decision-making compared to those with inadequate governance frameworks. Predictive analytics relies heavily on the accuracy and completeness of data, and HR departments often grapple with fragmented or inconsistent data sources. In many organizations, employee data is spread across different systems, making it difficult to integrate and ensure that the data is clean and reliable. Poor data quality can lead to incorrect predictions.
- *Integration:* Another challenge is the integration of predictive analytics into existing HR processes. Many HR departments still rely on traditional workforce planning

methods, which are often manual and reactive. The shift to predictive analytics requires a fundamental change in how data is collected, analyzed, and applied in decision-making. This transition can be complex and resource-intensive, requiring significant investments in technology and training. The integration process may face resistance from HR professionals accustomed to traditional approaches. They may be skeptical of relying on data-driven insights over their experience and intuition.

- *Resistance to Change:* Resistance to change is another critical barrier to successfully adopting predictive analytics in HR. Employees and managers may be hesitant to trust or embrace new technologies, particularly if they perceive them as a threat to their roles or as tools that could increase surveillance. Overcoming this resistance requires clear communication about the benefits of predictive analytics and training programs that empower HR professionals to use these tools effectively. Building a culture that values data-driven decision-making is essential for ensuring that predictive analytics can be successfully integrated into HR practices. Most HR professionals lack the analytical skills necessary to effectively utilize predictive models, interpret statistical results, or translate analytical insights into appropriate business decisions. Strategic leadership commitment represents the most critical factor in successful predictive HR analytics implementation.

- *Ethical Concerns:* Predictive analytics in HR raises important ethical considerations, particularly privacy and bias. Predictive models often rely on large amounts of personal data, including employee performance metrics, health records, and social media activity. Collecting and analyzing this data can lead to concerns about employee privacy and the potential to misuse sensitive information. Organizations must navigate these concerns carefully, ensuring their data practices comply with legal requirements and ethical standards. Organizations that prioritize ethical considerations build greater trust and acceptance among employees and stakeholders while reducing legal and reputational risks.
- *Bias:* Bias in predictive models is another significant ethical challenge. Predictive models can inadvertently perpetuate biases if they rely on biased historical data. Suppose the data used to train predictive models reflects historical biases or inequalities. In that case, the models may perpetuate or even exacerbate these issues. For example, a predictive model that identifies high-performing employees based on past data may inadvertently favor certain groups over others, leading to biased hiring, promotion, or training decisions.

Organizations are leveraging diversity and inclusion metrics to identify biases and ensure fair hiring and promotion practices.

- *Organizational Culture:* In the current economic climate, organizational culture is becoming increasingly critical. Managing a successful organizational culture influences team performance, talent attraction, and retention. While some companies adopt formal or informal work cultures, most integrate a combination of both. The importance of organizational culture in understanding the effectiveness of HR processes is particularly significant. To monitor the dynamics of changes in organizational culture and their impact on employee performance, the use of machine learning models is essential for overall improvement in organizational culture.
- *Transparency:* Transparency about data collection, storage, and use is crucial for maintaining employee trust. Transparency in how HR models operate allows businesses to make data-driven decisions without inadvertently perpetuating workplace inequalities. Employees may feel uneasy about predictive analytics if they do not understand how their data is used. Clearly communicate the purpose, benefits, and safeguards in place to foster trust.

- *Regulatory Compliance:* Regulatory compliance mechanisms ensure that predictive HR analytics implementations meet legal requirements across different jurisdictions while maintaining consistent analytical capabilities. Data privacy and compliance: HR analytics relies on collecting and analyzing sensitive employee data. Regulations such as GDPR and CCPA impose strict guidelines on data handling. Organizations must ensure that employee data is collected with their consent, used only for its intended purpose, and securely stored to prevent breaches. Security and privacy protection measures are integrated to ensure compliance with regulatory requirements and organizational policies across different jurisdictions.
- *Collaboration:* Organizations with strong collaboration between HR professionals, data scientists, IT specialists, and business stakeholders achieve better analytical solutions and higher user adoption rates. Collaboration best practices include establishing cross-functional project teams with clear roles and responsibilities, creating regular communication channels between different functional groups, developing shared understanding of business requirements, and implementing collaborative governance structures that facilitate joint decision-making.

10.7 FUTURE OF PREDICTIVE ANALYTICS IN HUMAN RESOURCES

Predictive analytics in HR is a rapidly evolving field that leverages artificial intelligence and data-driven decision-making to revolutionize the way HR decisions are made. Through predictive analytics, HR departments can forecast employee turnover, identify high-potential candidates, and even anticipate future skill gaps within the organization. Looking to the future, predictive analytics in HR offers exciting opportunities for continued innovation and improvement. Emerging trends, such as artificial intelligence and machine learning, also present new opportunities for predictive analytics in HR. Integrating artificial intelligence and machine learning into predictive models will likely enhance their accuracy and reliability as technology advances. These technologies can help HR departments understand complex patterns in employee behavior and customer demand, leading to more effective workforce planning and improved customer experiences. Predictive analytics is the future. Successful companies, such as Google, Netflix, and Cisco, have already implemented and developed HR predictive analytics tools to drive organizational growth [19].

10.8 CONCLUSION

At a time when data is considered synonymous with decision-making, predictive HR analytics could be the differentiating factor between the failure and success of an organization. Predictive analytics is an upcoming trend in human resources (HR). It is, in essence, a technology that learns from existing data, and it uses this to forecast individual behavior. It involves a set of various statistical (data mining) techniques that analyze historical data and outcomes. It is an important tool for businesses seeking to make data-driven decisions and gain a competitive edge. It can be used to predict what will happen in the future.

Predictive analytics applications in human resources have gained significant attention as organizations seek to move beyond historical reporting toward forward-looking insights. It is helping companies plan their workforce more effectively. Historical data helps to forecast hiring needs, skill gaps, and employee turnover, allowing organizations to prepare for future demands. Predictive analytics supports succession planning by identifying future leaders and ensuring a smooth transition when key employees depart [21]. Studies have demonstrated the effectiveness of predictive models in various HR applications, including recruitment optimization, retention prediction, and performance forecasting. More information on the integration of predictive analytics into human resources is available from the books in [21-24] and the following related journals:

- *Journal of Human Resource Management Perspectives*
- *International Journal of Research in Human Resource Management*
- *German Journal of Human Resource Management*
- *South Asian Journal of Human Resources Management*

REFERENCES

[1] "Predictive analytics: Why it matters for employee retention," April 2024, https://resources.workable.com/tutorial/predictive-analytics-and-employee-retention

[2] "Predictive analytics in HR: Forecasting workforce needs for 2025," April 2025, https://www.hrcloud.com/blog/predictive-analytics-in-hr-forecasting-workforce-needs

[3] M. N. O. Sadiku, P. A. Adekunte, and J. O. Sadiku, "Predictive analytics for human resources," *International Journal of Trend in Scientific Research and Development*, vol. 10, no. 2, March-April, 2026, pp. 103-110.

[4] "Supply chain predictive analytics: What is it and who's doing it?" https://riverlogic.com/?blog=supply-chain-predictive-analytics-what-is-it-and-whos-doing-it

[5] N. Babin, "AI and predictive analytics: Revolutionizing demand forecasting in supply chain management," https://www.linkedin.com/pulse/ai-predictive-analytics-revolutionizing-demand-supply-nicolas-babin-xrj2e/

[6] "The role of analytics in marketing: Types of analytics, marketing analytics process and tools," February 2024, https://www.sprinkledata.com/blogs/the-role-of-analytics-in-

marketing-types-of-analytics-marketing-analytics-process-and-tools

[7] "An overview of supply chain analytics," February 2023, Unknown Source.

[8] I. Tymchuk, "Big data and predictive analytics in supply chain: Success stories and tips," November 2020, https://www.n-ix.com/big-data-predictive-analytics-supply-chain-case-study/

[9] A. M. Căvescu and N. Popescu, "Predictive analytics in human resources management: Evaluating AIHR's role in talent retention," August 2025, https://www.mdpi.com/2673-9909/5/3/99

[10] "Examples of predictive analytics in the travel industry at Jordan Judah," https://asktheman.xyz/

[11] P. V. Vulpen, "Predictive analytics in human resources: Tutorial and 7 case studies," https://www.aihr.com/blog/predictive-analytics-human-resources/

[12] "How to use predictive analytics in human resources," https://businessanalyticsinstitute.com/how-to-use-predictive-analytics-in-human-resources/

[13] "Predictive analytics in HR: Use cases, examples & adoption guidelines," February 2025, https://www.itransition.com/predictive-analytics/hr

[14] O. Alabi et al., "Analytics in human resources: Enhancing workforce planning and customer experience," International *Journal of Research and Scientific Innovation,* vol. 11, no. 9, September 2024, pp. 149-158.

[15] K. Lewis, "Predictive analytics in healthcare: Current & future uses," April 2024, https://www.linkedin.com/pulse/predictive-analytics-healthcare-current-future-uses-kevin-lewis-gyckc

[16] M. O. Aduwo et al., "A predictive HR analytics model integrating computing and data science to optimize workforce productivity globally," *IRE Journals,* vol. 3, no. 2, August 2019, pp. 798-821.

[17] J. Fechter, "Predictive analytics in HR examples (complete guide)," February 2026, https://hr.university/analytics/predictive-analytics-hr/

[18] "The basics of predictive analytics: From data to insights," https://mailchimp.com/resources/predicitve-analytics/

[19] "Predictive HR analytics: What it is & how to use it in 2026," December 2025, https://factohr.com/predictive-hr-analytics/

[20] I. Kessavane, "HR analytics and predictive modeling," *International Journal for Multidisciplinary Research*, vol. 7, no. 2, March-April 2025, pp. 1-8.

[21] J. Fitz-enz and J. R. Mattox (eds.), *Predictive Analytics for Human Resources.* Wiley, 2014.

[22] M. S. Ng, *Predictive HR Analytics, Text Mining & Organizational Network Analysis with Excel.* Independently Published, 2019.

[23] S. Nijjer and S. Raj, *Predictive Analytics in Human Resource Management: A Hands-on Approach.* Routledge India, 2020.

[24] M. Edwards, K. Edwards, and D. Jang, *Predictive HR Analytics: Mastering the HR Metric.* Kogan Page, 3rd edition, 2024.

CHAPTER 11: PREDICTIVE ANALYTICS IN FRAUD DETECTION

"Seek ye first the political kingdom and all things shall be added unto you."

- Kwame Nkrumah

11.1 INTRODUCTION

Fraud is a global problem that affects nearly every industry. It is the act of deliberately deceiving someone to gain an unfair or unlawful advantage, often for financial or personal benefit. It usually involves false representation, concealment of facts, or abuse of trust to mislead individuals, organizations, or systems. Fraud can occur in many forms, such as financial fraud, identity theft, insurance fraud, or corporate misconduct, and often results in harm to victims, whether through financial loss, reputational damage, or compromised data. Fraud detection through predictive analytics has become a critical defense mechanism in today's digital landscape. Predictive analytics plays a transformative role in fraud detection and prevention by enabling organizations to identify, predict, and respond to fraudulent activities with greater precision and speed [1].

In an increasingly digital world, the sophistication and volume of fraudulent activities have reached unprecedented levels. Fraudsters are constantly evolving and finding new ways to get around the systems to commit fraudulent activities. Businesses today have to protect against constantly growing and evolving fraud threats. Predictive analytics refers to the use of historical and current data to make predictions by employing statistical modeling, data mining, and machine learning algorithms. It is a crucial component of predictive fraud analytics, a type of data analytics that uses current and historical data to forecast activity, behavior, and trends [2].

Predictive analytics is a powerful data-driven technique that leverages data, algorithms, and machine learning to identify the probability of future outcomes based on historical data. It represents a paradigm shift in the fight against fraud. It is an invaluable tool that has begun revolutionizing the world of fraud prevention. By transforming data into actionable intelligence, it empowers organizations to anticipate threats, streamline operations, and protect their assets with unprecedented precision. Predictive analytics in fraud detection has revolutionized the way financial institutions preemptively address and mitigate cyber threats, reducing the incidence of breaches and saving millions in potential losses [3].

In this chapter, we examine the multifaceted impact of predictive analytics on the fight against fraud or deceitful online activities. It begins by explaining predictive analytics. It describes predictive analytics in fraud detection and provides some of its applications. It highlights some benefits and challenges of predictive analytics in fraud detection. It predicts the future of predictive analytics in fraud detection. The last section concludes with comments.

11.2 WHAT IS PREDICTIVE ANALYTICS?

As its name implies, predictive analytics is about predicting future trends such as sales demand and exchange rates. and other important metrics. The technique relies on the application of statistical modeling and regression analysis to historical data to determine and understand trends and formulate future predictions. Strictly speaking, predictive analytics does not predict the future, but rather uses probability theories to determine what is likely to happen based on patterns and trends revealed by analyzing historical data [4]. Predictive analytics accurately anticipates customer demand, preventing overstocking and stockouts while adapting to market changes. Figure 11.1 illustrates predictive analytics [5], while Figure 11.2 shows different components of predictive analytics [6].

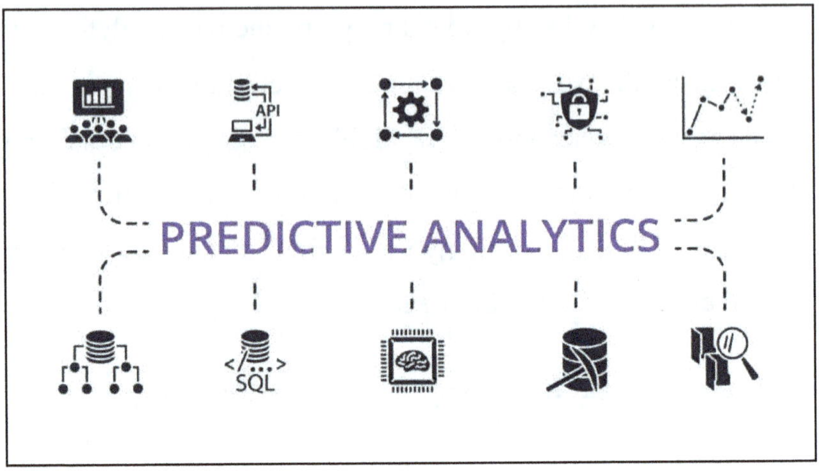

Figure 11.1 Predictive analytics [5].

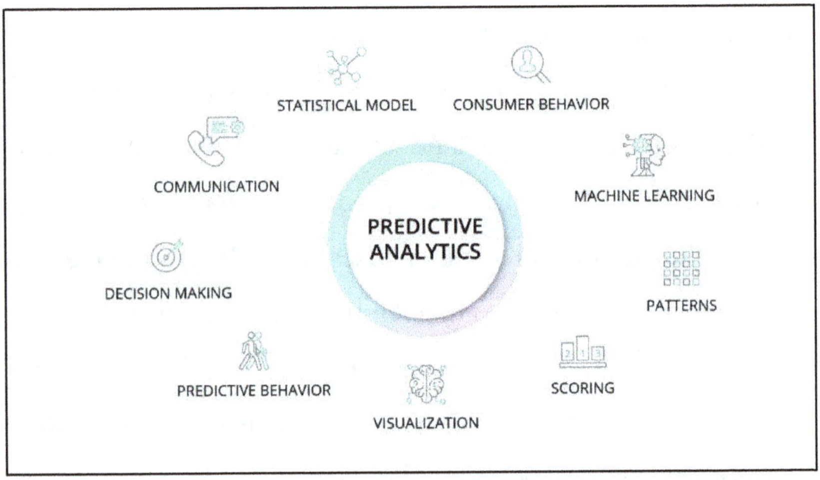

Figure 11.2 Different components of predictive analytics [6].

In general, analytics provides an efficient way to improve planning because it gives you better forecasts. There are different types of data analytics. They are briefly explained as follows [7]:

- *Descriptive Analytics:* Descriptive analytics examines what has happened over the years. They are capable of detecting trends in historical data. Analytics can uncover trends and postulate probable reasons for change by comparing the same data from various periods. It can be seen as the baseline of the industry, which basically assesses past and current data for more meaningful insights and delivers it to the people to use their own intelligence and knowledge to make decisions.
- *Predictive Analytics:* This assists businesses in predicting what might happen and the impact of various situations, such as possible supply chain bottlenecks. Managers can be proactive rather than responsive by pushing them to evaluate these prospective circumstances before they occur. Predictive analytics may be used to identify patterns and trends as well as anticipate breakdowns that may impact suppliers and, consequently, production processes. Predictive analytics for the supply chain leverages data, statistical algorithms, and machine learning techniques to identify the likelihood of future outcomes.

- *Prescriptive Analytics:* Prescriptive analytics builds on predictive analytics and dives deeper into predicting future insights on what can be done next. Prescriptive analytics uses the findings of descriptive and predictive analytics to recommend what measures a business should take to achieve its objectives. Because prescriptive analytics is increasingly complicated, they need more powerful software capable of rapidly processing and interpreting large amounts of data.
- *Cognitive Analytics:* Cognitive analytics attempts to mimic human thought and behavior, and it can assist companies in answering challenging, complex problems. Cognitive analytics does this by utilizing artificial intelligence (AI), which allows it to improve over time. With the use of AI in the industry, answering complex questions and draw out contextual conclusions on how humans would have interacted with the situation. It helps with more meaningful data and scales experience and knowledge with better decisions.
- *Diagnostics Analytics:* This gives the ability to identify the root cause. It is characterized by techniques such as drill-down, data discovery, data mining, and correlations. It involves analyzing overall performance and figuring out why errors, mistakes, and delays occur. It lets the manager know the delays, breakdowns, and disruptions

in the demand and supply processes and the reasons behind them.

Figure 11.3 shows these major types of data analytics [8]. Unlike diagnostic and descriptive analytics, which were designed to analyze situations after they happened, predictive analytics utilizes advanced data analytics techniques to forecast future outcomes. In the supply chain, the time has come to shift from mere descriptive and diagnostic analytics to predictive and prescriptive analytics. Predictive analytics is a branch of data analytics that makes predictions about future outcomes using historical data combined with statistical modeling, data mining techniques, and machine learning. Figure 11.4 shows how predictive analytics works [9].

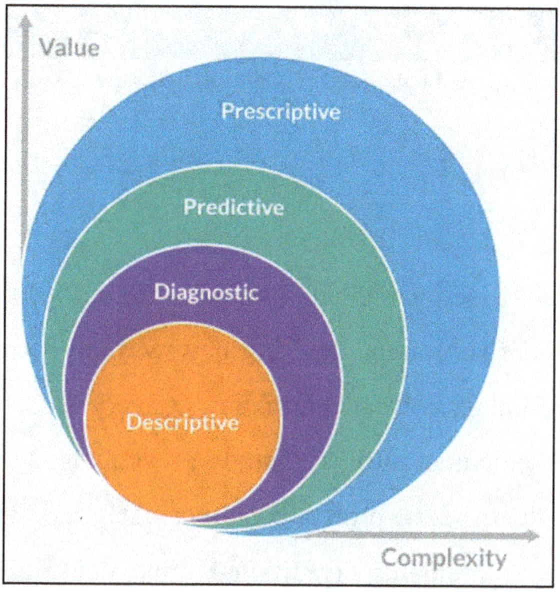

Figure 11.3 Types of data analytics [8].

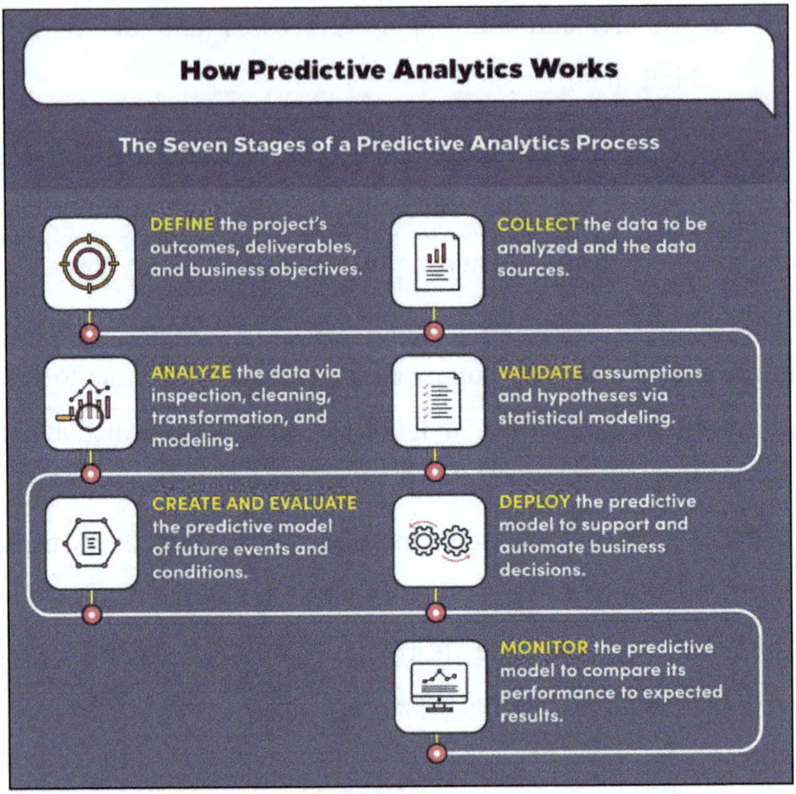

Figure 11.4 Predictive analytics process [9].

11.3 PREDICTIVE ANALYTICS IN FRAUD DETECTION

Fraud is a serious issue with long-lasting consequences. Fraudsters are constantly devising new ways to deceive online businesses and exploit vulnerabilities at every turn. Businesses need to implement robust fraud prevention strategies to safeguard their assets, protect customer data, and comply with regulatory requirements. Traditional fraud detection methods, which heavily rely on manual audits and reactive investigations, are rapidly becoming obsolete. They simply lack the speed, accuracy, and scalability required to combat modern cyber threats. As cybercriminals leverage advanced technologies to bypass security measures, organizations are turning to predictive analytics as a proactive defense mechanism. Predictive analytics leverages historical and current data to forecast future events or outcomes. By employing advanced statistical modeling, data mining, and machine learning algorithms, this technology identifies hidden patterns within vast datasets. The goal is to predict fraudulent actions with a high degree of accuracy so that organizations can take preventive or corrective actions before substantial damage occurs. The versatility of predictive analytics allows it to be tailored to the specific fraud challenges faced by various industries. From financial services to e-commerce, organizations are leveraging these advanced models to safeguard their operations and protect their customers. Advanced analytics and predictive analysis can help identify risks, improve claim assessment methodologies, and offer targeted insurance policies. Figure 11.5 shows fraud detection [10], while Figure 11.6 shows using predictive analytics to detect fraud [3].

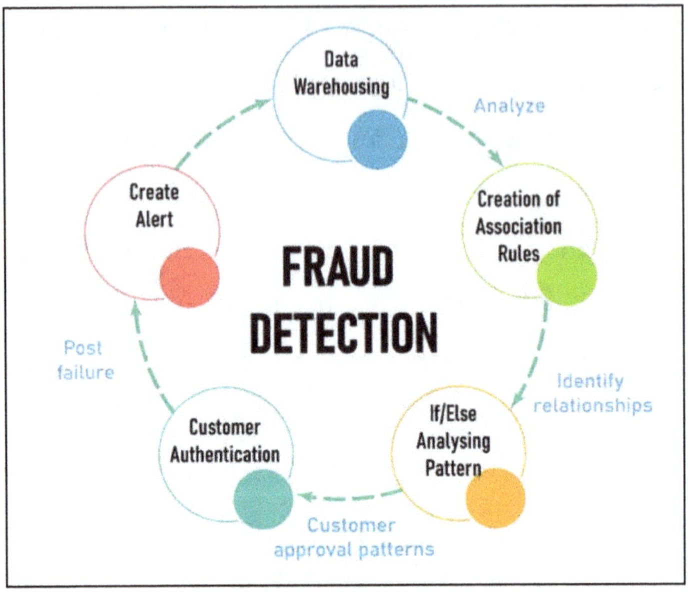

Figure 11.5 Fraud detection [10].

Figure 11.6 Using predictive analytics to detect fraud [3].

11.4 APPLICATIONS OF PREDICTIVE ANALYTICS IN FRAUD DETECTION

Predictive analytics offers a powerful defense against fraud, but it is not a "silver bullet." It enables proactive fraud detection by leveraging AI and machine learning to analyze extensive historical and real-time data. Common applications of predictive analytics in fraud detection include the following [2,10-12]:

- *Insurance:* Insurance is one of the highly competitive industries with very limited predictability. It is highly prone to risk and is dependent on statistics. In the insurance sector, predictive models analyze a claimant's history, the nature of the incident, and behavioral indicators to assign a risk score to each new claim. High-scoring claims are automatically routed to specialized investigation units, streamlining the claims process for legitimate customers while rigorously scrutinizing potential fraud. Insurance companies are increasingly adopting predictive analytics to flag fraudulent claims before they are paid. For example, Allstate Insurance uses machine learning algorithms to scrutinize claims data and identify patterns indicative of fraud.
- *Ecommerce Fraud:* Online retailers face constant fraudulent transaction threats, particularly through stolen

credit cards and identity theft. Predictive analytics helps ecommerce platforms fight back. Ecommerce predictive analytics fraud detection models can assess factors such as purchase history, device information, and geographic location to score transactions based on risk. Low-risk transactions are processed seamlessly, while high-risk ones are routed through manual checks. For example, ecommerce giants Amazon and Alibaba use predictive analytics to analyze buyer behavior in real-time.

- *Behavioral Analysis:* Predictive analytics uses behavioral analysis to assess the likelihood of fraud. For example, it can compare a user's current behavior with historical data, such as previous purchasing patterns or login locations, to identify discrepancies that may indicate fraud.
- *Fraud Data Analytics:* Fraud data analytics is one of the most sought-after practices for detecting and controlling unethical methods of acquiring sensitive data. It relies on accurate and comprehensive data sources for effective fraud detection. Such data may include transaction records, customer demographics, and behavior logs. Ensuring data quality and accuracy helps in creating predictive models that effectively identify potentially fraudulent activities. Developing robust predictive models for fraud prevention involves selecting appropriate

machine learning algorithms and incorporating relevant features to detect suspicious activities effectively.

- *Risk Management:* Enterprise risk management (ERM) is the process of identifying, analyzing, and treating the enterprise's exposure as visualized by the executive management. It includes looking at the various exposures, such as fraud, credit, finance, strategic, and operational matters. Despite being a significant organizational process, risk management processes and practices across the globe continue to be a challenging business aspect to manage. Traditional risk management approaches are highly subjective and are based on individual perceptions. To survive in this new digital era, businesses should identify the early indicators of risk events and act proactively to mitigate those risks before they become disruptions. Implementing predictive analytics across all asset classes, the entire credit lifecycle, and credit risk models will help you maximize your profits and contain credit risk within the risk portfolio. Figure 11.7 shows a representation of risk management [10].

Figure 11.7 A representation of risk management [10].

- *Predictive Risk Intelligence:* Predictive risk intelligence or risk monitoring involves using current and historical information to identify emerging and potential risks. Using ML and AI-empowered data analytics, you can discover hidden trends from the organizational risk data and get crucial insights about the future emergence of different types of risks. Predictive risk intelligence increases operational efficiency and resiliency and improves cost-effectiveness.
- *Anomaly Detection:* A key feature of predictive analytics is its anomaly detection capability, which identifies unusual behavior patterns signaling potential fraud. This includes spotting irregularities such as significant, unexpected transfers or a sudden spike in transaction

volume. By recognizing these deviations, predictive analytics can prompt timely interventions, mitigating potential fraud risks.

11.5 BENEFITS

Predictive analytics methodologies offer powerful tools for the detection of fraudulent activities. The integration of these advanced tools into organizations' fraud prevention measures has led to considerable improvements. It has redefined fraud prevention from a reactive analysis to a proactive approach. Other benefits of predictive analytics in fraud detection include the following [1,11]:

- *Cost Savings:* Fraud-related costs extend beyond direct financial losses to include legal expenses, regulatory penalties, and reputational damage. Data analytics helps organizations detect and prevent fraud early, reducing the frequency and severity of incidents. Over time, this leads to substantial cost savings by minimizing investigations, recovery efforts, and compliance-related expenses.
- *Proactive Detection:* The most significant advantage of predictive analytics is its shift from a reactive to a proactive stance. Unlike traditional systems that flag transactions based on pre-defined thresholds, predictive models analyze thousands of variables to assign a risk score to every event in real-time. This allows for

immediate intervention, such as blocking a suspicious credit card transaction or flagging an insurance claim for further review before payment is issued.

- *Operational Efficiency:* Efficiency is another significant benefit. Predictive analytics automates the labor-intensive process of manual auditing, allowing organizations to process and analyze vast amounts of data instantaneously. This automation not only accelerates the detection process but also significantly improves accuracy. This efficiency allows security teams to focus their resources on high-risk cases rather than wading through a sea of legitimate transactions.
- *Scalability:* As businesses scale, the sheer volume of data generated makes manual oversight impossible. Predictive analytics provides the scalability required to process millions of transactions per second. Predictive analytics provides the scalability necessary to handle the exponential growth in digital transactions. As businesses expand their online presence, the volume of data generated increases dramatically. Predictive models are designed to scale seamlessly, ensuring that fraud detection capabilities remain robust regardless of transaction volume.

11.6 CHALLENGES

Despite its profound benefits, the implementation of predictive analytics in fraud detection is not without challenges. Challenges such as evolving fraud tactics, false positives, model bias issues, transparency concerns, and ethical hurdles persist. The landscape of cybercrime is highly dynamic, with fraudsters continuously evolving their tactics to bypass security measures. Consequently, predictive models must be updated constantly to remain effective. Other challenges of predictive analytics in fraud detection include the following [1,11]:

- *Data Quality:* Predictive models are only as good as the data they are trained on, and poor-quality data can lead to inaccurate predictions. In the realm of fraud prevention, several data-specific issues create persistent obstacles. Ensuring that the data is clean, relevant, and representative of the current environment is critical for the success of predictive analytics.
- *Data Imbalance:* One of the most significant technical challenges is data imbalance. In a typical financial environment, fraudulent transactions represent a tiny fraction of the total volume. This scarcity makes it difficult for machine learning models to "learn" the characteristics of fraud effectively, as they are overwhelmed by the sheer volume of legitimate data. Standard algorithms may

achieve high accuracy by simply predicting that every transaction is legitimate, which is useless for fraud prevention.

- *Data Privacy:* The use of personal data for predictive analytics is strictly governed by regulations such as the General Data Protection Regulation (GDPR) and the California Consumer Privacy Act (CCPA). These laws impose constraints on how data is collected, stored, and processed. Balancing the need for deep data analysis with the requirement for consumer privacy is a delicate act that often limits the types of features a model can utilize.
- *False Alerts:* A persistent challenge in fraud prevention is the "false positive," a legitimate transaction that is incorrectly flagged as fraudulent. While missing a fraudulent transaction (False Negative) is costly, incorrectly flagging a legitimate one (False Positive) can be equally damaging. High false-positive rates not only frustrate customers but also lead to lost revenue and increased operational costs. They can overwhelm security teams, diverting their attention from genuine threats and leading to alert fatigue. Additionally, false positives can severely impact the customer experience, causing frustration when legitimate transactions are blocked or delayed. Balancing the sensitivity of predictive models to catch fraud while minimizing false alarms remains a

critical ongoing challenge for data scientists and security professionals.

- *Concept Drift:* Fraud is an adversarial game. As soon as a predictive model successfully identifies a specific fraud pattern, criminals adapt their tactics to bypass it. This phenomenon, known as concept drift, means that models trained on historical data can become obsolete very quickly. Maintaining the relevance of a model requires constant retraining and the ability to detect shifts in fraud patterns in near real-time.
- *Explainability:* Modern deep learning models are often "black boxes," providing highly accurate predictions without a clear explanation of why a specific transaction was flagged. This lack of explainability is a major hurdle for regulatory compliance, as many jurisdictions require financial institutions to provide reasons for adverse actions (e.g., declining a transaction). The complexity of the models used in predictive analytics can make them difficult to interpret, raising concerns about transparency and accountability.
- *Algorithmic Bias:* Predictive models can inadvertently inherit or amplify biases present in the training data. For example, if certain demographics have historically been flagged more often due to systemic factors, the model may continue to disproportionately target those groups, leading

to discriminatory fraud detection. Ensuring fairness and mitigating bias is a critical ethical and legal requirement that adds another layer of complexity to model development.

- *Collaboration:* Fraud is not confined to one organization or sector, which is why collaboration is becoming essential. Sharing anonymized threat intelligence across industries allows businesses to benefit from collective knowledge and spot fraud patterns faster. Working together, businesses, regulators, and law enforcement can stop fraud by sharing information and increasing detection efforts. Sharing data helps businesses work together, but they need to keep it private and secure. They must follow rules and protect customers' sensitive information.
- *Skills Gaps:* Many organizations lack the in-house expertise to properly implement predictive analytics. Data analytics consulting companies provide access to skilled data scientists and analysts who can fill this gap and guide organizations through the process of developing custom fraud prevention models.

11.7 FUTURE OF PREDICTIVE ANALYTICS IN FRAUD DETECTION

Predictive analytics involves gathering and analyzing large datasets to create models that forecast future behaviors or events. As technology continues to advance, predictive analytics will remain the cornerstone of a secure digital landscape, ensuring that businesses can innovate and grow without compromising the safety of their customers or the integrity of their operations.

As technology advances, so do the methods used by fraudsters. Fraud tactics continue to evolve, making it critical for organizations to adopt advanced technologies that stay ahead of emerging threats. Artificial intelligence is reshaping fraud detection by introducing powerful methods such as transformer-based models, explainable AI, and federated learning. The integration of artificial intelligence and machine learning will continue to enhance the capabilities of predictive analytics. Figure 11.8 shows the future trends in predictive analytics for fraud prevention [13].

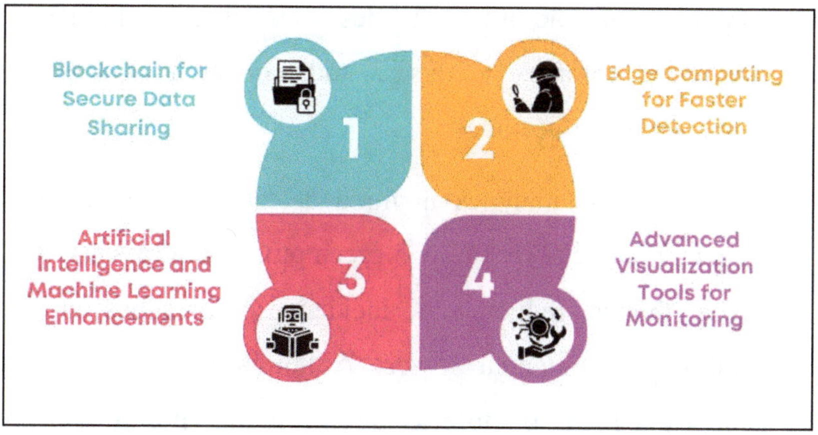

Figure 11.8 Future trends in predictive analytics for fraud prevention [13].

11.8 CONCLUSION

Costing billions of dollars a year and eroding public confidence in financial institutions, financial fraud represents a danger to both people and organizations. The more sophisticated the approaches that fraudsters use, the more difficult it is for standard detection tools to keep up. In a world where fraud is constantly evolving, data analytics and predictive models have become essential for proactive fraud detection. Predictive analytics has fundamentally transformed the paradigm of fraud detection, offering a powerful, proactive defense against increasingly sophisticated cyber threats. By leveraging historical data to anticipate and identify fraudulent activities, financial institutions can enhance their ability to detect and prevent fraud. By harnessing the capabilities of data mining, machine learning, and advanced statistical modeling, organizations across industries can identify hidden risks, automate complex analyses, and protect their assets with unprecedented accuracy.

Predictive analytics in fraud detection has revolutionized the way financial institutions preemptively address and mitigate cyber threats, reducing the incidence of breaches and saving millions in potential losses. Although predictive modeling implies a focus on forecasting the future, it can also predict outcomes, for example, the probability that a transaction is fraudulent. More information on the use of predictive analytics in fraud detection and prevention is available from the books in [14-18] and the following related journals:

- *Journal of Financial Crime*
- *Journal of Risk and Financial Management*

REFERENCES

[1] "Uncovering fraud with data analytics: 4 Cutting-edge techniques to detect anomalies," https://community.trustcloud.ai/docs/grc-launchpad/grc-101/compliance/uncovering-fraud-with-data-analytics-a-modern-approach/

[2] "Predictive analytics in fraud detection: Challenges and evolution in the face of sophisticated cyber threats," March 2026, https://financialcrimeacademy.org/predictive-analytics-in-fraud-detection/

[3] M. N. O. Sadiku, D. Padi, and J. O. Sadiku, "Predictive analytics in fraud detection," International Journal of Management and Organizational Research, vol. 5, no. 3, May-June, 2026, pp. 16-23.

[4] "Supply chain predictive analytics: What is it and who's doing it?" https://riverlogic.com/?blog=supply-chain-predictive-analytics-what-is-it-and-whos-doing-it

[5] N. Babin, "AI and predictive analytics: Revolutionizing demand forecasting in supply chain management," https://www.linkedin.com/pulse/ai-predictive-analytics-revolutionizing-demand-supply-nicolas-babin-xrj2e/

[6] "From insight to innovation: Why data analysis will define industry leaders in 2025,"

https://www.inkl.com/news/from-insight-to-innovation-why-data-analysis-will-define-industry-leaders-in-2025

[7] "An overview of supply chain analytics," February 2023, Unknown Source.

[8] I. Tymchuk, "Big data and predictive analytics in supply chain: Success stories and tips," November 2020, https://www.n-ix.com/big-data-predictive-analytics-supply-chain-case-study/

[9] "Predictive analytics in insurance: Types, tools, and the future," October 2020, https://online.maryville.edu/blog/predictive-analytics-in-insurance/

[10] K. Roy, "Data science for risk management," https://www.datatobiz.com/blog/data-science-for-risk-management/

[11] https://manus.im

[12] "The role of predictive analytics in fraud prevention," https://www.fraud.com/post/predictive-analytics-in-fraud-prevention

[13] N. Saini, "The role of predictive analytics in fraud prevention," January 2025, https://www.hashstudioz.com/blog/the-role-of-predictive-analytics-in-fraud-prevention/

[14] A. Bari, M. Chaouchi, and T. Jung, Predictive Analytics For Dummies. For Dummies, 2nd edition, 2016.

[15] B. Baesens, V. V. Vlasselaer, and W. Verbeke, Fraud Analytics Using Descriptive, Predictive, and Social Network Techniques: A Guide to Data Science for Fraud Detection. Wiley, 2015.

[16] Innoware PJP, Unveiling Deception: Leveraging AI and Predictive Analytics for Fraud Detection in Finance. Kindle Edition, 2024.

[17] Innoware PJP, Harnessing AI and Predictive Analytics for Healthcare Fraud Detection. Independently Published, 2024.

[18] D. D. Spann, Fraud Analytics: Strategies and Methods for Detection and Prevention. Wiley, 2013.

CHAPTER 12: PREDICTIVE ANALYTICS IN RISK MANAGEMENT

"You can't let your failures define you. You have to let them teach you."

– Barack Obama

12.1 INTRODUCTION

Risks are inherent in much of everything in today's global economic scenario. Uncertainty is the new normal in today's business world. From market volatility and cybersecurity threats to supply chain issues and changing regulations, companies are constantly navigating risks that can disrupt operations and damage their reputation. Predictive analytics, an advanced method utilizing data, machine learning, and statistical algorithms, has emerged as a transformative force in risk management. Predictive analytics involves analyzing historical and real-time data to forecast potential risks. Unlike traditional models that focus on risk mitigation after an event occurs, predictive analytics proactively identifies patterns and anomalies that signal potential threats [1].

In an increasingly complex and data-rich world, organizations face a myriad of risks that can impact their financial stability, operational efficiency, and overall reputation. Traditional risk management approaches, often reliant on historical data and expert intuition, tend to be reactive, addressing issues only after they have materialized. However, the advent of predictive analytics has ushered in a new era, enabling organizations to proactively identify, assess, and mitigate potential risks before they escalate. From financial institutions assessing credit risk to healthcare providers predicting disease outbreaks, predictive analytics is reshaping the way organizations approach uncertainty. Predictive modeling is now the heart of risk management [2].

Risk is an inherent and inevitable part of every business operation. Risk management has always been at the core of organizational strategy, safeguarding assets, reputation, and long-term viability. Traditionally, companies relied on historical data and reactive strategies to manage risk. Risk management has been largely reactive, focusing on mitigating threats after they materialize. Predictive analytics, a subset of data analytics, empowers organizations to anticipate risks by analyzing historical and real-time data to identify patterns and trends. It enables organizations to foresee threats, enhance strategic planning, and manage the delicate equilibrium between personalization and privacy. In the realm of risk management, predictive analytics serves as a cornerstone. The transition from reactive to proactive risk mitigation is reshaping the business landscape [3].

This chapter will explore how predictive analytics has revolutionized risk management across various industries. It begins by explaining predictive analytics. It describes predictive analytics in risk management and provides some of its applications. It highlights some benefits and challenges of predictive analytics in risk management. It predicts the future of predictive analytics in risk management. The last section concludes with comments.

12.2 WHAT IS PREDICTIVE ANALYTICS?

As its name implies, predictive analytics is about predicting future trends such as sales demand and exchange rates. and other important metrics. The technique relies on the application of statistical modeling and regression analysis to historical data to determine and understand trends and formulate future predictions. Strictly speaking, predictive analytics does not predict the future, but rather uses probability theories to determine what is likely to happen based on patterns and trends revealed by analyzing historical data [4]. Predictive analytics accurately anticipates customer demand, preventing overstocking and stockouts while adapting to market changes. Figure 12.1 illustrates predictive analytics [5], while Figure 12.2 shows different components of predictive analytics [6].

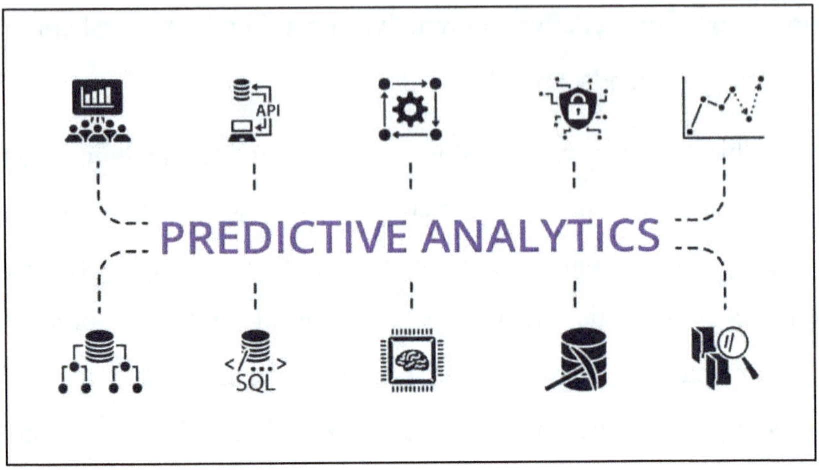

Figure 12.1 Predictive analytics [5].

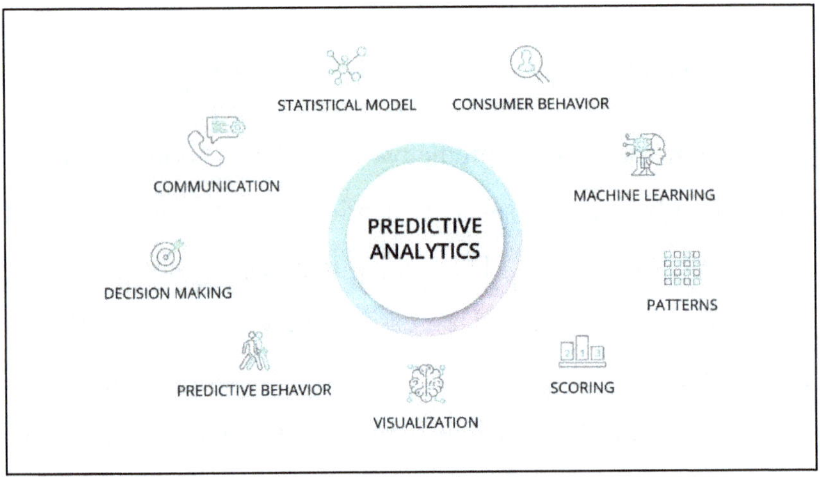

Figure 12.2 Different components of predictive analytics [6].

In general, analytics provides an efficient way to improve planning because it gives you better forecasts. There are different types of data analytics. They are briefly explained as follows [7]:

- *Descriptive Analytics:* Descriptive analytics examines what has happened over the years. They are capable of detecting trends in historical data. Analytics can uncover trends and postulate probable reasons for change by comparing the same data from various periods. It can be seen as the baseline of the industry, which basically assesses past and current data for more meaningful insights and delivers it to the people to use their own intelligence and knowledge to make decisions.
- *Predictive Analytics:* This assists businesses in predicting what might happen and the impact of various situations, such as possible supply chain bottlenecks. Managers can be proactive rather than responsive by pushing them to evaluate these prospective circumstances before they occur. Predictive analytics may be used to identify patterns and trends as well as anticipate breakdowns that may impact suppliers and, consequently, production processes. Predictive analytics for the supply chain leverages data, statistical algorithms, and machine learning techniques to identify the likelihood of future outcomes.

- *Prescriptive Analytics:* Prescriptive analytics builds on predictive analytics and dives deeper into predicting future insights on what can be done next. Prescriptive analytics uses the findings of descriptive and predictive analytics to recommend what measures a business should take to achieve its objectives. Because prescriptive analytics is increasingly complicated, they need more powerful software capable of rapidly processing and interpreting large amounts of data.
- *Cognitive Analytics:* Cognitive analytics attempts to mimic human thought and behavior, and it can assist companies in answering challenging, complex problems. Cognitive analytics does this by utilizing artificial intelligence (AI), which allows it to improve over time. With the use of AI in the industry, answering complex questions and draw out contextual conclusions on how humans would have interacted with the situation. It helps with more meaningful data and scales experience and knowledge with better decisions.
- *Diagnostic Analytics:* This gives the ability to identify the root cause. It is characterized by techniques such as drill-down, data discovery, data mining, and correlations. It involves analyzing overall performance and figuring out why errors, mistakes, and delays occur. It lets the manager know the delays, breakdowns, and disruptions in the

demand and supply processes and the reasons behind them.

Figure 12.3 shows these major types of data analytics [8]. Unlike diagnostic and descriptive analytics, which were designed to analyze situations after they happened, predictive analytics utilizes advanced data analytics techniques to forecast future outcomes. In the supply chain, the time has come to shift from mere descriptive and diagnostic analytics to predictive and prescriptive analytics. Predictive analytics is a branch of data analytics that makes predictions about future outcomes using historical data combined with statistical modeling, data mining techniques, and machine learning. Figure 12.4 shows how predictive analytics works [9].

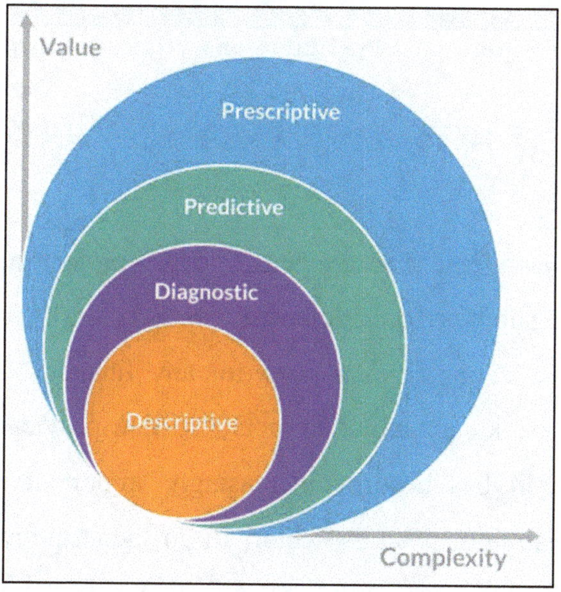

Figure 12.3 Types of data analytics [8].

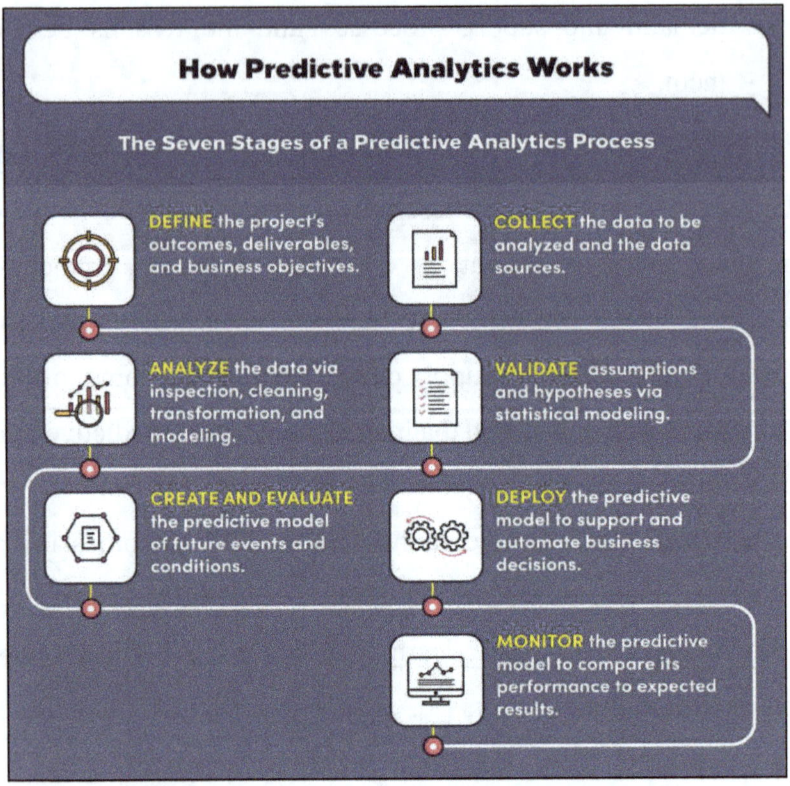

Figure 12.4 Predictive analytics process [9].

12.3 PREDICTIVE ANALYTICS IN RISK MANAGEMENT

Risk management is relevant for every project that seeks to avoid and suppress unanticipated costs, basically calling for pre-emptive action. It is a need for any financial institution, including banks, insurance companies, loan providers, trading firms, etc. It has become increasingly important in today's rapidly changing business sector. In an increasingly complex and volatile business landscape, effective risk management is paramount for organizational resilience and sustained success. Traditional risk management approaches, often reactive in nature, are proving insufficient to navigate the dynamic landscape of modern threats. This has led to the emergence of predictive analytics as a pivotal tool, leveraging statistical models, machine learning algorithms, and historical data to forecast future events and potential risks. By leveraging advanced statistical algorithms, machine learning models, and vast datasets, predictive analytics offers a transformative approach to risk management, yielding significant benefits across various sectors.

For years, we have relied on historical patterns, reactive strategies, and instinct when facing business uncertainties. But now, predictive analytics has changed the game entirely, giving us powerful new ways to identify risks before they materialize and transform how we protect our organizations. Predictive analytics, leveraging statistical algorithms and machine learning techniques, has emerged as a transformative force in risk management across various industries, as illustrated in Figure 12.5 [2]. From identifying potential threats to developing effective mitigation strategies, predictive analytics offers a holistic approach to risk management. Predictive analytics risk management uses internal, external, and alternative data to identify, assess, and mitigate risks. Using predictive analytics can assist companies in overcoming different challenges and enhance their risk management practices. Predictive data can provide early warning signs of potential risks, allowing decision-makers to take the necessary actions to prevent them before they cause any damage [10].

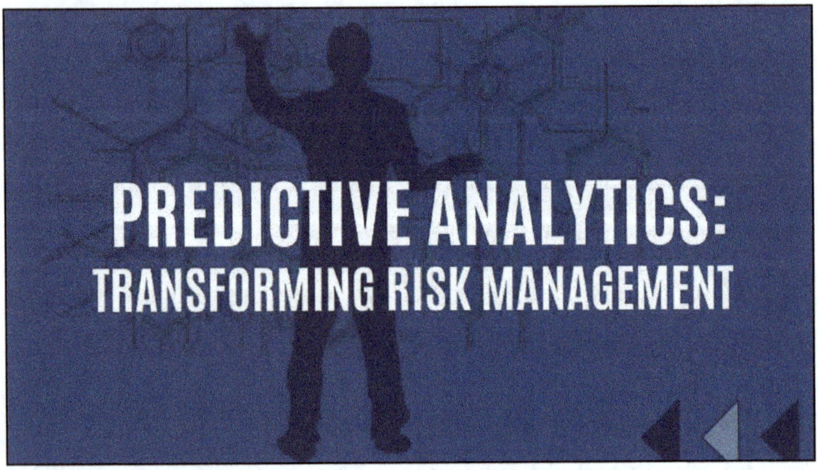

Figure 12.5 Predictive analytics transforms risk management [2].

12.4 APPLICATIONS OF PREDICTIVE ANALYTICS IN RISK MANAGEMENT

Predictive analytics (PA) has emerged as an indispensable tool in modern risk management, empowering organizations to move beyond traditional reactive strategies to a proactive, data-driven approach. Across finance, operations, and healthcare, its applications have enabled organizations to anticipate threats, optimize decision-making, and build greater resilience. By enhancing risk identification, assessment, and mitigation, PA offers significant benefits in terms of precision, efficiency, and cost savings across diverse sectors like banking and finance, supply chain, healthcare, manufacturing, and cybersecurity. Common applications of predictive analytics in risk management include the following [11,12]:

- *Risk Management Analytics:* Being competitive in today's market is always challenging due to various factors such as changes in customer expectations, technological advances, policy-level changes from the government, and more. Predictive risk analysis leverages past and present data to predict what is likely to happen, and this can help organizations to respond to variables and ultimately determine the probability of growth or decline. Risk management analytics involves the use of data analytics techniques to identify, assess, manage, and mitigate risks within an organization. By integrating data from various sources and employing predictive models, organizations can forecast potential future risks and develop strategies to minimize negative impacts. This approach enhances decision-making, efficiency, and regulatory compliance, providing a proactive means to manage risks across financial services, healthcare, manufacturing, retail, and energy sectors. Properly leveraging predictive risk analytics helps organizations evolve and become more agile, enabling faster execution of risk mitigation controls and effective organizational changes.

- *Financial Risk Management:* Banking and financial services were probably one of the earliest industries that started adopting and realizing the value that predictive risk analytics can offer. The financial sector has been at the forefront of adopting predictive analytics, recognizing its immense potential in mitigating diverse financial risks. One of the most significant applications is in credit risk assessment. Historically, credit decisions relied on static credit scores and limited historical data. Predictive analytics, however, moves beyond these traditional methods by analyzing dynamic, behavior-based data, including transaction histories, spending patterns, and even social media activity. This allows financial institutions to assess creditworthiness more accurately, identify potential defaults earlier, and even expand access to credit for underserved populations while simultaneously mitigating default risks. Financial institutions employ predictive models to identify potential customers who might default on their loans. With this information, they are developing risk mitigation strategies, such as offering different types of loans based on the customer's risk profile. Figure 12.6 is a representation of PA in financial risk management [13].

Figure 12.6 A representation of PA in financial risk management [13].

- *Supply Chain Risk:* Supply chains are inherently vulnerable to various disruptions, from natural disasters to geopolitical instability. Traditional supply chain risk management relies heavily on historical data, manual monitoring, and reactive responses. While this approach can work for static or low-risk environments, it quickly falls apart under emerging risks like cyber threats, pandemics, and climate change. Predictive analytics is revolutionizing supply chain risk management, enabling smarter decisions, greater agility, and stronger resilience in the face of uncertainty. It enables organizations to forecast potential disruptions by analyzing factors such as weather patterns, supplier performance, and geopolitical events. In the realm of supply chain optimization, predictive analytics helps organizations navigate the complexities of global logistics. It identifies potential bottlenecks, assesses supplier risks, and anticipates demand volatility. By integrating data from various sources, including weather patterns, geopolitical events, and transportation networks, companies can gain real-time visibility into their supply chains. This enables them to proactively reroute shipments, diversify suppliers, and adjust inventory levels to mitigate disruptions caused by unforeseen events

- *Healthcare Risk Management:* The healthcare sector, with its critical focus on patient well-being and operational efficiency, is increasingly leveraging predictive analytics to manage risks. In healthcare, predictive analytics assists in managing both financial and operational risks. In clinical risk assessment, predictive models are used to identify high-risk patients for early intervention. This includes forecasting patient readmissions, predicting the onset of conditions, and tracking the progression of chronic diseases. By flagging at-risk individuals, healthcare providers can tailor personalized care plans, leading to improved patient outcomes and reduced healthcare costs. Predictive analytics can forecast patient inflow, optimize hospital bed utilization, and manage staffing levels more effectively. This ensures that resources are allocated appropriately, reducing wait times, preventing overcrowding, and improving the overall patient experience. Furthermore, predictive analytics plays a vital role in public health and population management. By analyzing epidemiological data, environmental factors, and demographic information, models can predict disease outbreaks, identify high-risk cohorts within a population, and inform public health interventions. This proactive approach enables health authorities to allocate resources efficiently, implement preventative measures, and respond more effectively to health crises.

- *Cybersecurity Risk Management:* With the ever-evolving threat landscape, cybersecurity risk management is a critical application area. Predictive analytics models can identify patterns indicative of cyber threats and potential breaches before data exfiltration occurs, allowing security teams to implement preventative measures and strengthen defenses. While predictive analytics has revolutionized cybersecurity threat detection, its applications extend far beyond protecting digital assets.
- *Manufacturing:* Beyond finance, predictive analytics has become indispensable in enhancing operational and supply chain resilience. In manufacturing and industrial settings, predictive maintenance is a prime example. By

continuously monitoring equipment performance data, such as temperature, vibration, and pressure, and analyzing historical maintenance records, predictive models can forecast potential equipment failures before they occur. Predictive maintenance models analyze equipment performance data to foresee failures, reducing downtime and repair costs.

- *Fraud Detection:* Fraud detection and prevention have also been profoundly transformed. Traditional rule-based systems often struggled to keep pace with evolving fraud tactics, leading to significant losses. Real-time predictive analytics, powered by AI and machine learning, can analyze vast streams of transactional data instantaneously to detect anomalies and suspicious patterns that indicate fraudulent activity. This includes identifying sophisticated schemes like synthetic identity fraud, where criminals combine real and fake information, and account takeover fraud, which is detected through deviations in typical login and transaction behaviors. The shift to real-time analysis not only strengthens security but also improves customer trust by reducing false positives and streamlining authentication processes.

12.5 BENEFITS

The benefits of predictive analytics in risk management are manifold. The primary advantage of predictive analytics lies in its ability to shift risk management from a reactive to a proactive paradigm. Instead of merely responding to past events, organizations can now forecast future outcomes with greater accuracy, anticipating potential threats and opportunities. Predictive analytics enhances the precision and accuracy of risk assessments. The enhanced accuracy translates directly into cost reductions, as organizations can avoid the financial repercussions of operational disruptions, legal liabilities, reputational damage, and non-performing assets. This leads to more refined credit scoring, more effective fraud detection, and more accurate demand forecasting, among other improvements. Other benefits of predictive analytics in risk management include the following [11,14]:

- *Automation:* Predictive analytics drives efficiency by automating and streamlining many aspects of risk assessment and monitoring. This automation frees up human resources to focus on more strategic tasks, improving overall operational effectiveness.
- *Cost Reduction:* Early detection of risks reduces financial losses associated with crisis management and remediation. By preventing incidents and minimizing their impact,

predictive analytics can save companies significant resources. The ability to prioritize risks based on potential impact and probability ensures that organizations focus efforts where they are needed most, avoiding unnecessary expenses.

- *Enhanced Decision-making:* Predictive analytics empowers businesses of all sizes and industries to make well-informed decisions. Utilizing data and analytical tools has allowed decision-making to become more controlled, but the large volume of data makes it riskier to handle. Predictive analytics enables scenario modelling and interconnectivity analysis for decision-making. Predictive models provide data-backed insights that empower decision-makers to evaluate various risk scenarios with greater accuracy. These models can simulate outcomes under different conditions, helping companies choose the best course of action. For example, in the insurance sector, predictive analytics can assess policyholder risk profiles to set premiums more accurately and reduce fraud.
- *Demand Forecasting:* Poor demand planning leads to overstocking, stockouts, and missed revenue. Predictive analytics uses past sales, seasonality, and external signals (e.g., economic indicators, weather) to accurately forecast demand, reducing inventory risk.

- *Risk Monitoring:* Modern predictive analytics tools can process and analyze data in real time, offering instant alerts and continuous monitoring. This dynamic approach is crucial in sectors like cybersecurity, where threats evolve rapidly, and response times are critical. By using real-time predictive analytics, companies can identify anomalies that may indicate a breach and act swiftly to contain the damage.
- *Regulatory Compliance:* One of the most compelling reasons to adopt predictive analytics in compliance programs is the ability to make better-informed decisions about where to allocate your resources. With regulations constantly evolving, staying compliant is a challenge. Predictive analytics can help organizations anticipate changes in regulatory environments and adapt accordingly. Moreover, it can identify compliance risks by detecting patterns of non-compliance before audits or penalties occur. Predictive analytics can streamline the generation of regulatory reports, ensuring that institutions meet deadlines and provide accurate, comprehensive data to regulators. For example, financial institutions use predictive models to monitor transactions for anti-money laundering (AML) compliance, significantly reducing the risk of regulatory violations.

12.6 CHALLENGES

Despite its transformative potential, the application of predictive analytics in risk management is not without its challenges, which can undermine its effectiveness and lead to unforeseen consequences. The challenges include data privacy, data quality, algorithmic bias, model risk, model interpretability, model generalizability, integration, human element, and ethical considerations. These challenges are discussed as follows [2,11,15]:

- *Data Privacy:* Data privacy and security are paramount concerns. As predictive models rely on vast amounts of personal and sensitive data, organizations must navigate stringent regulations like GDPR and ensure robust data protection measures. Techniques such as anonymization, tokenization, and federated learning are crucial for extracting meaningful insights while safeguarding individual privacy.
- *Data Quality*: Data quality and integration remain foundational challenges. Predictive models are only as good as the data they are trained on; hence, the adage "garbage in, garbage out" holds. The effectiveness of predictive models heavily relies on the accuracy, completeness, and relevance of the data used for training. Incomplete, inaccurate, or inconsistent data can lead to flawed insights and unreliable

predictions. Organizations must invest in robust data governance frameworks, ensure data accuracy, and integrate disparate data sources to create a unified and reliable foundation for their analytics initiatives.

- *Ethical Concerns:* The deployment of predictive analytics in risk management also raises critical ethical considerations, particularly concerning privacy, bias, and fairness. Organizations must ensure that their models are developed and used ethically, respecting individual rights and avoiding discriminatory outcomes.
- *Bias:* Another critical challenge is algorithmic bias. Predictive models, trained on historical data, can inadvertently perpetuate or even amplify existing societal biases. This can lead to discriminatory outcomes, such as unfair credit scoring or biased risk assessments in healthcare. The investigation into the Apple Card algorithm for potential gender bias highlights the real-world implications of algorithmic bias and the need for rigorous auditing and fairness assessments. Ensuring that predictive models are equitable and do not disproportionately disadvantage certain groups is a complex but essential challenge that organizations must address. Continuous testing for "unintended consequences" and ensuring fairness in algorithmic decision-making are essential to mitigate these risks.

- *Interpretability:* The increasing complexity of advanced predictive models, particularly those based on deep learning, presents a significant challenge to interpretability. While complex models often achieve higher predictive accuracy, their inner workings can be opaque, leading to a lack of transparency in how decisions are made. In high-stakes environments like risk management, understanding the rationale behind a model's prediction is crucial for trust, accountability, and regulatory compliance. The trade-off between accuracy and interpretability is a persistent dilemma.
- *Model Generalizability:* Another significant challenge is model generalizability and the potential for model degradation over time. A model trained on data from a specific location, demographic, or time period may not perform well when applied to a different context. Furthermore, the environment in which the model operates is rarely static. Changes in market conditions, consumer behavior, or regulatory landscapes can render previously accurate models obsolete. Continuous monitoring, evaluation, and retraining are essential to ensure models remain relevant and effective, adding to the operational burden of maintaining predictive analytics systems.
- *Human Element:* While predictive analytics provides powerful insights, it is crucial to remember that these tools

should augment, not replace, human judgment. It is critical to remember that AI and human expertise must function in tandem. The most effective risk management strategies combine data-driven insights with experienced decision-making and industry expertise. Organizations must adopt a balanced approach, recognize the limitations of predictive models, and supplement them with human expertise, robust governance frameworks, and continuous monitoring. As a business leader, your role is to ensure your organization maintains this balance – leveraging technology to enhance decision-making while recognizing situations where human insight and experience are irreplaceable.

- *Collaboration:* Effective collaboration between AI and human decision-making drives better stakeholder engagement. Senior leadership, board members, and even frontline employees need reassurance that someone with a nuanced understanding of the business and its regulatory landscape oversees compliance activities.
- *Change Management*: Successful implementation of predictive analytics necessitates a cultural transformation within organizations. Overcoming resistance to change and fostering a data-driven culture are crucial steps in realizing the full potential of this technology.
- *Computational Resources:* Predictive analytics, particularly when applied to large datasets, demands

substantial computational resources. Organizations often require specialized hardware or cloud-based solutions to handle the intensive processing requirements associated with these models.

Figure 12.7 shows five challenges and limitations of predictive analytics in risk management [2].

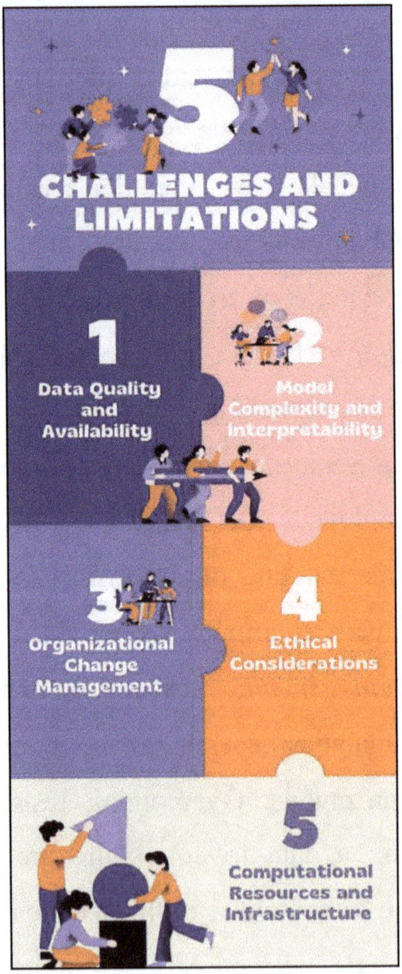

Figure 12.7 Five challenges and limitations of predictive analytics in risk management [2].

12.7 FUTURE OF PREDICTIVE ANALYTICS IN RISK MANAGEMENT

The trajectory of predictive analytics in risk management points towards even more sophisticated and integrated applications. The future will see a seamless integration with prescriptive analytics, moving beyond merely predicting "what will happen" to providing actionable recommendations on "what should we do." This synergy will enable organizations to not only foresee risks but also to automatically implement optimal mitigation strategies. As technology continues to evolve, so too will the capabilities of predictive analytics. As the field evolves, organizations must prepare for the next frontier: prescriptive analytics and integrated risk ecosystems.

AI-powered APIs and real-time insights will become the norm, transforming how financial institutions, for example, interact with customers. APIs will analyze spending behavior, predict cash flow issues, and suggest personalized investment opportunities in real-time. This shift towards instantaneous, automated risk mitigation will redefine customer relationships, moving from transactional interactions to deeply embedded financial advisory.

12.8 CONCLUSION

Predictive analytics is no longer a futuristic concept; it is already delivering measurable value in supply chains across the globe. It has become a strategic imperative for organizations seeking to thrive in an increasingly complex and uncertain world. It has undeniably ushered in a new era of risk management, transforming it from a reactive necessity into a proactive strategic advantage. By harnessing the power of data and predictive analytics, businesses can move from reactive to proactive risk management, safeguarding their assets and reputation. Large enterprises from different industries are adopting predictive analytics to identify, analyze, and plan against future business risks. Today, industries, including healthcare, ecommerce, governments, manufacturing, and supply chains, use predictive analytics to drive growth, profitability, and mitigate business challenges and risks.

The increasing complexity of the US financial sector and the growing demands of regulatory compliance have necessitated the adoption of more sophisticated risk management tools. As business environments in the global context continue to become more uncertain and complex, organizations have been turning to AI-based predictive analytics to help them improve their abilities to manage risk. Predictive analytics represents a pivotal step forward in risk management, offering unparalleled insights and proactive capabilities. It empowers financial institutions to take a proactive approach to risk management [16]. Predictive data analytics and risk management come together to help you catch risks with any strategy or plan that is not working as expected. More information on the use of predictive analytics in risk management is available from the books in [17-22].

REFERENCES

[1] "The future of risk management: Predictive analytics and beyond," https://www.erm-academy.org/publication/risk-management-article/the-future-of-risk-management-predictive-analytics-and-beyond/

[2] "Predictive analytics: Transforming risk management," August 2024, https://codersperhour.com/predictive-analytics-transforming-risk-management/

[3] M. N. O. Sadiku, S. A. Ajayi, and J. O. Sadiku, "Predictive analytics in risk management," International Journal of Trend in Scientific Research and Development, vol. 10, no. 2, March-April, 2026, pp. 1444-1453.

[4] "Supply chain predictive analytics: What is it and who's doing it?" https://riverlogic.com/?blog=supply-chain-predictive-analytics-what-is-it-and-whos-doing-it

[5] N. Babin, "AI and predictive analytics: Revolutionizing demand forecasting in supply chain management," https://www.linkedin.com/pulse/ai-predictive-analytics-revolutionizing-demand-supply-nicolas-babin-xrj2e/

[6] "From insight to innovation: Why data analysis will define industry leaders in 2025,"

https://www.inkl.com/news/from-insight-to-innovation-why-data-analysis-will-define-industry-leaders-in-2025

[7] "An overview of supply chain analytics," February 2023, Unknown Source.

[8] I. Tymchuk, "Big data and predictive analytics in supply chain: Success stories and tips," November 2020, https://www.n-ix.com/big-data-predictive-analytics-supply-chain-case-study/

[9] "Predictive analytics in insurance: Types, tools, and the future," October 2020, https://online.maryville.edu/blog/predictive-analytics-in-insurance/

[10] "Predictive analytics for risk management: Uses, types & benefits," https://predikdata.com/predictive-analytics-for-risk-management/

[11] https://manus.im

[12] "How predictive analytics can transform risk management," June 2024,

https://10xds.com/blog/predictive-analytics-for-risk-management/

[13] "Predictive analytics in financial risk management: Building models with R," October 2024,

https://imarticus.org/blog/predictive-analytics-in-financial-risk-management/

[14] "How predictive analytics can transform risk management," https://sixmexico.com/blog/how-predictive-analytics-transforms-risk-management

[15] T. Fox, "Next-generation predictive analytics for risk management," March 2025, https://www.linkedin.com/pulse/next-generation-predictive-analytics-risk-management-thomas-fox-lofsc/

[16] J. I. Azubuike, "The role of predictive analytics in automating risk management and regulatory compliance in the U.S. financial sector," European Journal of Accounting, Auditing and Finance Research, vol.12, no. 10, October 2024, pp.19-31.

[17] A. Bari, M. Chaouchi, and T. Jung, Predictive Analytics For Dummies. For Dummies, 2nd edition, 2016.

[18] Innoware PJP, Harnessing AI and Predictive Analytics for Risk Management in Finance. Independently Published, 2024.

[19] S. Castillo, Predictive Analytics & Risk Modeling: For Insurance and Actuarial Science. Kindle Edition, 2025.

[20] D. Covington, Analytics & Probability: Data Science, Data Analysis and Predictive Analytics for Business & Risk

Management, Statistics, Combinations, and Permutations for Business. Kindle Edition, 2020.

[21] A. C. Tatto, AI in Credit Risk Management: Predicting Default with Precision. Kindle Edition, 2025.

[22] W. H. Hsu, Emerging Methods in Predictive Analytics: Risk Management and Decision-making. IGI Global, 2014.

CHAPTER 13: PREDICTIVE ANALYTICS IN CUSTOMER RELATIONSHIP MANAGEMENT

"A wise man speaks because he has something to say; a fool because he has to say something."

- Plato

13.1 INTRODUCTION

Customer relationship management (CRM) has become the cornerstone of modern business strategy, playing a critical role in achieving long-term success and sustainability. The significance of CRM lies in its ability to enhance customer satisfaction, foster loyalty, and ultimately drive revenue growth. One of the primary benefits of CRM is its ability to provide a comprehensive view of the customer [1].

However, the landscape of CRM is undergoing a profound transformation, largely driven by the integration of artificial intelligence (AI) and predictive analytics. For decades, traditional CRM systems served as the backbone of customer relationship management. Traditional CRM systems excel at telling you what happened yesterday. While this historical perspective is valuable, it is inherently reactive. CRM systems possess inherent limitations that often hinder businesses from truly understanding and anticipating their customers' evolving needs. A primary shortcoming is their reactive nature, designed to respond to customer interactions after they occur, rather than proactively preventing potential issues. Furthermore, traditional CRM systems often fall short in accurately forecasting future customer actions. The integration of AI-powered predictive analytics fundamentally reshapes CRM capabilities, offering a multitude of benefits that address the shortcomings of traditional systems. A significant number of companies recognize predictive analytics as essential for delivering personalized customer experiences [2].

In today's competitive business landscape, understanding your customers is no longer enough; you must anticipate their needs before they even articulate them. Customer relationship management (CRM) systems have long served as the central repository for customer data, tracking interactions, purchases, and preferences. Predictive analytics is a transformative technology that shifts CRM from a reactive record-keeping tool into a proactive engine for growth. It leverages historical data, statistical algorithms, and machine learning techniques to identify the likelihood of future outcomes based on past patterns. When integrated into a CRM system, predictive analytics empowers businesses to forecast customer behavior, optimize marketing strategies, and significantly enhance customer retention. CRM Predictive analytics is changing the way businesses interact with their customers [3].

This chapter explores the transformative role of predictive analytics in customer relationship management (CRM) systems. It begins by explaining predictive analytics. It describes predictive analytics in CRM and provides some of its applications. It highlights some benefits and challenges of predictive analytics in CRM. It predicts the future of predictive analytics in CRM. The last section concludes with comments.

13.2 WHAT IS PREDICTIVE ANALYTICS?

As its name implies, predictive analytics is about predicting future trends such as sales demand and exchange rates. and other important metrics. The technique relies on the application of statistical modeling and regression analysis to historical data to determine and understand trends and formulate future predictions. Strictly speaking, predictive analytics does not predict the future, but rather uses probability theories to determine what is likely to happen based on patterns and trends revealed by analyzing historical data [4]. Predictive analytics accurately anticipates customer demand, preventing overstocking and stockouts while adapting to market changes. Figure 13.1 illustrates predictive analytics [5], while Figure 13.2 shows different components of predictive analytics [6].

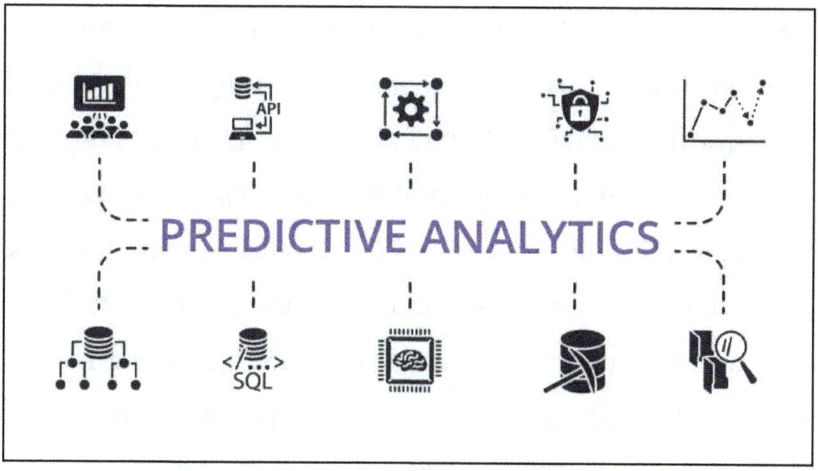

Figure 13.1 Predictive analytics [5].

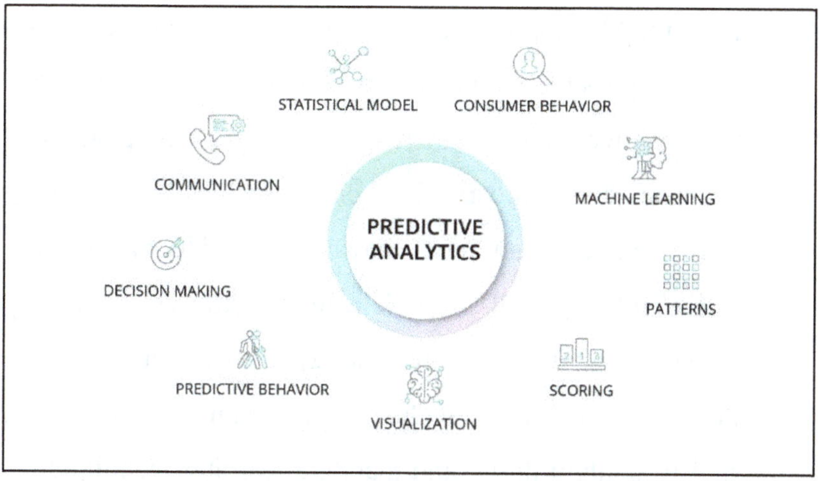

Figure 13.2 Different components of predictive analytics [6].

In general, analytics provides an efficient way to improve planning because it gives you better forecasts. There are different types of data analytics. They are briefly explained as follows [7]:

- *Descriptive Analytics:* Descriptive analytics examines what has happened over the years. They are capable of detecting trends in historical data. Analytics can uncover trends and postulate probable reasons for change by comparing the same data from various periods. It can be seen as the baseline of the industry, which basically assesses past and current data for more meaningful insights and delivers it to the people to use their own intelligence and knowledge to make decisions.
- *Predictive Analytics:* This assists businesses in predicting what might happen and the impact of various situations, such as possible supply chain bottlenecks. Managers can be proactive rather than responsive by pushing them to evaluate these prospective circumstances before they occur. Predictive analytics may be used to identify patterns and trends as well as anticipate breakdowns that may impact suppliers and, consequently, production processes. Predictive analytics for the supply chain leverages data, statistical algorithms, and machine learning techniques to identify the likelihood of future outcomes.
- *Prescriptive Analytics:* Prescriptive analytics builds on predictive analytics and dives deeper into predicting future insights on what can be done next. Prescriptive analytics uses the findings of descriptive and predictive analytics to recommend what measures a business should take to

achieve its objectives. Because prescriptive analytics is increasingly complicated, they need more powerful software capable of rapidly processing and interpreting large amounts of data.

- *Cognitive Analytics:* Cognitive analytics attempts to mimic human thought and behavior, and it can assist companies in answering challenging, complex problems. Cognitive analytics does this by utilizing artificial intelligence (AI), which allows it to improve over time. With the use of AI in the industry, answering complex questions and draw out contextual conclusions on how humans would have interacted with the situation. It helps with more meaningful data and scales experience and knowledge with better decisions.
- *Diagnostic Analytics:* This gives the ability to identify the root cause. It is characterized by techniques such as drill-down, data discovery, data mining, and correlations. It involves analyzing overall performance and figuring out why errors, mistakes, and delays occur. It lets the manager know the delays, breakdowns, and disruptions in the demand and supply processes and the reasons behind them.

Figure 13.3 shows these major types of data analytics [8]. Unlike diagnostic and descriptive analytics, which were designed to analyze situations after they happened, predictive analytics utilizes advanced data analytics techniques to forecast future outcomes. In the supply chain, the time has come to shift from mere descriptive and diagnostic analytics to predictive and prescriptive analytics. Predictive analytics is a branch of data analytics that makes predictions about future outcomes using historical data combined with statistical modeling, data mining techniques, and machine learning. Figure 13.4 shows how predictive analytics works [9].

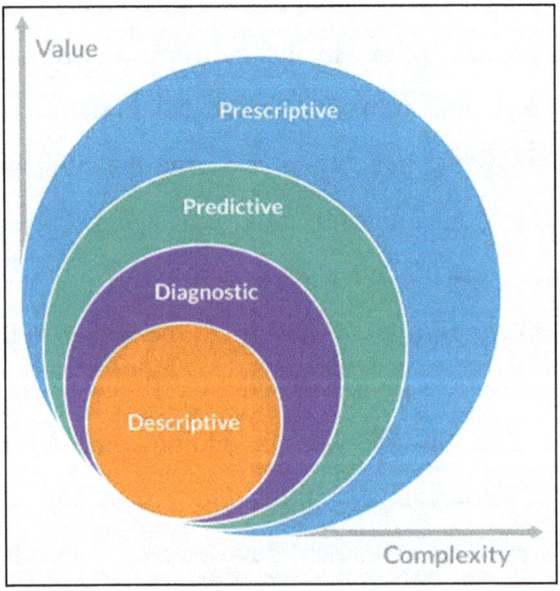

Figure 13.3 Types of data analytics [6].

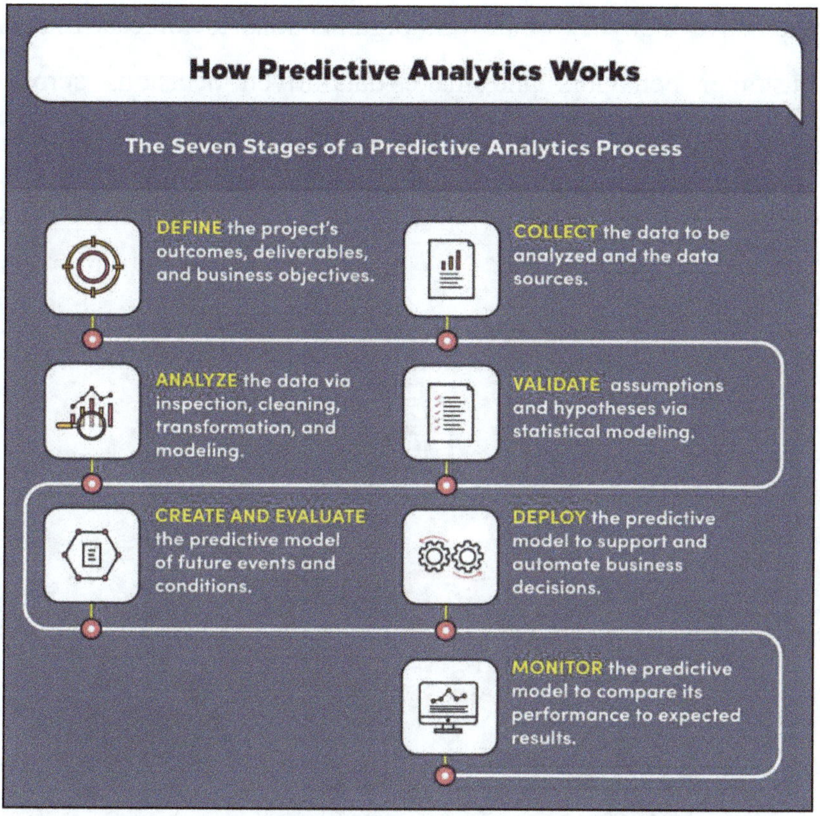

Figure 13.4 How predictive analytics works [9].

13.3 PREDICTIVE ANALYTICS IN CUSTOMER RELATIONSHIP MANAGEMENT

Customer relationship management (CRM) systems have long served as the central repository for customer data, tracking past interactions and purchases. However, the integration of predictive analytics is transforming these systems from reactive databases into proactive engines of growth. By leveraging statistical algorithms, machine learning, and historical data, predictive analytics empowers organizations to forecast future customer behaviors and make data-driven decisions across sales, marketing, and customer service. Figure 13.5 shows different components of CRM [10].

Figure 13.5 Components of CRM [10].

Traditional customer relationship management (CRM) systems were initially developed to support basic contact management and data storage, aiming to centralize customer information and streamline communication within organizations. Traditional CRM's data-centric approach provided an essential foundation for businesses by organizing and storing customer information, but it fell short in delivering insights that could drive customer [11]. The traditional approach to sales often relies heavily on intuition and manual analysis of past performance. Predictive analytics introduces a scientific rigor to the sales process, enabling teams to focus their efforts where they are most likely to yield results. Predictive CRM analytics combines data science, AI, and customer relationship management tools to forecast future customer actions. It uses historical data such as sales patterns, engagement metrics, and support interactions to identify trends and generate probability-based insights [12].

13.4 APPLICATIONS OF PREDICTIVE ANALYTICS IN CUSTOMER RELATIONSHIP MANAGEMENT

Predictive analytics offers a diverse range of practical applications within CRM, transforming how businesses interact with their customers and optimize their strategies. The application of predictive models, which analyze patterns in customer data to anticipate future behavior, has become essential in developing loyalty programs, personalized marketing strategies, and customer segmentation. Common applications of predictive analytics in CRM include the following [1,13]:

- *Lead Scoring*: One of the most impactful applications is predictive lead scoring. Instead of treating all incoming leads equally, predictive models analyze historical data to identify the characteristics of leads that have successfully converted in the past. The CRM system then automatically assigns a score to new leads based on their similarity to these successful profiles. This allows sales representatives to prioritize high-value prospects, significantly improving conversion rates and reducing time wasted on unqualified leads. Moving beyond basic demographic data, predictive models assess a lead's engagement, historical interactions, and other factors to assign a score indicating their conversion probability. This streamlines sales processes and improves conversion rates.
- *Personalization:* Marketing teams are constantly striving to deliver the right message to the right person at the right time. Predictive analytics makes this level of hyper-personalization achievable at scale. Predictive analytics plays a pivotal role in enhancing customer satisfaction by personalizing interactions based on individual preferences. Analyzing customer data allows businesses to deliver tailored experiences that make customers feel valued and understood, thereby driving engagement and loyalty. Leveraging real-time data processing, predictive analytics enables the delivery of highly personalized

customer journeys. This means tailoring communications, offers, and experiences to individual preferences, leading to stronger customer relationships. By analyzing a customer's purchase history and comparing it to similar customer profiles, the CRM can predict which additional products or services a customer is most likely to buy next. This allows marketers to tailor their recommendations, increasing the average order value and deepening the customer relationship.

- *Churn Prediction:* This is a cornerstone application, allowing businesses to pinpoint customers exhibiting behaviors indicative of potential churn. Customer churn is a significant challenge for businesses across all industries. Early detection facilitates targeted retention campaigns and personalized outreach. Customer acquisition is significantly more expensive than retention, making churn a major concern for any business. Predictive models analyze behavioral patterns, such as decreasing engagement levels, unresolved support tickets, or changes in purchasing frequency, to identify customers who are at a high risk of leaving. Armed with this foresight, marketing and customer success teams can proactively intervene with targeted retention campaigns or personalized offers before the customer actually churns.

- *Sentiment Analysis:* Sentiment analysis, also known as opinion mining, is a widely used technique that applies natural language processing (NLP) and machine learning (ML) to assess customer emotions, opinions, and attitudes from textual data sources such as reviews, social media, and customer feedback. Businesses use sentiment analysis to gauge customer satisfaction, identify pain points, and respond proactively to issues. Sentiment analysis tools analyze customer reviews, social media interactions, and online reviews and measure the state of the customer's sentiment so that companies can take correct actions, and service quality will increase. By analyzing customer feedback, social media interactions, and support tickets, predictive analytics can gauge customer sentiment, identifying potential issues or areas for improvement before they escalate. When a customer submits a support ticket, predictive models can instantly analyze the text to determine the category, urgency, and sentiment of the issue.
- *Demand Forecasting:* Particularly relevant in retail and ecommerce, predictive analytics can forecast future demand for products and services, optimizing inventory management, pricing strategies, and marketing campaigns.

- *Sales Forecasting:* Predictive analytics enhances sales forecasting accuracy. Traditional forecasting often struggles with subjective inputs and static models. Predictive analytics revolutionizes sales forecasting. Instead of relying on intuition or simple historical averages, sales leaders can use predictive models to forecast revenue with high accuracy. Predictive CRM tools can generate dynamic, real-time revenue projections by analyzing open opportunities, historical win rates, deal sizes, and sales cycle lengths. This provides sales leaders with a more reliable view of the pipeline, enabling better resource allocation and strategic planning.

13.5 BENEFITS

The integration of predictive analytics into CRM systems offers a multitude of benefits across various business functions, from sales and marketing to customer support. Predictive analytics in customer relationship management (CRM) focuses on enhancing customer engagement, satisfaction, and retention strategies. Integrating predictive analytics into modern CRM systems can offer personalized experiences that improve customer engagement, satisfaction, and retention. Other benefits of predictive analytics in CRM include the following [2,3]:

- *Proactive Customer Support:* Customer support is traditionally a reactive function, waiting for a customer to report an issue before taking action. Predictive analytics enables a proactive approach. By analyzing product usage data and historical support tickets, companies can anticipate when a customer might encounter a problem or require assistance. This proactive approach significantly enhances customer satisfaction.
- *Customer Satisfaction:* In the realm of customer service, predictive analytics shifts the paradigm from reactive problem-solving to proactive issue resolution. This not only improves operational efficiency but also significantly enhances customer satisfaction. Predictive analytics helps businesses understand customer behaviors, preferences, and needs. This allows companies to offer better products, services, and communication. This leads to stronger relationships and more loyal customers.
- *Efficiency:* Predictive analytics helps businesses deliver more value and relevance to customers. This improves the overall effectiveness of their marketing efforts. This leads to greater efficiency and a higher return on investment. Predictive analytics provides data-driven insights into where customer success efforts will yield the greatest impact. This allows for tailored approaches to specific customer segments, ensuring that resources are allocated

efficiently and effectively, delivering the right support at the opportune moment.

- *Proactive Engagement:* Instead of reacting to problems, predictive analytics empowers businesses to anticipate potential issues. For example, if historical data indicates a surge in support tickets after a specific product update, businesses can proactively provide helpful resources or explainer videos to new users, preventing frustration and enhancing overall customer satisfaction.
- *Reduced Customer Churn:* Acquiring a new customer is notoriously more expensive than retaining an existing one. Predictive analytics provides a powerful solution by identifying customers who are at a high risk of leaving. It identifies customers likely to churn by analyzing engagement patterns, purchase frequency, and satisfaction scores. By analyzing engagement patterns, purchase frequency, support ticket history, and even sentiment analysis from social media, predictive models can flag at-risk accounts. This early warning system allows customer success teams to intervene proactively with targeted win-back campaigns, personalized offers, or dedicated support. Predictive analytics enables the early identification of at-risk customers, allowing businesses to intervene with personalized support and targeted solutions before customers decide to leave. This proactive retention

strategy fosters a more stable customer base and a healthier revenue stream.

- *Precise Sales Forecasting:* Sales teams often struggle with prioritizing leads, wasting valuable time on prospects who are unlikely to convert. Predictive lead scoring solves this problem by assigning a numerical value to each lead based on their probability of closing. The algorithm considers factors such as demographic data, firmographics, website behavior, and past interactions to identify the most promising opportunities. Sales and marketing teams use predictive analytics to forecast revenue and plan resources.
- *Product Recommendations:* In the era of the empowered consumer, personalization is not a luxury; it is an expectation. Predictive analytics enables marketers to deliver hyper-personalized experiences at scale. A prime example of this is predictive product recommendations. Predictive algorithms analyze purchase histories to recommend products or services customers are most likely to buy. This approach drives cross-selling and upselling opportunities while improving the customer experience. Ecommerce giants like Amazon have built their success on algorithms that analyze purchase histories and browsing behavior to suggest products that customers are highly likely to buy. This approach allows businesses to

recommend products or services that align perfectly with customer needs, significantly boosting their overall value to the company.

- *Enhanced Lead Scoring:* Sales teams rely on predictive analysis to score leads based on their likelihood to convert. High-quality leads receive priority, improving the efficiency of sales efforts and enabling a more strategic allocation of resources. By analyzing various data points, predictive analytics can accurately score leads based on their likelihood of conversion, enabling sales teams to prioritize their efforts on the most promising prospects.

13.6 CHALLENGES

While the benefits of predictive analytics in CRM are substantial, successful implementation is not without challenges. Major challenges include issues of data privacy, data quality, data silos, regulatory compliance, ethical issues, algorithm bias, ambiguity of human language, sarcasm detection, and integration complexity of AI with existing CRM systems. These challenges necessitate strict data protection and ethical handling practices. Predictive analytics in CRM is not a plug-and-play solution but a complex, ongoing strategic journey. Effective implementation depends on a balance between technical innovation and adherence to ethical standards in data management. Other challenges of predictive analytics in CRM include the following [2,3,14]:

- *Ethical Concerns*: As predictive analytics becomes more pervasive, the ethical and legal implications have taken center stage. Ethical data handling is no longer just about compliance; it is a prerequisite for customer trust. Organizations must balance the drive for personalization with the fundamental right to privacy.
- *Data Quality:* The foundation of any predictive model is data. Predictive models are only as good as the data they are trained on. Therefore, organizations must ensure their CRM data is clean, comprehensive, and well-integrated across all touchpoints. Incomplete or inaccurate data will inevitably lead to wrong predictions. Data often resides in disparate silos across marketing, sales, and customer support departments, leading to a fragmented view of the customer journey. Organizations must ensure their CRM data is clean, accurate, and comprehensive. Businesses need to comply with various data protection regulations, such as GDPR and CCPA, before implementing AI-driven solutions.
- *Data Silos:* Another significant challenge is the prevalence of data silos. Customer data frequently remains scattered across disparate departments, systems, and channels, making it difficult to construct a unified, holistic view of

the customer. This fragmentation often results in inconsistent and ineffective customer experiences. Companies grappling with siloed data structures experience a decrease in customer satisfaction and a reduction in customer retention.

- *Resistance to Change*: Adopting predictive analytics requires a cultural shift within the organization. Teams must be trained not only to use the new tools but also to trust the data-driven insights over traditional intuition. Even when a model is technically sound, it often faces resistance from the very people it is meant to help. Overcoming resistance to change and fostering a culture that embraces data is crucial for maximizing the return on investment in predictive CRM technologies.
- *Skill Shortage:* Technology is only half the battle; the human component of predictive analytics is equally challenging. There is a persistent scarcity of talent capable of bridging the gap between complex data science and practical business application.
- *Bias:* There is the growing concern of algorithmic bias. Predictive models are trained on historical data, which may contain inherent human biases. If left unchecked, these models can inadvertently discriminate against certain customer segments, leading to reputational damage and legal liability.

- *Integration:* The integration of predictive analytics with existing CRM systems is challenging. It requires huge investment in infrastructure and expertise to implement AI in legacy CRM systems and is a laborious process for companies with legacy systems.

13.7 FUTURE OF PREDICTIVE ANALYTICS IN CUSTOMER RELATIONSHIP MANAGEMENT

The integration of predictive analytics into CRM systems represents a fundamental shift in how businesses manage customer relationships. The future of CRM is intrinsically linked with the continued evolution of AI and predictive analytics. Emerging trends, such as the synergy between generative AI and predictive analytics, promise even more sophisticated and tailored customer experiences. The emphasis will increasingly be on real-time data processing, enabling instant responses to subtle shifts in customer behavior. As technology advances, CRM systems will continue to break free from traditional data silos, integrating seamlessly with a broader ecosystem of emerging technologies to create truly intelligent and adaptive customer relationship management platforms. By harnessing the power of data to forecast future outcomes, businesses can cultivate deeper customer relationships, optimize operational efficiencies, and secure a competitive edge in the dynamic marketplace. The future of CRM is proactive, personalized, and powered by prediction [2].

Modern CRM systems integrate machine learning models that automatically detect correlations across datasets. These models continuously learn from every customer interaction to improve predictions over time. As machine learning algorithms become more sophisticated and data integration improves, predictive analytics will undoubtedly become an indispensable tool for any business seeking to thrive in the modern, customer-centric economy.

13.8 CONCLUSION

Predictive analytics is not just an enhancement to CRM; it is a fundamental paradigm shift. In the realm of customer service, predictive analytics shifts the paradigm from reactive problem-solving to proactive issue resolution. Moreover, predictive analytics enables proactive support. Using predictive analytics effectively can unlock deeper customer insights, streamline operations, and drive sustainable growth. Predictive analysis in customer relationship management (CRM) has been widely explored in recent years, driven by the increasing need for companies to harness large datasets and derive actionable insights for customer engagement. It is transforming how businesses understand and engage customers. For businesses looking to maintain a competitive edge, integrating predictive analytics into their CRM strategy is no longer optional.

In the modern landscape of customer relationship management (CRM), predictive analytics has been hailed as the "holy grail" of business strategy. Predictive analytics is no longer a luxury for CRM; it is becoming necessary for businesses aiming to remain competitive. Predictive analytics transforms CRM from a system of record into a system of intelligence. By anticipating customer needs and behaviors, businesses can build stronger, more profitable relationships that stand the test of time. More information on the use of predictive analytics in customer relationship management is available from the books in [15-18] and a related journal: *Journal of Business Venturing, AI and Data Analytics.*

REFERENCES

[1] C. S. Odionu, B. Bristol-Alagbariya, and R. Okon, "Big data analytics for customer relationship management: Enhancing engagement and retention strategies," International Journal of Scholarly Research in Science and Technology, vol. 5, no. 2, 2024, pp. 50-67.

[2] https://manus.im

[3] M. N. O. Sadiku, S. A. Ajayi, and J. O. Sadiku, "Predictive analytics in customer relationship management," International Journal of Trend in Scientific Research and Development, vol. 10, no.2, March-April, 2026, pp. 1454-1462.

[4] "Supply chain predictive analytics: What is it and who's doing it?" https://riverlogic.com/?blog=supply-chain-predictive-analytics-what-is-it-and-whos-doing-it

[5] N. Babin, "AI and predictive analytics: Revolutionizing demand forecasting in supply chain management," https://www.linkedin.com/pulse/ai-predictive-analytics-revolutionizing-demand-supply-nicolas-babin-xrj2e/

[6] "From insight to innovation: Why data analysis will define industry leaders in 2025," https://www.inkl.com/news/from-insight-to-innovation-why-data-analysis-will-define-industry-leaders-in-2025

[7] "An overview of supply chain analytics," February 2023, Unknown Source.

[8] I. Tymchuk, "Big data and predictive analytics in supply chain: Success stories and tips," November 2020, https://www.n-ix.com/big-data-predictive-analytics-supply-chain-case-study/

[9] "Predictive analytics in insurance: Types, tools, and the future," October 2020, https://online.maryville.edu/blog/predictive-analytics-in-insurance/

[10] O. Nguyen, "How to look for the best CRM management software," June 2022, https://www.digital-marketingsolutions.com/best-crm-management-software/

[11] A. R. Khan, S. Akter, and R. Islam, "Big data analytics and predictive analysis in enhancing customer relationship management (CRM): A systematic review of techniques," Journal of Machine Learning, Data Engineering and Data Science, vol. 1, no. 1, November 2024, pp.83-99.

[12] N. Rowan, "Predictive CRM analytics: How AI forecasts customer behavior and boosts retention," https://www.business-software.com/blog/predictive-crm-analytics-how-ai-forecasts-customer-behavior-and-boosts-retention/

[13] R. Khatoon and M. S. I. Chowdhury, “Predictive analytics in customer relationship management in the USA,” Journal of Business Venturing, AI and Data Analytics, vol. 1, no. 1, August 2024, pp. 37-43.

[14] Y. Gaidhani et al., “AI-driven predictive analytics for CRM to enhance retention, personalization and decision-making,” International Journal of Advanced Computer Science and Applications, vol. 16, no. 4, 2025, pp. 552-563.

[15] A. Bari, M. Chaouchi, and T. Jung, Predictive Analytics For Dummies. For Dummies, 2nd edition, 2016.

[16] V. Kumar, Customer Relationship Management (Legend in Marketing). Vibrant Publishers, 2024.

[17] A. Sathi, Customer Experience Analytics: The Key to Real-Time, Adaptive Customer Relationships. MC Press, 2011.

[18] A. Chorianopoulos, Effective CRM Using Predictive Analytics. Wiley, 2015.

CHAPTER 14: PREDICTIVE ANALYTICS IN ENTERTAINMENT

"The only man who never makes a mistake is the man who never does anything."

- Theodore Roosevelt

14.1 INTRODUCTION

The entertainment industry has historically been viewed as a bastion of creative intuition, where "gut feelings" and artistic vision dictated the success of blockbusters and chart-topping hits. However, the digital revolution has ushered in a paradigm shift, integrating predictive analytics into every facet of the creative process. Predictive analytics involves the use of historical data, statistical algorithms, and machine learning techniques to identify the likelihood of future outcomes. By converting raw information into actionable insights, predictive analytics is revolutionizing how content is created, distributed, and consumed across film, streaming, music, and live events. In entertainment, this translates to forecasting audience preferences, optimizing production budgets, and personalizing user experiences to an unprecedented degree [1].

Gone are the days when entertainment decisions were primarily based on guesswork and intuition. With data science, entertainment companies can rely on objective data to drive their decision-making. Technological advancements have made data science an integral part of the entertainment industry. Data science is at the intersection of technology and entertainment, enabling the industry to leverage data-driven decision-making. It has revolutionized marketing strategies in the entertainment industry. It also enables entertainment companies to identify and capitalize on emerging trends. Figure 14.1 shows some data scientists [2]. By analyzing vast amounts of data, entertainment companies can gain valuable insights into audience preferences and tailor their content accordingly.

Figure 14.1 Some data scientists [2].

The entertainment industry is always at the forefront of adopting new technologies. The industry has historically been driven by intuition, creative vision, and a degree of unpredictability. For decades, studio executives, music producers, and event organizers relied on instinct and past experiences to determine which projects would resonate with audiences. However, the digital age has ushered in a paradigm shift, transforming entertainment. At the forefront of this transformation is predictive analytics, the use of statistical techniques, machine learning, and historical data to forecast future outcomes [3].

This chapter examines the transformative role of predictive analytics in entertainment. It begins by explaining predictive analytics. It describes predictive analytics in entertainment and provides some of its applications. It highlights some benefits and challenges of predictive analytics in entertainment. It predicts the future of predictive analytics in entertainment. The last section concludes with comments.

14.2 WHAT IS PREDICTIVE ANALYTICS?

As its name implies, predictive analytics is about predicting future trends such as sales demand and exchange rates. and other important metrics. The technique relies on the application of statistical modeling and regression analysis to historical data to determine and understand trends and formulate future trends.

Strictly speaking, predictive analytics does not predict the future, but rather uses probability theories to determine what is likely to happen based on patterns and trends revealed by analyzing historical data [4]. Predictive analytics accurately anticipates customer demand, preventing overstocking and stockouts while adapting to market changes. Figure 14.2 illustrates predictive analytics [5], while Figure 14.3 shows different components of predictive analytics [6].

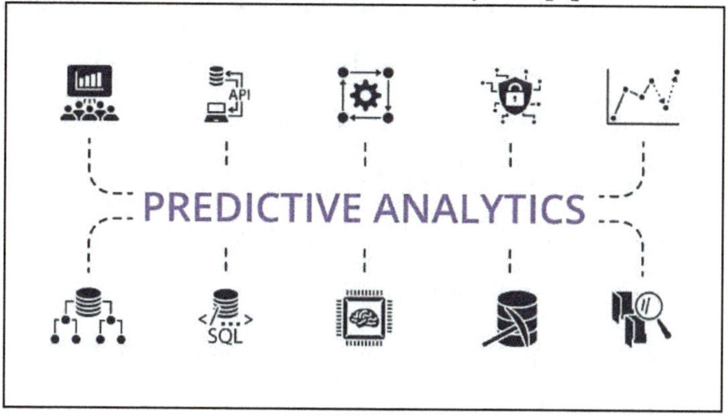

Figure 14.2 Predictive analytics [5].

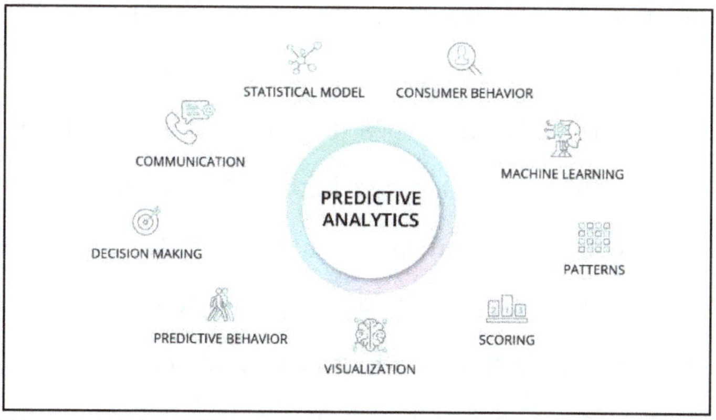

Figure 14.3 Different components of predictive analytics [6].

In general, analytics provides an efficient way to improve planning because it gives you better forecasts. There are different types of data analytics. They are briefly explained as follows [7]:

- *Descriptive Analytics:* Descriptive analytics examines what has happened over the years. They are capable of detecting trends in historical data. Analytics can uncover trends and postulate probable reasons for change by comparing the same data from various periods. It can be seen as the baseline of the industry, which basically assesses past and current data for more meaningful insights and delivers it to the people to use their own intelligence and knowledge to make decisions.
- *Predictive Analytics:* This assists businesses in predicting what might happen and the impact of various situations, such as possible supply chain bottlenecks. Managers can be proactive rather than responsive by pushing them to evaluate these prospective circumstances before they occur. Predictive analytics may be used to identify patterns and trends as well as anticipate breakdowns that may impact suppliers and, consequently, production processes. Predictive analytics for the supply chain leverages data, statistical algorithms, and machine learning techniques to identify the likelihood of future outcomes.

- *Prescriptive Analytics:* Prescriptive analytics builds on predictive analytics and dives deeper into predicting future insights on what can be done next. Prescriptive analytics uses the findings of descriptive and predictive analytics to recommend what measures a business should take to achieve its objectives. Because prescriptive analytics is increasingly complicated, they need more powerful software capable of rapidly processing and interpreting large amounts of data.
- *Cognitive Analytics:* Cognitive analytics attempts to mimic human thought and behavior, and it can assist companies in answering challenging, complex problems. Cognitive analytics does this by utilizing artificial intelligence (AI), which allows it to improve over time. With the use of AI in the industry, answering complex questions and draw out contextual conclusions on how humans would have interacted with the situation. It helps with more meaningful data and scales experience and knowledge with better decisions.
- *Diagnostic Analytics:* This gives the ability to identify the root cause. It is characterized by techniques such as drill-down, data discovery, data mining, and correlations. It involves analyzing overall performance and figuring out why errors, mistakes, and delays occur. It lets the manager know the delays, breakdowns, and disruptions in the demand and supply processes and the reasons behind them.

Figure 14.4 shows these major types of data analytics [8]. Unlike diagnostic and descriptive analytics, which were designed to analyze situations after they happened, predictive analytics utilizes advanced data analytics techniques to forecast future outcomes. In the supply chain, the time has come to shift from mere descriptive and diagnostic analytics to predictive and prescriptive analytics. Predictive analytics is a branch of data analytics that makes predictions about future outcomes using historical data combined with statistical modeling, data mining techniques, and machine learning. Figure 14.5 shows how predictive analytics works [9].

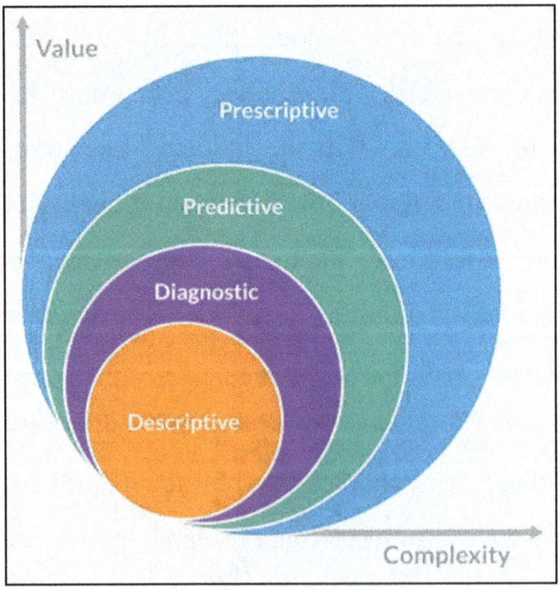

Figure 14.4 Types of data analytics [8].

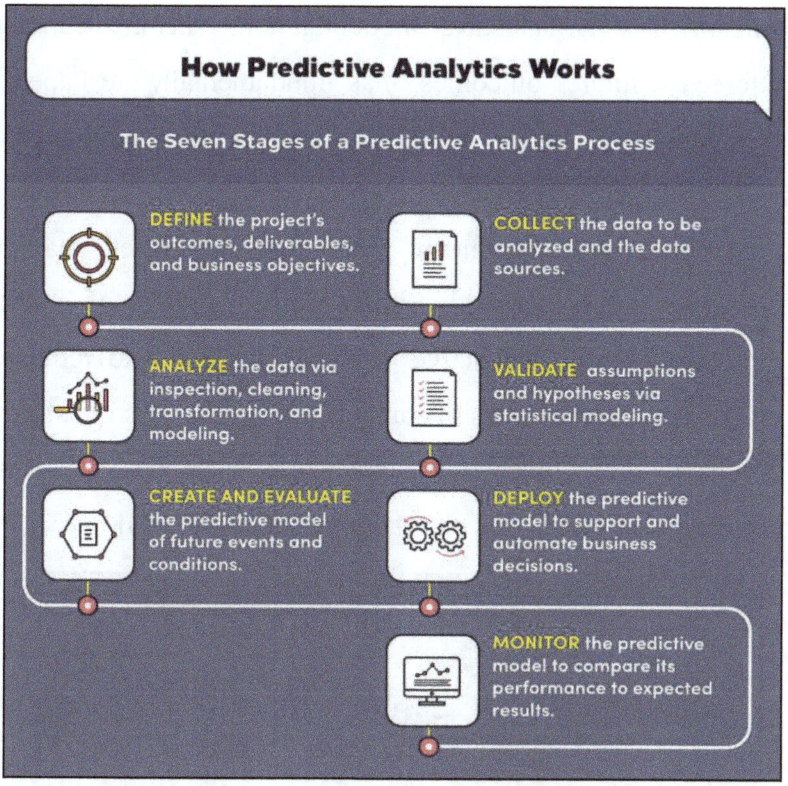

Figure 14.5 Predictive analytics process [9].

14.3 PREDICTIVE ANALYTICS IN ENTERTAINMENT

Perhaps no sector has been more profoundly transformed by predictive analytics than the entertainment industry. The entertainment industry, once governed primarily by creative intuition and "gut feelings," has undergone a radical transformation through the integration of predictive analytics. Predictive analytics, the branch of advanced analytics that uses historical data, statistical modeling, and machine learning to forecast future outcomes, has fundamentally reshaped the entertainment landscape. By leveraging predictive analytics, entertainment companies have significantly reduced the inherent risks of content production, optimized marketing strategies, and created unprecedented levels of audience personalization. Predictive analytics promises to reduce the inherent financial risks of content production. It is transforming the landscape of the entertainment and media industries. Figure 14.6 shows media and entertainment analysts [10].

Figure 14.6 Media and entertainment analysts [10].

In entertainment and media, predictive analytics can optimize content creation, improve audience targeting, and enhance marketing strategies. By leveraging data-driven insights, organizations can anticipate trends and audience preferences, ultimately driving engagement and profitability.

By analyzing data on production timelines, resource allocation, and audience reception, entertainment companies can identify areas for improvement and streamline their operations. Predictive analytics utilizes historical data, statistical algorithms, and machine learning techniques to identify the likelihood of future outcomes. In the media and entertainment sector, this translates to forecasting audience preferences and predicting content performance.

14.4 APPLICATIONS OF PREDICTIVE ANALYTICS IN ENTERTAINMENT

Predictive analytics has become an indispensable tool for film studios, influencing decisions from the initial greenlighting of a script to the final marketing push. Common applications of predictive analytics in entertainment include the following [1,11,12]:

- *Music Industry:* The music industry has similarly embraced predictive analytics, fundamentally altering how talent is discovered and how artists connect with fans. In the realm of Artists and Repertoire (A&R), record labels utilize data analytics to identify emerging talent with viral potential. By analyzing streaming metrics, social media growth, and playlist inclusions, predictive models can spot rising stars long before they achieve mainstream success. For example, Spotify's algorithm combines collaborative filtering with natural language processing (analyzing music blogs and news articles) and raw audio analysis to curate a highly personalized playlist for each user every week. In the music industry, data-driven tools can assist in harmonic layering or even synthesize "phantom" voices that complement human performances. Songs are increasingly structured to capture attention within the first few seconds to satisfy streaming algorithms, leading to a loss of complex narrative structures.

- *Gaming Industry*: The gaming industry has become a leader in the application of predictive tools, particularly within the "freemium" model. Developers use churn prediction models to identify players who are likely to stop playing based on their recent behavior, such as a decrease in session frequency. Once identified, these players can be targeted with specific incentives, such as in-game currency or exclusive content, to maintain engagement. Furthermore, analytics helps optimize in-game purchases by predicting which players are most likely to become "high-value" users, allowing for a more tailored monetization strategy.
- *Streaming Platforms:* Perhaps the most visible application of predictive analytics in entertainment is found within streaming platforms like Netflix, Amazon Prime, and

Spotify. These services rely heavily on recommendation engines to keep users engaged and reduce churn rates. The core objective is to predict what a user will want to watch or listen to next, often before the user even knows it themselves. These recommendation systems are powered by a complex interplay of behavioral and contextual signals.

- *Personalization:* Predictive analytics has revolutionized the way audiences discover and consume content through personalized recommendation engines. Personalization in content delivery is vital in a digital age that prioritizes user experience. The level of personalization extends beyond mere content suggestions. It enhances user engagement and retention, as consumers are more likely to remain loyal to a platform that consistently provides high-quality, relevant content. Mature streaming platforms utilize predictive models to customize the user interface itself, tailoring rows, thumbnails, and previews to individual preferences. For instance, a user who frequently watches romantic comedies might see promotional artwork highlighting the romantic elements of a film, while a fan of action movies might see artwork emphasizing explosive sequences for the same title. This hyper-personalization significantly boosts session length and overall retention.

- *Forecasting:* AI-driven trend forecasting is transforming the entertainment industry. It is revolutionizing how the entertainment industry anticipates and responds to audience preferences. In the rapidly evolving media and entertainment landscape, staying ahead of trends is essential for success. Artificial intelligence (AI) has emerged as a powerful tool for predictive analytics, enabling companies to anticipate audience preferences, optimize content strategies, and make data-driven decisions. As AI technology continues to advance, we can expect even more sophisticated trend forecasting capabilities.
- *Sentiment Analysis:* A common outcome for sentiment analysis is positive, negative, or neutral sentiment. The sentiment of a document, sentence, or word is classified with positive, negative, or neutral labels. Impressions publicized by consumers can be a valuable source of insight into the opinions of broader audiences. These insights, when employed in real time, can be used to significantly enhance audience engagement.

14.5 BENEFITS

Predictive analytics plays a crucial role in audience segmentation and marketing optimization. In live entertainment, predictive analytics is reshaping tour planning and ticketing. The data-driven approach can lead to more efficient production, reducing costs and increasing overall productivity. Other benefits of predictive analytics in entertainment include the following [1,10,11]:

- *Increased Efficiency:* AI can process and analyze vast amounts of data much faster than human analysts. Companies can allocate resources more effectively and adjust campaigns in real-time to enhance revenue potential. The data-driven strategies ensure that content reaches its potential audience efficiently.
- *Enhanced Audience Understanding:* AI provides deeper insights into audience preferences and behaviors, enabling more targeted content creation and marketing. Predictive analytics offers insights into viewer behaviors and preferences, enabling precise targeting. By understanding when and where to place ads, businesses can maximize engagement and conversion rates.
- *Improved Decision-making:* Predictive analytics assists stakeholders in entertainment and media by providing insights into audience preferences and viewing habits. Using data from various sources, analysts can forecast future trends, enabling informed decisions on content creation and marketing.
- *Inclusion:* Beyond commercial success, predictive analytics offers significant potential for advancing

Diversity, Equity, and Inclusion (DEI) within the entertainment industry. By carefully analyzing viewing patterns, organizations can identify gaps in representation and better understand the content preferences of underrepresented groups. Predictive models can forecast how inclusive content will perform across various demographics, providing data-driven justification for diverse storytelling.

14.6 CHALLENGES

While the benefits of predictive analytics are clear, the entertainment industry faces significant challenges. As the industry leans more heavily on algorithms, it faces profound challenges ranging from technical data limitations to the existential threat of cultural homogenization. One of the most significant technical hurdles in predictive analytics is the "cold start" problem. Other challenges of predictive analytics in entertainment include the following [1,10,11]:

- *Ethical Concerns:* There is a need to balance data-driven decisions with creative intuition and diverse storytelling. We need to examine ethical considerations related to data and AI, including bias, privacy, and fairness.
- *Privacy Concerns*: The use of predictive analytics raises significant ethical and privacy concerns. The extensive collection of personal data required to fuel predictive

models raises significant privacy concerns. As platforms track increasingly granular details of user behavior, the balance between a "personalized experience" and "intrusive surveillance" becomes a critical point of debate for both regulators and consumers. Entertainment companies must balance utilizing data to enhance their operations and protecting consumer privacy.

- *Bias:* One primary concern is algorithmic bias, where models trained on historical data may inadvertently reinforce existing prejudices, potentially limiting opportunities for diverse creators or underrepresented stories. If historical data contains biases (e.g., under-representation of minority groups), the predictive models will perpetuate these biases, making it harder for marginalized creators to receive funding or visibility. There is also the growing fear of content homogenization. If every creative decision is dictated by what the data suggests will be "safe" or "successful," the industry risks losing the very "risky" and original ideas that often lead to cultural breakthroughs.
- *Data Quality:* The accuracy of predictions depends on the quality and relevance of input data. Maintaining data quality and integrity is crucial. To develop high-quality models, the dataset needs to be relevant, complete, and large enough to support model training. The quality of the

training data is often considered more important than the machine learning algorithms for performance improvement. Businesses may benefit from regular audits and cleansing processes to eliminate inaccuracies that could mislead predictive models.

- *Data Infrastructure:* In sports, movies, video games, and theme parks, the entertainment industry uses this data to understand audiences, predict trends, and create more engaging experiences. Data is integrated, formatted, transformed, and enriched for modeling purposes. A strong data infrastructure is paramount for effective predictive analytics. Organizations need to ensure they have systems in place to collect, store, and process large volumes of data from diverse sources such as audience behavior, content performance, and market trends.
- *Skill Shortage*: Companies need skilled data scientists and AI specialists to implement and manage these systems effectively. Instructors impart their years of knowledge and experience to teach and inspire the next generation of innovators.
- *Unpredictability of Culture*: Entertainment is uniquely susceptible to the "Black Swan" theory, the occurrence of highly improbable events that have a massive impact. Culture is not a closed system; it is influenced by sudden

shifts in political climate, social movements, and viral trends that no historical data can fully anticipate.

- *Human Element*: The challenges of predictive analytics in entertainment do not suggest that data is the enemy of art. Rather, they highlight the limitations of a purely algorithmic approach. The future of the industry lies in a "Human-in-the-Loop" model, where data provides the map, but human intuition remains the compass. Predictive analytics should be used to handle the "logistics" of entertainment, while leaving the "magic" of creation to human artists. AI tools should work alongside human creators to develop innovative content ideas based on predicted trends.

14.7 FUTURE OF PREDICTIVE ANALYTICS IN ENTERTAINMENT

The future of entertainment lies not in the replacement of human intuition with algorithms, but in a collaborative synergy where data informs rather than dictates. Maintaining this balance will be essential to ensuring that the industry remains as innovative and diverse as the audiences it serves. The integration of artificial intelligence into production workflows will drive automation and efficiency, streamlining the creative process from scriptwriting to post-production.

Looking ahead, the integration of predictive analytics in entertainment is poised to deepen. Experts anticipate a shift toward hyper-personalization, where content curation occurs in real-time, tailored to a user's specific context and mood at any given moment. While the entertainment industry will always rely on the intangible magic of human creativity, predictive analytics provides a powerful compass. As predictive models continue to evolve, the challenge for the industry will be to maintain a symbiotic balance between the precision of data science and the irreplaceable spark of human creativity [1].

Data science in the entertainment industry has significantly impacted content creation, marketing strategies, and decision-making. In the future, data science will play an even more significant role as artificial intelligence, machine learning, and predictive analytics are further integrated into the industry's workflows. As the industry moves forward, data science will continue to shape its future, bringing forth emerging trends and technologies while addressing potential challenges and ethical considerations [2].

14.8 CONCLUSION

Predictive analytics has undoubtedly become an indispensable tool in the entertainment industry, offering a bridge between the unpredictability of human creativity and the demands of commercial viability. The integration of predictive analytics has provided the entertainment industry with a robust framework for navigating an increasingly complex and competitive market. By leveraging AI for predictive analytics, entertainment companies can make informed decisions that drive engagement, revenue, and growth. As technology advances and data science continues to evolve, the future of the entertainment industry holds exciting possibilities. To remain competitive in this fast-paced industry, media and entertainment companies must embrace AI-powered predictive analytics as a core component of their strategy. Embracing predictive analytics provides organizations with the tools they need to make informed decisions and adapt to market changes swiftly. More information on the use of predictive analytics in entertainment is available from the books in [13-15].

REFERENCES

[1] https://manus.im

[2] "The impact of data science in the entertainment industry," December 2023,

https://www.institutedata.com/us/blog/data-science-in-the-entertainment-industry/

[3] M. N. O. Sadiku, M. Oteniya, and J. O. Sadiku, "Predictive analytics in entertainment," International Journal of Trend in Scientific Research and Development, vol. 10, no.3, May-June, 2026, pp. 214-221.

[4] "Supply chain predictive analytics: What is it and who's doing it?" https://riverlogic.com/?blog=supply-chain-predictive-analytics-what-is-it-and-whos-doing-it

[5] N. Babin, "AI and predictive analytics: Revolutionizing demand forecasting in supply chain management," https://www.linkedin.com/pulse/ai-predictive-analytics-revolutionizing-demand-supply-nicolas-babin-xrj2e/

[6] "From insight to innovation: Why data analysis will define industry leaders in 2025," https://www.inkl.com/news/from-insight-to-innovation-why-data-analysis-will-define-industry-leaders-in-2025

[7] "An overview of supply chain analytics," February 2023, Unknown Source.

[8] I. Tymchuk, "Big data and predictive analytics in supply chain: Success stories and tips," November 2020, https://www.n-ix.com/big-data-predictive-analytics-supply-chain-case-study/

[9] "Predictive analytics in insurance: Types, tools, and the future," October 2020, https://online.maryville.edu/blog/predictive-analytics-in-insurance/

[10] J. Upadhyaya, "Predictive analytics for entertainment & media: Consult synergylabs for expert guidance," https://www.synlabs.io/post/predictive-analytics-for-entertainment-media-consult-synergylabs-for-expert-guidance

[11] "AI-driven trend forecasting in entertainment industry success," https://developerlinkai.com/ai-driven-trend-forecasting-in-entertainment-industry-success/

[12] "Building media & entertainment predictive analytics solutions on AWS," March 2021, https://d1.awsstatic.com/whitepapers/Analytics/ME%20Advanced%20Analytics%20on%20AWS.pdf

[13] A. Bari, M. Chaouchi, and T. Jung, Predictive Analytics For Dummies. For Dummies, 2nd edition, 2016.

[14] C. Friesz, How to Win with AI in Sport: How Data, Analytics and Machine Learning Are Transforming

Performance, Coaching, Talent Development and Fan Experience. Kindle Edition, 2025.

[15] G. Wallner, Data Analytics Applications in Gaming and Entertainment. Boca Raton, FL: CRC Press, 2019.

INDEX

Accounting, 76

Accuracy, 53,83,178

Adaptability, 212

Advertising, 108

Algorithmic bias, 119, 335

Algorithmic trading, 138

Anomaly detection, 330

Audience understanding, 413

Auto insurance, 234

Automation, 81,114,145,242,272,359

Automotive industry, 174

Banking, 75

Behavioral analysis, 328

Bias, 53,247,307,363,393,415

Business, 11,64

Business intelligence, 79

Capacity planning, 208

Change management, 182,300,365

Churn prediction, 109,241,385

Claims management, 237

Claims processing, 243

Clinical decision support, 49

Clustering techniques, 109

Collaboration, 88,309,336,365

Communication, 274

Competitive advantage, 83,116,245

Complexity, 86,183

Computational resources, 365

Concept drift, 335

Cost reduction, 47,209,359

Cost savings, 114,272,331

Cost-effectiveness, 81

Costs, 146,275,304

Credit scoring, 80

Customer churn, 84,389

Customer education, 270

Customer experience, 20,115

Customer feedback, 274

Customer relationship management (CRM), 16,80,374

Customer retention, 116,238,244,271

Customer satisfaction, 147,176,211,273,388

Customer segmentation, 108

Customer sentiment, 272

Customer service, 17,211,258

Customer support, 270,388

Cybersecurity, 50,150

Cybersecurity risk management, 357

Data acquisition, 300

Data bias, 22,277

Data imbalance, 333

Data infrastructure, 416

Data privacy, 52,179,213,246,276,304,334,362

Data quality, 22,52,86,118,149,179,213,247,276,305,333,362,392,415

Data silos, 393

Debt collection, 142

Decision-making, 18,82,116,146,176,210,245,273,299,360,413

Demand forecasting, 46,111,173,202,360,386

Demand prediction, 269

Detection, 331

Digital divide, 248

Disasters, 300

Disease management, 42

Disease prevention, 48

Disruption management, 206

Earnings prediction, 143

Ecommerce, 268

Ecommerce fraud, 327

Economic reality, 54

Efficiency, 19,82,177,211,388,413

Employee engagement, 296

Employee performance, 297

Employee retention, 297

Engagement, 389

Entertainment, 400

Ethical concerns, 21,53,85,246,277,307,363,392,414

Explainability, 55,335

False alerts, 334

Finance, 14,75,127

Financial forecasting, 140

Financial risk management, 354

Financial services, 269

Forecasting, 15,77,412

Fraud data analytics, 328

Fraud detection, 16,45,77,138,174,208,237,317,358

Gaming industry, 410

Global adaptation, 300

Global reach, 88

Health insurance, 233

Healthcare, 9,29,268,295

Healthcare risk management, 356

High initial costs, 180

Human element, 250,364

Human errors, 56

Human resources (HR), 18,285

Improvement, 274

Inclusion, 413

Information overload, 275

Insurance, 16,80,144,223,327

Insurance claims, 45

Integration, 87,120,151,180,214,248,277,305,394

Interoperability, 23,35,119

Interpretability, 215,364

Inventory costs, 209

Inventory management, 203

Inventory optimization, 172,204

Knowledge management, 300

Last-mile delivery, 206

Lead scoring, 112,384,391

Life insurance, 235

Logistics, 207

Loss, 147

Maintenance costs, 178

Manufacturing, 15,160,357

Market complexities, 150

Market expansion, 238

Market volatility, 205

Marketing, 13,75,97,269

Model generalizability, 364

Music industry, 409

Operational efficiency, 245,332

Order management, 174

Organizational culture, 54,308

Over-reliance on technology, 87,215

Patient care, 40

Patient stratification, 44

Performance management, 298

Performance monitoring, 300

Personalization, 20,83,114,148,212,244,384,411

Personalized medicine, 42

Personalized support, 273

Pharmaceutical manufacturing,174

Physician adoption, 55

Population health management, 43

Portfolio optimization, 143

Predicting customer behavior, 110

Predictive analytics, 1

Applications of, 9

Definition of, 3,31,66,99,129,162,193,225,260,287,319,345,376,402

Word cloud for, 2

Predictive analytics for customer service, 258-280

Applications of, 268

Benefits of, 272

Challenges of, 275

Future of, 278

Predictive analytics for human resources, 285-312

Applications of, 294

Benefits of, 299

Challenges of, 304

Future of, 310

Predictive analytics in business, 64-91

Applications of, 73

Benefits, 81

Future of, 89

Predictive analytics in customer relationship management, 374-396

Applications of, 383

Benefits of, 387

Challenges of, 391

Future of, 394

Predictive analytics in entertainment, 400-419

Applications of, 409

Benefits of, 412

Challenges of, 414

Future of, 417

Predictive analytics in finance, 127-154

Applications of, 137

Benefits of, 145

Challenges of, 149

Future of, 152

Predictive analytics in fraud detection, 317-339

Applications of, 327

Benefits of, 331

Challenges of, 333

Future of, 336

Predictive analytics in healthcare, 29-58

Applications of, 39

Benefits of, 46

Challenges of, 51

Future of, 56

Predictive analytics in insurance, 223-253

Applications of, 232

Benefits of, 242

Challenges of, 246

Future of, 250

Predictive analytics in manufacturing, 160-186

Applications of, 169

Benefits of, 175

Challenges of, 179

Future of, 183

Predictive analytics in marketing, 97-122

Applications of, 106

Benefits of, 113

Challenges of, 118

Future of, 120

Predictive analytics in risk management, 343-369

Applications of, 352

Benefits of, 359

Challenges of, 362

Future of, 367

Predictive analytics in supply chain, 191-218

Applications, 201

Benefits of, 208

Challenges of, 212

Future of, 216

Predictive intelligence, 242

Predictive maintenance, 78,170,205

Predictive modeling, 40

Predictive SEO, 112

Price optimization, 172,204

Pricing optimization, 110,241

Privacy, 22,85,118,414

Product recommendations, 390

Production planning, 173

Profitability, 146

Property insurance, 235

Quality control, 171

Readmission prevention, 49

Regulations, 249

Regulatory compliance, 55,142,278,309,361

Reliability, 181

Resistance to change, 182,214,248,306,393

Resource allocation, 48,147

Resource optimization, 43

Restaurants, 296

Retail, 12,74,107

Return on investment (ROI), 115

Revenue growth, 147

Risk assessment, 78,236

Risk intelligence, 330

Risk management, 17,139,173,204,210,243,329,343

Risk management analytics, 353

Risk monitoring, 361

Risk prediction, 44

Risk reduction, 20

Risks, 342

Sales, 75

Sales forecasting, 111,387,390

Scalability, 84,181,300,332

Security, 22

Sentiment analysis, 144,386,412

Sentiment prediction, 110

Skill shortage, 393,416

Skilled professionals, 149

Skills gap, 88,120,180, 181,214,249,336

Stock market forecasting, 142

Stock trading, 80

Stock volatility, 143

Streaming platforms, 410

Supply chain disruptions, 183

Supply chain optimization, 171

Supply chain risk, 355

Supply chain visibility, 206

Supply chains, 15,76,191

Talent acquisition, 296

Telecommunication, 268

Training, 151

Transparency, 88,119,308

Underwriting processes, 238

Unpredictability of culture, 416

Waste, 177

Waste reduction, 209

Workforce planning, 298

www.ingramcontent.com/pod-product-compliance
Lightning Source LLC
LaVergne TN
LVHW050754061126
851857LV00012B/556